INTIMATE OUTSIDERS

OBJECTS/HISTORIES:
CRITICAL PERSPECTIVES ON ART, MATERIAL
CULTURE, AND REPRESENTATION

A series edited by Nicholas Thomas

PUBLISHED WITH THE ASSISTANCE
OF THE GETTY FOUNDATION

INTIMATE
Outsiders

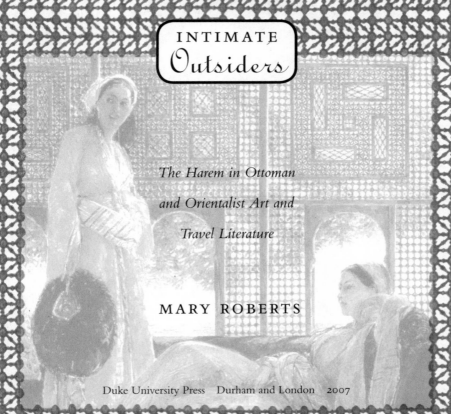

The Harem in Ottoman
and Orientalist Art and
Travel Literature

MARY ROBERTS

Duke University Press   Durham and London   2007

To John and Gwenneth Roberts

In memory of
Hilda Roberts (1900–1994)

Contents

Illustrations

FIGURES

Acknowledgments

In the course of writing this book, I have been encouraged and inspired by numerous colleagues and friends to whom I owe an inestimable debt. From its earliest stages, I was enthusiastically supported by my colleague Jill Beaulieu; her insightful readings and creative thinking and our engaging dialogues about nineteenth-century art have greatly enhanced this book. Another crucial interlocutor for my research has been Roger Benjamin, who has always provided a model of scholarly erudition. I am sincerely grateful for his astute advice and encouragement throughout the project. I am indebted to my research assistant, Hannah Williams, who worked with me in the last three years of this project; her industriousness and acute editorial eye have been invaluable. I am grateful to Zeynep Çelik for her support and advice on matters of interpretation; this and her good humour have been crucial to the development of this project. The feedback on drafts of this manuscript from Reina Lewis, Zeynep Çelik, and the anonymous readers from Duke University Press has greatly enriched and refined my ideas in this book. I am also grateful to Ken Wissoker and Nicholas Thomas for seeing the place of *Intimate Outsiders* in the Objects/Histories Series, and to Ken, Courtney Berger, and the editorial team at Duke for their professionalism in bringing this manuscript to fruition. My thanks also to Alexandra Kaufman for her careful copyediting and Jenni Carter for her skilled photography.

This book has entailed a peripatetic research adventure encompassing archival work in the United Kingdom, Turkey, Egypt, Japan, Denmark, and the United States. I want to thank the following for their assistance with research and translation along the way: in Japan, Satako Asada; in Denmark, Anne-Mette Villumsen and Neil Stanford; and in Istanbul, the tenacious young translators who have worked with me over many years: Evra Günhan, Pınar Öztamur, and Berfu Aytaç. I would also like to thank Marcus Barry and Samuel Williams for Turkish translations; Laurent Mignon for Ottoman translations; Kate Daniels for Arabic translations; Hannah Williams, Gay McAuley, and Chiara O'Reilly for French translations. As so much of the research for this book took place in Turkey I am also indebted to the support I have received from the Turkish consul general in Sydney, Mr. Nihat Erşen, and his wife, Berren Erşen.

I would like to express my gratitude to all the librarians and curators who assisted with this project at the following libraries and museums: Dolmabahçe Palace Museum; Topkapı Palace Museum Archive and Library; Museum of Painting and Sculpture, Mimar Sinan University; Atatürk Library of Istanbul Municipality; Istanbul University Library and Archive; IRCICA; the Directorate of the National Palaces of Turkey; Boğaziçi University Library; the Istanbul Library; Sadberk Hanım Museum; German Archaeological Institute in Istanbul; the French Anatolian Research Institute, Istanbul; the Swedish Consulate Library, Istanbul; the School of Oriental and African Studies, University of London; the British Library; the National Art Library; Witt Library; Courtauld Institute of Art, the Paul Mellon Centre for Studies in British Art; the Victoria and Albert Museum; Christies London; Sotheby's London; Tate Britain; the Royal Academy of Arts; the Fine Art Society; Staffordshire Record Office; the Bodleian Library, Oxford; the Ashmolean Museum, Oxford; Fitzwilliam Museum, Cambridge; Leicester City Art Gallery; Birmingham City Council Museums and Art Gallery; Southampton City Gallery; Laing Art Gallery, Newcastle-upon-Tyne; the Cecil Higgins Art Gallery, Bedford; Leeds City Art Gallery; the Bristol City Art Gallery; Harris Museum and Art Gallery, Preston; Walker Art Gallery, Liverpool; Whitworth Art Gallery, University of Manchester; City of Manchester Art Gallery; Yale Center for British Art, New Haven; and the Royal Library, Copenhagen. I am also grateful to the late Major-General Michael Lewis for his generous encouragement and support in the earliest years of my work on John Frederick Lewis. My special thanks to John Spencer and Peter Wright at the Schaeffer Library; and Anthony Green and Nicholas Keyzer at the Power Institute Image Library, as well as Helena Poropat and Deborah Rodrigo. I would like to thank staff at all of the public museums, private auction houses, libraries, and archives in which are held the works that are at the center of this study, and to the private collectors who have generously consented to having works from their collections reproduced here. For their assistance with tracking down illustrations, I would like to thank Briony Llewellyn, Ken Jacobsen, Roger Benjamin, Chiara O'Reilly, Hannah Williams, Lynne Thornton, Max Donnelly at the Fine Art Society, and Brian MacDermot at the Mathaf Gallery.

A project such as this, requiring international research, would not have been possible without the generous financial support of several funding bodies. My research trips and invaluable resources were made possible through the financial assistance of the Australian Research Council's Discovery Grants Scheme and a Yale Centre for British Art Visiting Fellowship. In addition, the University of Sydney's RIHSS Writing Fellowship in 2006 enabled me to complete the manuscript. I am grateful to my former head of school, Adrian Mitchell, and to Roger Benjamin and the Power Institute Foundation for Art and Visual Culture for the provision of additional funding for the illustrations in this volume.

Several academics and scholars have provided the collegial support that has contributed to the making of this book: Caroline Jordan, Deborah Cherry, Tim Barringer, Geoff Quilley, Julie Codell, Luke Gartlan, Douglas Fordham, Janice Helland, Anita Callaway, Michael Carter, Jos Hackforth-Jones, Aykut Gürçağlar, Şehnaz Tahir-Gürçağlar, Virginia Spate, Alison Inglis, Chiara O'Reilly, Jennifer Barrett, Carol Ockman, Charles Newton, Philip Mansel, Sema Öner, and my colleagues in the Department of Art History and Theory at the University of Sydney. My thinking about the ideas in this book has been constantly enriched by dialogues with my students over the years. I would like to warmly thank John Schaeffer for his unique vision, his support for my scholarship and teaching, and his valuable contribution to the study of nineteenth-century art in Australia today.

Such an all-consuming project would not have been possible without the nurturing support and encouragement of my friends. I have mentioned many of them already, but I am also sincerely grateful to Anne Brennan, Barbara Campbell, Gavin Harris, Gordon Bull, Helen Ennis, Nicole Mahony, Julieanne Mahony, Kate Sands, Anne Ferran, Gavin Harris, David Williams, Marjorie Gadsden, and Peter Black. Finally, for their unwavering support throughout, I would like to thank my family: Lindy, Rob, Timothy, Sarah, Kevin, Rachel, Howard, Sophia, Geoffrey, Kathy, and Lucy.

This book is dedicated with heartfelt thanks to my parents, John and Gwenneth, and in loving memory of my grandmother Hilda Roberts.

 INTIMATE OUTSIDERS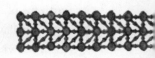

As Elisabeth Jerichau-Baumann drew into the port of Istanbul in October 1869, she was utterly enchanted by her first glimpse of the ancient capital. The sight of Seraglio Point and Topkapı Palace behind the formidable sea walls encapsulated the beauty and mystery of the Ottoman city, inspiring a flight of fancy in which she imagined the palace as a seductive odalisque: it "lay stretched out in the morning mist, lightly veiled, gleaming pink in the early light like a made-up odalisque, with poison hidden under her fingernails."[1] The artist's anthropomorphic reverie was, however, suddenly disrupted upon disembarkation from the steamer by the sober realities of border crossing in the form of an encounter with an Ottoman customs official.

This customs officer, who was charged with the task of luggage inspection, cast a concerned eye over one unusual item among her baggage: a large crate of Jerichau-Baumann's paintings. To her total dismay, this crate was dismembered and its contents strewn over the dirty pavement, attracting a crowd of curious onlookers. In order to secure the safe passage of her art and allay the suspicions of this official, Jerichau-Baumann declared that her portrait of the Princess of Wales was a present for the sultan. This lie momentarily had the desired effect, as the authority of the Ottoman sultan solicited a respectful reaction from the official. Yet her troubles were not over. As she recalls in her travelogue, "[My portrait was] hoisted up on the shoulders of a ragged, brown Turk, and away he ran with his plunder, while my lovely Danish girls in church, my portrait of Sir John Bawring, my own small daughters and my husband's portraits, together with others of my pictures, lay spread out on the dirty pavement, surrounded by the gaping multitude." Faced with the unhappy prospect of losing some of her artwork, her "most prized possessions," because they were being separated from one another, Jerichau-Baumann had no choice but to leave those still lying on the dock in the charge of a fellow passenger while she took up the chase "after the Turk who had kidnapped the Princess." This impulsive decision led her on a terrifying journey through the dirty labyrinthine alleys of the foreign city, where she was uncertain of the dangers that awaited her or her artwork around each corner. Her frightening chase after the "princess thief" concluded when they both emerged into an open square, where the ragged man presented her portrait of Princess Alexandra to yet another customs official with the mistaken explanation, "Her Highness belong[s] in the Sultan's harem." While awaiting the Ottoman official's pronouncement about her art, Jerichau-Baumann saw the humor in this situation, in which her portrait was mistakenly cast as one of the sultan's odalisques. This bizarre interpretation is somehow emblematic of the otherness she felt upon her arrival, just as the entire event encapsulates the strangeness that she and her art represented to the Ottoman officials. To her great relief, approval was quickly granted with a brusque "all right" from the stern official.[2]

Jerichau-Baumann's rationale for taking this unusual step of bringing so many of her paintings to Istanbul was not, in fact, to gift them to Sultan Abdülaziz. Instead, her intention was to use them to attract lucrative commissions from the upper echelons of Ottoman society. Indeed, her ultimate ambition was to paint portraits of women inside elite Ottoman harems. She also equipped herself for this mission with a letter of introduction from one of her European patrons, the Danish Princess Alexandra, and she brought several elegant dresses, which she had been advised were "the female artist's principal allies when visiting the ladies of the harem."[3] Jerichau-Baumann's dockside encounter upon entering Istanbul began this long and complicated process of negotiation that ultimately led to commissions for a number of portraits of the Ottoman princess Nazlı Hanım.

Rarely in the history of Orientalist painting is any consideration given to the logistics of border crossing for an artist. And yet such accounts can provide great insight into the shifting cultural position of the European artist abroad. Borders are transitional zones between cultures as well as sites of negotiation between local authorities and those seeking entry. Jerichau-Baumann provides us with a lively account of such a transition between European and Ottoman cultures. The dockside vulnerability of her art, for instance, provides a compelling metaphor for the precariousness of her position as a foreigner entering Ottoman Istanbul and the uncertainties of her unusual quest as a traveling artist. Her lively account of her initial encounter with the Ottoman bureaucracy also focuses us on Ottoman culture as a site of reception for her art and provides a counterpoint to the oft-assumed authority of the Western Orientalist. One wonders how her dockside Ottoman audience interpreted her canvases. Confronted by the hostility of the first customs official, the artist manages to protect her cargo by invoking the authority of the sultan. This is a canny strategy, and yet it serves to underscore the fact that she is dependent for their safe passage upon a local system of authority over which she has very little control, as later, inside the elite Ottoman harems, she is also beholden to the goodwill of her Ottoman patrons and their interest in her art to ensure the success of her mission. Jerichau-Baumann's tale of border crossing is exemplary of the processes of negotiation and exchange in the formation and reception of visual culture with which this book is engaged.

The focus in this book is on harem representations that were created as the result of cross-cultural exchanges. Throughout, I explore the entanglements of Western fantasies of the harem with the alternative desires of modernizing Ottoman elites whose engagement with Western visual culture facilitated a refashioning of their self-image. In the second half of the nineteenth century, while many Western artists were looking to the

East as an exotic refuge from industrial modernity, Ottoman elites were renegotiating their cultural identity, embracing the challenge of modernization and engagement with the West. As I argue, representations of the harem were not immured from these profound social changes within Ottoman culture.

To date, most art historical analyses of harem imagery have proceeded from the assumption of an unassailable distance between Western artists' imaginings about the harem and the lived experience of Ottoman women. By focusing on European and Ottoman artists, writers, and patrons who had some form of privileged relationship to the Ottoman harem, I look at the ways these encounters impinged upon their visual representations. While recognizing the persistence of Orientalist myth making, I bring into play the Ottoman context in which such myth making was forged in order to assess the impact that it had on the resulting images. My study therefore explores the ways in which two seemingly incompatible concepts of the harem, the Western fantasy and the Ottoman social institution, can in fact be interpreted as mutually defining ideas.

The historical reach of this book is from 1839 to the end of the nineteenth century, its geographical scope is the urban centers of Istanbul and Cairo, and its demographic focus is the elite harems of those cities. In particular I focus on the harems of the sultans in Istanbul, the Egyptian khedives in Cairo, and the modernizing urban elites in both cities. My focus is also on Europeans who spent extended periods of time in these cities, expatriate artists, travel writers, and governesses who were more familiar than their countrymen with the cultural life, particularly Ottoman domestic culture, in these two urban centers. Rather than survey the period, I focus on selected case studies to explore the movement of ideas across cultural boundaries and the ways these Westerners became authoritative interpreters of Ottoman culture for their European audiences. I am particularly interested in how their experiences were transmuted into representations that both challenged and refashioned extant harem fantasies. This book is also the first to analyze the ways Ottoman elites, particularly Ottoman women, engaged with these Western visitors to their cities in order to fashion their representations.

Throughout this period, under the reign of four successive sultans, Abdülmecit (1839–61), Abdülaziz (1861–76), Murat V (1876), and Abdül-hamit II (1876–1909), major transformations occurred at all levels of Otto-man society in an effort to secure the political survival of the empire. The Ottoman rulers and the newly emergent urban elite class, some of whom were educated in France, instated political, economic, and social reforms based on Western models. The period was characterized by increasing cen-tralization and efforts to develop modern Ottoman industry.[4] In a period marked by European (particularly British and French) global imperial am-bitions, the Ottoman Empire became increasingly economically beholden to those Western powers while remaining politically independent.

This noncolonial status ensured a significant difference in attitude to Western culture among the indigenous elites from the imposed Western-ization in colonial situations such as India and Algeria. To overlook these differing political circumstances and the distinctive indigenous responses to western European culture risks repeating the generalizing effect of much nineteenth-century European Orientalist art and literature. The difference, for instance, between colonial Algiers and Ottoman Istanbul in the nineteenth century was profound and continues to differentially inflect contemporary attitudes to the legacy of nineteenth-century Euro-pean representations of these cities.

The Turkish novelist Orhan Pamuk encapsulates this distinction in his recent book *Istanbul: Memories of a City* when he writes, "If Western trav-ellers embroider Istanbul with illusions, fantasies about the East, there is in the end no harm done to Istanbul—we were never a Western colony." Citing the example of Théophile Gautier's writings on Istanbul, he notes, "I might disagree entirely with what he says, but I still don't feel badly wronged. The disservice is done *elsewhere*."[5] This defiance, in which Pamuk asserts a distance from negative European stereotypes of his culture, is part of a complex meditation on the identity of the city and its inhabitants, a self-portrait that reflects the entangled legacy of the Ottoman Empire, Turkish Westernization, and European representations, but one which is self-consciously forged on the basis of Istanbul's noncolonial status.[6] In this respect, Pamuk's approach to Istanbul contrasts markedly with the contested colonial and postcolonial reinscriptions of place that Zeynep Çelik has so cogently explored in her analysis of the city of Algiers.[7] What becomes evident through this comparison is that the differing relationship to European culture in these cities has resulted in quite distinctive connections between identity, memory, and place.

At an earlier moment in Turkey's history, the period addressed in this book, before the downfall of the Ottoman Empire was a fait accompli, there was a consciousness among the Ottoman elites of the urgent necessity for change to ensure the empire's survival. For many of these elites based in the empire's capital in the nineteenth century, political pragmatism was coupled with an enthusiasm for European culture. Such enthusiasm was not universally shared. Nonetheless, by the end of the century this engagement had led to major changes in the built environment, particularly in Istanbul, which became the major focal point for urban renewal based on planning principles derived from European models.[8] The Ottoman palace and the urban elites led a top-down reform process that was not always enthusiastically received by the populace but which was vigorously debated within a newly emergent popular press and within contemporary literature.[9]

Cairo was also the focus for intense Westernizing reform in the period. Attitudes toward European culture varied, but modernization remained central to the political agenda of Muhammad Ali Paşa (ruled 1805–48) and a number of his successors.[10] Muhammad Ali entered Cairo as a lieutenant commander of an Albanian contingent in the Ottoman army to oust the French. Yet as soon as he secured the governorship, he shrewdly looked toward France and Britain as models for the military, educational, and industrial reforms that he instituted in order to guarantee his power base and to realize his aspiration to develop Egypt into a significant regional power.[11] The reforms that Muhammad Ali introduced enabled him to embark on territorial conquests that extended beyond Egypt's borders and, at the height of his powers, threatened the Ottoman sultanate itself. Yet opening up the Egyptian economy to European markets ultimately made Egypt vulnerable to the European powers, and the increasing economic imbalance created the political climate that led to British occupation in 1882 and the creation of the "veiled protectorate."[12] Nonetheless, the Egyptian ruling family increasingly embraced elements of Western culture. The axis of their political and cultural life was, however, focused as much on the Ottoman rulers in Istanbul as on Europe.

In 1841 Muhammad Ali established the basis for a ruling dynasty by securing an agreement from Sultan Abdülmecit for hereditary governorship. The challenge for his successors was to consolidate and maintain their dynastic legitimacy and to secure the terms of their qualified autonomy within the Ottoman Empire. Although remaining part of the empire, Muhammad Ali's nineteenth-century successors maneuvered for increased independence from the Ottoman sultans. While they were still required to pay a tribute to the Ottoman state and were subject to various restrictions that curbed their external powers, including limitations imposed upon the size of the army,[13] the Egyptian rulers had far greater autonomy than governors of other provinces within the empire. Ismail Paşa achieved recognition of this distinct status in 1867, when he was granted permission from Sultan Abdülaziz to use the old Persian title "khedive."

Although at various junctures the Ottoman-Egyptian rulers struggled against their vassal status within the Ottoman Empire, culturally they were Ottomans, and in defining their dynastic image the elite looked to the sultanate in Istanbul as a model. Unlike the vast majority of the population of Egypt, Muhammad Ali's family and the small group of elites who ruled Egypt throughout the nineteenth century were Ottomans, not Arabs. Over the century they increasingly established a distinctive Ottoman-Egyptian identity, but there remained a continued sense of strong cultural connections with Istanbul.[14] Some of the Ottoman-Egyptian elites sent their children to the Ottoman capital for their schooling, and a number, including the Khedive Ismail and his family, maintained luxurious palaces on the Bosporus, to which they relocated in the hottest summer months.[15] The structure of the Egyptian dynastic households, including their harems, followed the Ottoman precedent, and as a result these elite harems were very similar to those in Istanbul. Like them, they selectively embraced Western cultural influences.

The impact of modernizing reforms on the lives of the Ottoman women of Istanbul and Cairo was variable. As Donald Quataert argues, within Ottoman society women were only slowly included in the Tanzimat reformist ideals of equality between citizens.[16] Improvements were made in women's education throughout the century, and yet many of women's property rights under Islamic law disappeared. Within the palace harem and in many of the homes of the modernizing reformers in Istanbul and Cairo, ideals of modernization were having a significant impact on their daily lives. These were women from the highest echelons of society, and their experiences were by no means representative of that of the vast majority of Ottoman women. As Quataert argues, their homes were often the "testing ground" for changes that were later embraced more broadly.[17] In the second half of the century a number of these women were educated in European languages, some by British or French governesses; many more selectively adopted Western fashions and introduced elements of European furnishings into their homes. Such cultural appropriations were selectively adopted to conform with the continuing observance of conventions of feminine seclusion. Women of this social stratum had historically been trained in the arts, and the most powerful palace women were important patrons. As Leslie Peirce has shown, historically the most senior women of the sultans' harems played an important role in dynastic image making through religious endowments, imperial ceremonies, and cultural patronage,[18] and they continued to do so in the nineteenth century. The female patrons that I address in this book emerged from within this powerful stratum of Ottoman society.

Visual culture played an important role in mediating the processes of modernization within Ottoman culture. Recent revisionary studies have examined the developments in Ottoman photography, painting, town planning, architecture, and museology.[19] In doing so, they have reassessed the contribution of Ottoman architects, museum administrators, photographers, artists, and patrons to the refashioning of the empire's self-image in this period. Visual culture proved an effective tool for projecting a modern Ottoman identity within the empire and for contesting its negative image abroad. Contemporary reassessments have addressed the varied ways in which such work drew on Western forms while using them to fashion a local identity. One well-known example is Sultan Abdülhamit's photographic albums given to the American government in 1893 that were deliberately used to present a modernized image of the empire to an Occidental audience.[20] In her recent study of the development of the Ottoman museum, Wendy Shaw argues that Osman Hamdi Bey and those who worked with him to create and extend the Ottoman archaeology museum adopted the form of the European museum while rejecting its metanarratives.[21] In these groundbreaking studies, it is primarily the contribution of Ottoman men to art in the public realm that comes into view. In this book, I extend our understanding of the impact of modernization on visual culture by examining the private realm of the Ottoman households and reassessing the power of elite Ottoman women in relation to visual culture. My research in this area demonstrates that gender segregation did not prevent elite Ottoman women from participating in the patronage of Western painting in the nineteenth century.

At the same time as the modernizing imperative was having a profound impact on the everyday life of the Ottoman elites in Istanbul and Cairo, more and more Europeans were traveling to these cities. With the developing infrastructure of modern travel and mass tourism, Turkey and North Africa were becoming more accessible to middle-class Europeans. So too the harem was becoming accessible in a new way for bourgeois women travelers who were invited in increasing numbers to visit these secluded domains. The particular appeal of their harem accounts was premised on the notion that they conveyed the truth about this mysterious world of women, even though the accounts they produced often threatened cherished fantasies.[22] The desire to know about the harem, an ethnographic imperative, had historically been coterminous with the harem fantasy.[23] The fact that harems were real places, from which Western men were prohibited, had served to make the fantasy all the more enticing to them. For this reason Seraglio Point, the location of the Ottoman sultan's harem until the mid-nineteenth century, held a special place in the Western imaginary. The prohibitions associated with this most famous of Ottoman harems had always conferred a special authority on those with any kind of access; the accounts of male piano tuners and clockmakers were enthusiastically received back in Europe no matter how restricted their access to the Topkapı Palace harem actually was. Other male travelers who had even less contact with Ottoman harems often, as Ruth Yeazell puts it, pretended to a "familiarity in excess of [their] experience."[24] Such a fiction was easier for European expatriates to sustain because of their greater knowledge of the cultures among which they lived.

In the sphere of nineteenth-century Orientalist art, this ethnographic imperative manifested itself through realism. As Linda Nochlin has argued, Orientalist realism was selectively coded to maintain a notion of the exotic Orient. Carefully observed details were accumulated on the canvases of artist-travelers such as Jean-Léon Gérôme, announcing to their European audiences that this was the real Orient.[25] Modernization in the East was kept at bay in order to sustain this fiction of the "real" exoticism of the Orient. Realist harem paintings such as those by Gérôme, John Frederick Lewis, and Henriette Browne created powerful new fictions of access to this exotic world. Yet, as the reception of Browne's *Une Visite (Intérieur de Harem, Constantinople, 1860)* of 1861 (Plate 12) demonstrates, such realist harem images, in this case because of its prosaic domesticity, could also threaten to extinguish the fantasy.[26] These European artists who visited Istanbul and Cairo were not oblivious to the social changes taking place in these cities, including the changes within elite Ottoman harems. Yet, in their art, the myth of a timeless exotic realm proved to have remarkable tenacity. Back home, the demand for the fantasy persisted and their artistic reputations were forged on this basis. For many of the travel writers and artists whose work I examine, the very notion of the modernizing harem was anathema to their fantasy. Yet their fantasies of the harem coexisted with this seemingly incompatible context of Ottoman modernization. Through the case studies in this book, I examine how processes of cultural change within Ottoman culture impinged upon their representations.

Each of the artists and writers addressed in this book had some form of privileged access, or in some cases perceived access, that conferred upon them an authority to represent the Ottoman harem. They are intimate outsiders. Characterizing them as such emphasizes the tension between the two ideas, intimacy and outsideness, in their lives and cultural production. Sometimes marginal within their own culture, and often obscured from the art historical record because a large part of their careers were spent in the East, these intimate outsiders nonetheless occupied a position of privileged intimacy within Ottoman circles. At times this intimacy has a fictional dimension; it can be constructed, represented, and reestablished, with nostalgia playing an important role in its retrospective evocation. Throughout this book I attend to the various ways visual language facilitates such fictional intimacy for the viewer of the work of art. Outsideness, by contrast, suggests an inability to assimilate, or that which establishes some form of distance or difference. Outsideness, however, does not necessarily equate with powerlessness. Although Ottoman women were outsiders in relation to European culture, they occupied positions of considerable prestige within their own culture, and for them a selective intimacy with Western culture served their own ends.

In this book I focus on the role of intimate outsiders in cultural exchange, in mediating between cultures. To date, the notion of cultural exchange has seemed foreign to the analysis of harem paintings because the Western fantasy of the seraglio has been seen as the archetype for Western appropriation of the Orient. Attending to the movement of ideas and images across cultural boundaries focuses us instead on the processes by which authority is established. It allows us to attend to the influx of ideas within Ottoman culture as well as the shift in the other direction, back to Europe. This mediation takes differing forms, sometimes encompassing collaboration, at other times involving betrayals and lacunas between seemingly incompatible ideas of the harem.

The harem paintings of the British realist John Frederick Lewis, analyzed in the first part of this book, are particularly compelling examples of the persistence of the harem myth in the face of the realist ethnographic imperative and Ottoman modernization. They also demonstrate the power of such a myth to create an elision of art and life. In this case, the identity and authority of the Orientalist painter was intimately bound up with the perpetuation of a "realist" harem fantasy. The mythology of Lewis going native in Cairo during his decade there in the 1840s, establishing a traditional Cairene home and simulating harem life, has lent an unchallenged veracity to his harem paintings. In turn, these paintings, along with William Makepeace Thackeray's laconic travel narrative, have functioned to confirm the fiction of Lewis's intimacy with harem life. This fictional coalescence of art and life, which was uncritically accepted back in Britain, is paradigmatic of the authority that the expatriate could accrue as an intermediary for his Western audience. The example of Lewis also reveals the continuing power of such myth making within art historical narratives. My project disrupts this uncritical elision of Lewis's art and life by distinguishing between his situation as an expatriate in Muhammad Ali's modernizing Cairo and Thackeray's myth of the artist as the "languid lotus-eater." This interpretation also reveals how, despite the desire to create an intimacy with the harem through his art, Lewis's harem paintings remind us that he was an outsider to the private world of Ottoman women.

All but one of his ethnographic harem paintings were produced after his return to England, and in the ensuing decades he became more and more inventive with his aesthetic strategies to create a fictional intimacy with the harem. Yet in some of these works the logic of Lewis's ethnographic harem narrative reminds us of the impossibility of his gaining access to Cairene harems; in others, the repetition of costume and setting reveal that his harems were a fiction constructed and performed in the artist's studio in Surrey.

Unlike Lewis, British women who visited Istanbul and Cairo in this period were able to visit Ottoman harems. With the right contacts within the Ottoman community or European diplomatic circles, they could access elite harems, and from midcentury onward they did so in droves, writing about their experiences in their published travelogues. So popular was this phenomenon that a distinct subgenre of the "harem visit" emerged in women's travel writing. In the second part of this book I examine the ways in which the exigencies of these visits resulted in unique harem fantasies. Women travelers had to negotiate the hiatus between their preconceived ideas of the exotic, timeless harem and the transitional social realms that they encountered. Their travelogues are a testament to the remarkable persistence of Western fantasy and its capacity for transformation in response to such encounters inside modernizing harems. Selectively overlaying fantasy and experience, women travelers imagined themselves as protagonists in harem adventures, and their proximity to the harem lent tangibility to such fantasies. In a period when it was presumed the harem fantasy was anathema to the respectability of the Victorian lady, these travelogues prove a sustained alternative that challenges us to revise this presumption. The conditions of the visit precluded the anonymity of voyeuristic looking (a mainstay of the masculine harem fantasy); instead, women travelers took pleasure in a range of alternative scopic pleasures facilitated by these intimate encounters, including the reciprocity of seeing and being seen.

My approach to nineteenth-century women's harem literature is indebted to the work of many feminist writers, such as Billie Melman, Sara Mills, and Reina Lewis.[27] These scholars have alerted us to the richness of this travel writing and critically examined the multifarious ways in which women who visited Ottoman harems contested masculine fantasies. My approach to this corpus of Victorian women's harem literature, however, differs in its emphasis. My concern is with a feminine harem fantasy and its entanglements with these ethnographic claims. As an art historian I am particularly attentive to the moments when these texts inscribe distinctive pleasures in looking. I am also interested in the points at which those distinctive bourgeois female pleasures were challenged and put under strain by the alternative priorities of the Ottoman women whose harems they were visiting. Such moments of contestation provide us with insights into differing ways of seeing from within Ottoman harems, while also revealing, even more clearly, the parameters and investments of the British women travelers in their own particular fantasies of the harem.

The Ottoman women who orchestrated these visits controlled what European women saw inside their homes, often challenging their misapprehensions about harem life. One of the remarkable things about these travelogues is the ways they register such resistant indigenous voices. For Ottoman women, inviting European women into their homes was their most direct means of engagement with European culture. These were not the acquiescent odalisques of Western myth; they were powerful elite women for whom visiting rituals facilitated an extension of their influence beyond the confines of the harems in which they lived.[28] In the third part of this book, I examine a number of these elite women who exercised that power in their patronal role, commissioning portraits from European women artists. To date, these harem women and their honorific portraits have been absent from the field of art historical study.

Most of the recent postcolonial studies of harem imagery have premised their critique on the idea of the absence of harem women from participation in visual culture of the nineteenth century and the early twentieth. For Malek Alloula, in his study of French postcards from the very different context of colonial Algeria, it was precisely this occlusion of an indigenous oppositional gaze from the historical record that motivated his postcolonial critique, a project that he characterizes as retrospectively returning the clichéd French colonial harem postcards to their sender.[29] For her part, Joan DelPlato, in her important iconographic study of British and French harem imagery, drawing on Gayatri Chakravorty Spivak, acknowledges the role of imperialist and patriarchal discourses in silencing harem women.[30] The Ottoman women patrons from Istanbul and Cairo that I analyze in this part of the book belie such a notion of their categorical absence from history. Taking their contribution to visual culture into consideration requires us to rethink this issue of indigenous women's agency.

The archival sources that have enabled me to explore elite Ottoman women's engagement with portraiture in the mid- to late nineteenth century have been pieced together through a painstaking process of tracking between archives in Turkey, Denmark, and Britain. Although these sources are scattered and fragmentary, they still enable us to register these Ottoman women's cultural interventions. Such artifacts and accounts remind us that there were other players inside Ottoman harems whose voices and aesthetic preferences have left their mark on visual culture. The fact that they remained hidden for so long, with many of these portraits continuing to elude our gaze, is itself a testament to the power of these Ottoman women and their effectiveness in quarantining their representations from circulating in a foreign visual economy. A number of Ottoman women of the next generation would take quite a different approach, embracing a far more public mode of engagement across cultures by collaborating with British women to publish their travel writing and memoirs. In the very different political climate of the early twentieth century, as Reina Lewis has recently shown, these Ottoman women adopted a self-conscious emancipatory perspective forged in the context of the major political transition from Ottoman Empire to Turkish Republic and through their knowledge of the women's movement abroad.[31]

The Ottoman women I analyze, by contrast, assumed their individual privilege as members of the Ottoman elite, and were affronted when European women failed to recognize them as such. These portrait patrons ranged from the very highest echelons of the Ottoman court, such as Sultan Abdülmecit's daughter Fatma Sultan, Princess Nazlı of the powerful Muhammad Ali dynasty, and the wives of the Ottoman elites. They shared the view that their engagement with portraiture was compatible with Ottoman tradition, and in order to ensure this they rigorously controlled how they would be represented and where their portraits would be seen. Some even intervened in the process of painting, ensuring that the work was modified to reflect the influence of the miniature tradition. Most of them chose to be represented in a fusion of Ottoman and Parisian fashions. These sartorial preferences, like the choice to commission their portraits, reflect a desire to project a modern self-image. Through an analysis of these harem portrait sittings, my study profoundly challenges a prevalent notion of the silent or subaltern status of Ottoman women by revealing the complex ways in which they negotiated a new self-image through their sartorially and aesthetically hybrid portraits. These alternative harem representations, most of which remained exclusively within the private realm of the Ottoman family, bring to light a visual economy very different from the familiar Western paintings of the seraglio. The shift from the anonymous harem scene to the individualizing genre of portraiture involves an inversion of power relations because it is the harem women who exercise control over their representations and it is their aesthetic and cultural concerns that come to the fore. As a consequence, their inclusion within the history of nineteenth-century harem imagery expands the genre and profoundly challenges its hierarchies.

The structure of this book establishes a narrative trajectory from a dominant masculine fantasy that is appropriated and refashioned by British women into a feminine harem fantasy, and that is in turn contested by Ottoman women through their honorific portrait commissions. These are divergent representations of the harem inflected by cultural and gender distinctions. Yet by drawing these differing representations together we can also see parallels and resonances. For instance, I am struck by the remarkable consonance between some of Lewis's later harem paintings and the feminine fantasies articulated in women's travelogues. Interpreting the resonances between these texts and images enables me to push the debates on gendered spectatorship within art history. My analysis of the harem diaries also reveals an unlikely alliance between the British harem governess Emmeline Lott and the harem eunuchs who colluded to thwart masculine fantasy through a satirical narrative. Further mutually beneficial and yet ambivalent alliances are evident in my study of the patronal relationship between Elisabeth Jerichau-Baumann and the Egyptian Princess Nazlı mentioned at the beginning of this introduction. The European artist's painting sessions inside the princess's harem produced alternative honorific portraits, inspiring Nazlı's lifelong involvement in the visual arts, while at the same time providing an experience that sustained Jerichau-Baumann's fantasy of the harem. My intention in drawing these together is to challenge a notion of the exclusivity of Western myth in visual representations of the harem that has held sway within the discipline of art history. By establishing the dialogue between these divergent representations by intimate outsiders, this domain emerges as a more complex, contested web of representations, encompassing both masculine and feminine harem fantasies as well as the challenge of harem women as art patrons.

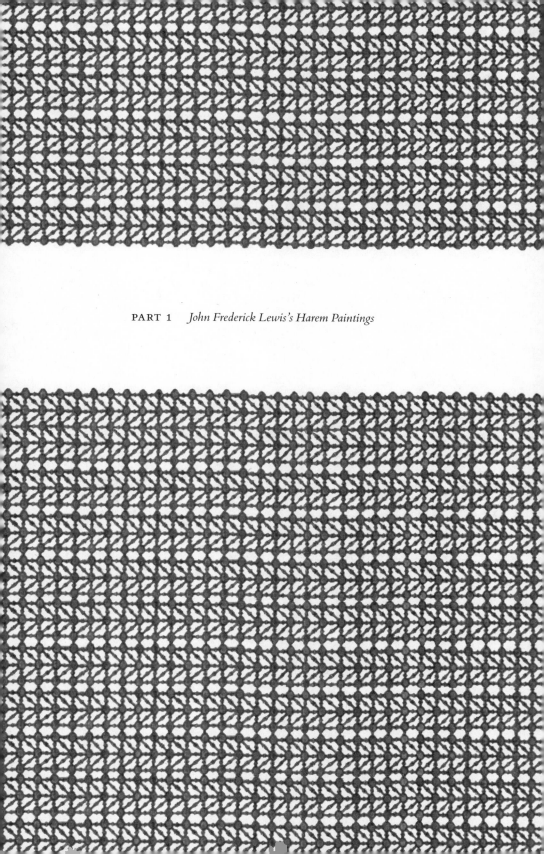

PART 1   *John Frederick Lewis's Harem Paintings*

Chapter One

 ## THE LANGUID LOTUS–EATER

It was the infrastructure of mass travel and modern tourism that brought William Makepeace Thackeray to Cairo in 1844, and yet the wry humor of his travelogue reflects his misgivings about the value of the experiences it yielded. Distinguishing between the casual traveler and the expatriate, Thackeray privileged the latter as having the more profoundly transformative experience. While the writer's own experience was that of the casual visitor, his admiration is evident in his account of the artist John Frederick Lewis, who was by contrast a long-term resident of the city. Thackeray stayed in Cairo no more than one week, and the ancient city was one of dozens of destinations on his three-month voyage.[1] He moved around at breakneck speed visiting the most important sites: the pyramids, the mosque of Sultan Hasan, and the Citadel. In his writing about these experiences his enthusiasm for the picturesque scenes of daily life in the ancient city was in counterpoint to an undertone of amused disenchantment. The freneticism of tourism seemed to dull his responses and those of his fellow travelers. At the first site of the pyramids from his Nile steamer, Thackeray felt no sense of awe but rather a dull sensation of having seen them before. Noticing that his fellow travelers were more absorbed in their victuals than the sight of one of the world's ancient wonders, he concluded that, like himself, "nobody was seriously moved."[2] The sheer speed of modern travel to the East seemed responsible for this disenchantment, and the parodic figure of Waghorn (an undisguised reference to the man who had organized the Egyptian part of the journey for the P & O company) became the focus for his misgivings about this experience.[3] "Lieutenant Waghorn is bouncing in and out of the [Cairo hotel] courtyard full of business. He only left Bombay yesterday morning, was seen in the Red Sea on Tuesday, is engaged to dinner this afternoon in the Regent's Park, and (as it is about two minutes since I saw him in the courtyard) I make no doubt he is by this time at Alexandria or at Malta, say, perhaps, at both." Thackeray playfully compares Napoleon's failed conquest of Egypt to Waghorn's triumph: "[He has] conquered the Pyramids themselves; dragged the unwieldy structures a month nearer England than they were, and brought the country along with them."[4]

In contrast to his critique of the experience of modern tourism, Thackeray had a great deal more respect for a more thoroughgoing immersion in local culture. It is for this reason that he wrote so admiringly about John Frederick Lewis and the lifestyle he led as an expatriate artist. Lewis had been resident in Cairo for three years when Thackeray visited him, and he stayed for a further seven years before returning to England. In Thackeray's opinion Lewis had completely assimilated to local life by living in the Arab quarter, far from the tourist hotels. Thackeray's laconic description promoted the notion of Lewis as a "languid lotus-eater," dressed à la turque, who lived as a wealthy Ottoman, thus implying that he had an insider's knowledge of harem life. This mythology tapped into a cherished European myth about cultural cross-dressing and lent a veracity to Lewis's Orientalist paintings.[5] Thackeray's account of Lewis was first published while the artist was still resident in Cairo and it was well-known to his British audience by the time Lewis initiated his career as an Orientalist painter by exhibiting *The Hhareem* (Plate 1) at the Old Watercolour Society in 1850. Given the brevity of Thackeray's visit to Cairo, these were very much first impressions of Lewis's life; however, the writer created an appealing mythology of Lewis going native that was to have a lasting impact, being reiterated in all subsequent art historical accounts. Lewis's intimacy with life in Cairo, resulting from his residence there for almost a decade, distinguishes the artist from other British Orientalist painters of his generation, and for many, the veracity of his Orientalist paintings are attributed to the life he led there.[6]

What interests me is the effect of this coalescence of art and life because it is paradigmatic of the authority that the expatriate artist could accrue in his home country as a result of his experiences abroad. Going native gave Lewis an authority, in the eyes of his British audience, to represent the harem. In turn, the realistic visual language of his painting established a fictional intimacy for the male viewer by offering a point of identification with the artist's viewpoint. Through this ethnographic mode, Lewis found an acceptable way of representing a fantasy of the harem to his Victorian audience. In this chapter I examine these early years of Lewis's Orientalist career, contrasting Thackeray's mythology with the exigencies of Muhammad Ali's Cairo of the 1840s, thereby historicizing Lewis's Cairo years. Shifting from Cairo to England, I examine the critical fortunes of Lewis's first and most popular harem painting, which establishes a model of spectatorship fusing ethnography with fantasy. This forms a counterpoint to the alternative harem fantasies of his later paintings and the representations of the harem by women Orientalists that I take up in the chapters that follow. When we track the shift of the artist and his work from Cairo to England, what comes into focus are the processes of translation and transformation that occur: of translation across cultures as the expatriate accrues authority as an intermediary for his British audience and a transformation of the idea of the harem into a convincing visual fiction: the realist fantasy.

Lewis's life in Cairo remains enigmatic because he provided no written commentary on this period. The most significant evidence we have from the artist himself is the profound impact the journey had upon his art. Although Lewis's artistic career was well established before he left England for his long sojourn abroad in 1837, he was primarily known in these early years for animal paintings and genre scenes. Preceding his Orientalist career, in the 1830s he was referred to as "Spanish Lewis" because of the numerous paintings of Spanish subjects he completed after traveling through Spain between 1832 and 1834.[7] But his trip to Cairo via Istanbul, which the painter embarked upon in 1837, was to transform his practice entirely. This journey set him on a path as a painter who was almost exclusively preoccupied with Orientalist subjects for the remainder of his life. Not only was he one of the few British artists to spend such a lengthy period of time in North Africa, but he was also the only British Orientalist who consistently painted harem scenes. Other major painters, such as Frederick Goodall, Frederick Leighton, and David Roberts, included the harem among the variety of Eastern themes they depicted, but none painted it so often, and none became so completely synonymous with it in the eyes of the art public.

In lieu of a first-person narrative, Thackeray's account of Lewis, published in his *Notes on a Journey from Cornhill to Grand Cairo*, has held sway. The particular appeal of Thackeray's account lies in its vivid construction of Lewis's Oriental masquerade and its masterful performance of the artist's cultural assimilation. In Cairo, Thackeray discovered the artist living in the Arab quarter, away from the expatriate community, transformed from the dandy of the London club, living "a hazy, lazy, tobaccofied life" in the "most complete Oriental fashion." Setting the scene, Thackeray characterized Lewis's courtyard and house as picturesque and quintessentially Oriental:

> We made J.'s quarters; and, in the first place, entered a broad covered court or porch, where a swarthy, tawny attendant, dressed in blue, with white turban, keeps a perpetual watch. Servants in the East lie about all the doors, it appears; and you clap your hands, as they do in the dear old "Arabian Nights," to summon them. This servant disappeared through a narrow wicket, which he closed after him; and went into the inner chambers to ask if his lord [J. F. Lewis] would receive us.[8]

A slippage between fantasy and realist observation in this text ensures that contemporary Cairo becomes synonymous with the Arabian Nights fantasy, a device through which Thackeray imagines himself as a visitor to Lewis as Eastern lord. The erotic possibilities of this identification are augmented by Thackeray's description of a woman inside Lewis's house observing the writer through the lattice screens: "There were wooden lattices to those arched windows, through the diamonds of one of which I saw two of the most beautiful, enormous, ogling, black eyes in the world, looking down upon the interesting stranger."[9] The entire narrative entertains an image of Lewis as harem master with slaves at his beck and call, and this allusion to his serving girl encourages the reader to imagine what transpires in the private quarters of the house, which seem veiled in all the mystery of the Oriental harem.

The emphasis on transformation is further enhanced when Lewis emerges to greet him. Thackeray suggests that Lewis looks like and lives as an Orientalized gentleman. The writer gives us a vivid picture of his first encounter:

> J—— appeared. Could it be the exquisite of the "Europa" and the "Trois Frères?" A man—in a long yellow gown, with a long beard somewhat tinged with gray, with his head shaved, and wearing on it first a white wadded cotton nightcap, second, a red tarboosh—made his appearance and welcomed me cordially. It was some time, as the Americans say, before I could "realise" the *semillant* J. of old times. He shuffled off his outer slippers before he curled up on the divan beside me. He clapped his hands, and languidly called "Mustapha." Mustapha came with more lights, pipes, and coffee; and then we fell to talking about London, and I gave him the last news of the comrades in that dear city. As we talked, his Oriental coolness and languor gave way to British cordiality; he was the most amusing companion of the ——club once more. He has adopted himself outwardly, however, to the Oriental life. When he goes abroad he rides a gray horse with red housings, and has two servants to walk beside him. He wears a very handsome, grave costume of dark blue, consisting of an embroidered jacket and gaiters, and a pair of trousers, which would make a set of dresses for an English family. His beard curls nobly over his chest, his Damascus scimitar on his thigh. His red cap gives him a venerable and Bey-like appearance. There is no gewgaw or parade about him, as in some of your dandified young Agas. I should say that he is a Major-General of Engineers, or a grave officer of State. We and the Turkified European, who found us at dinner, sat smoking in solemn divan.[10]

Thackeray designates a particular social positioning for Lewis, conveying the artist's intimacy with Cairo society and construing him as an expert at the Orientalist's game of semblance. So convincing is Lewis's charade (even down to the precision of his mannerisms) that it is some time before Thackeray can unmask the disguise and identify Lewis's "British cordiality." Although it is unlikely that Lewis's costume worked as camouflage, Thackeray entertained this notion and was particularly impressed by its success in the public sphere, enabling Lewis to blend into his environment as "venerable" and "Bey-like." The descriptive emphasis on Lewis's clothing reinforces the assertion of his assimilation and thereby his capacity to avail himself of exotic pleasures. Thackeray's account of Lewis's Eastern masquerade combines artistic practicality and erotic fascination, because Lewis's clothing facilitates his intimate knowledge of his subject matter.

For Thackeray, Lewis's masquerade signals his transformation from dandy to Oriental. He prefaces his description by entreating his reader to recall Lewis's previous life in London: "You remember J——, and what a dandy he was, the faultlessness of his boots and cravats, the brilliancy of his waistcoats and kid gloves; we have seen his splendour in Regent Street, in the Tuileries, or on the Toledo."[11] This description of Lewis's precision in dress has its parallel in Simon Rochard's portrait of the young Lewis (Fig. 1). In this fashionable portrait, Lewis is self-styled as the immaculately groomed dandy. Each element of dress is carefully considered and worn with self-conscious precision, from the starched dress shirt, the carefully folded black silk stock around his neck, and the neatly tailored black coat with patterned vest, to the jaunty watch chain. Together they convey an image of a fashionable gentleman of urban refinement.[12] The theatricality of this self-presentation is further emphasized by the staged conceit of the backdrop and the dramatically withdrawn curtain. This representation of the young Lewis as man about town forms a vivid contrast to Thackeray's word-portrait of Lewis as the reclusive "languid lotus-eater" in Cairo and its appealing image of the artist's exotic refuge from modernity. And yet there are some significant similarities in approach to dress in Rochard's young dandy and Lewis's Oriental masquerade. Both are premised upon a notion of dress as artifice and a theatrical performance of the self is paramount. Indeed, the dandy, whose sartorial mode is characterized by a

FIGURE 1. Simon Jacques Rochard, *Portrait of J. F. Lewis, R.A.*, c. 1826.
Private Collection, England. Photograph by Jenni Carter.

meticulous attention to detail, seems particularly suited to the practice
of cross-cultural disguise.[13] The performative aspect of dandyism enables
Lewis to assume his Oriental guise. I would argue that Lewis's Eastern
costume operates as a supplementary layer in the dandy's cultivation of artifice, and that Lewis, as the dandy masquerading in Eastern dress, became
a surrogate for Thackeray and other British men in his intimate experience
of domestic life in Cairo.

Thackeray offers a specific social designation for Lewis as a local digni-
tary working in a civil capacity—as a "Major-General of Engineers, or a
grave officer of State." His costume, large home, and the servants in his em-
ploy all identify him as a member of the ruling Ottoman elite who occupied the senior military and administrative positions during Muhammad
Ali's reign. By implication, Lewis enjoyed all the social privileges that such

wealth and social position entailed.[14] While situating Lewis within this elite class of Ottoman administrators, Thackeray distinguishes him from those Ottomans in Cairo who had adopted elements of European dress, whom he refers to as the "dandified young Agas."[15] From 1829, legislation for men's dress was introduced by Sultan Mahmut II, making the fez and Western jacket and trousers mandatory for civilian men throughout the empire, thus extending the clothing reforms introduced into the Ottoman military the previous year.[16] Significantly the only element of this dress reform that Lewis adopted was the tarboosh (or fez), which had Eastern, not Western origins. It was this element of Lewis's dress in particular that, according to Thackeray, marked him out as "venerable and Bey-like."[17] For Thackeray, the Europeanized dress of the "dandified young agas" in Cairo was at odds with Orientalist exoticism.

In contrast with his celebration of Lewis's assimilated position, Thackeray was deeply disenchanted with the Ottoman elite he encountered in Cairo. The author disdained all the visible signs of engagement with European culture that he observed in Alexandria and Cairo, and as a tourist he lamented being unable to get beyond what he determined were the superficialities of this imported European culture. His admiration for Lewis stems from the perception that this expatriate resident had penetrated traditional culture and escaped the constraints of civilization by creating for himself a lifestyle and an abode that was comparable to traditional Ottoman domestic life. Thackeray plays a crucial role as a witness whose testimony affirms Lewis's cultural assimilation. For Thackeray, the appeal of this lifestyle resides in the retreat from the stifling pressures of modern urban life, encapsulated in the physical constraints imposed by formal clothing: "He was away from evening-parties . . . he needn't wear white kid-gloves, or starched neckclothes, or read a newspaper."[18]

There are a number of parallels between Thackeray's word-portrait of Lewis in 1844 and Lewis's own portrayal of the Egyptian ruler Muhammad Ali Paşa painted in the same year (Plate 2), particularly in the choices of dress and interior furnishings. Lewis's portrait of Muhammad Ali conveys an exotic image of Egypt's ruler to a Western viewer. Wearing traditional dress, Muhammad Ali is seated cross-legged on a divan rather than in the chair that was chosen for his portrait painted three years earlier by David Wilkie (Plate 3), a detail which brings Wilkie's portrait in line with those of European dignitaries.[19] For a Western viewer, the choices of costume and pose lend an air of exotic informality to Lewis's painting. Indeed, this representation of the ruler is situated somewhere between a portrait and a genre scene. The paşa is dwarfed by the large curtain that dominates the upper two-thirds of the canvas, and the expanse of divan beneath creates a strong horizontal counterpoint across the bottom of the work. This exotic setting is corroborated by the landscape vistas in the distance. On the left the pyramids, and on the right the mosque of Sultan Hasan unequivocally locate the scene in exotic Cairo. Given these parallels, it is tempting to suggest that Lewis modeled his Eastern masquerade on Egypt's leader. Closer analysis, however, reveals telling differences and highlights the disparities between the Egyptian leader's aspirations seen in his portrait and Lewis's own desire to live as an Eastern lord.

Despite the obvious similarities in costume, Muhammad Ali's dress is chosen for vastly different reasons from that of the Westerner going native. Here Lewis's sartorial masquerade with its overtones of Orientalist exoticism contrasts starkly with Muhammad Ali's choice of dress, which stems from regional Ottoman political differences. Muhammad Ali's dress expresses his deliberate refusal to conform to the Ottoman sultan's sartorial reforms of 1829 and his desired independence from his Ottoman suzerains, with whom he was locked in a power struggle throughout his reign.[20] After his initial entry into Cairo in 1801 as a relatively junior soldier (he was the second in command of a small Albanian contingent) and part of the Ottoman–British alliance that routed Napoleon's occupying forces from Egypt, Muhammad Ali quickly rose to become the powerful leader of Egypt. Despite his continuing allegiances to his Ottoman sovereign throughout Muhammad Ali's long rule, he struggled against his status as vassal and his expansionary military policies posed a serious threat to the Ottoman sultans.[21] The dress he wears in his portraits was a deliberate choice that distinguished Muhammad Ali from the Ottoman sultans, whose own portraits in adopted European military uniform were to become such a public and, at times, controversial tool in promoting their modernizing reforms in this period.[22]

Muhammad Ali's choice of traditional dress was not, however, a sign of his turning away from European culture (as Lewis sought to temporarily achieve); indeed, it was quite the opposite. Throughout his rule, from 1805 to 1848, Muhammad Ali introduced major reforms into Egypt, profoundly changing the country's social, educational, economic, and military infrastructure, adopting industrial technology from Europe in an effort to rebuild his adopted country as a powerful international player. Despite the mixed successes of these efforts, he aspired to respond to the dominant European powers as an equal. He held French culture in particularly high regard, and yet his engagement with the West continued to be pragmatic and strategic, primarily serving his aspirations to rebuild Egypt.[23]

The period in which Lewis was resident in Cairo was during the later phase of Muhammad Ali's rule.[24] In the first two decades of his reign, Muhammad Ali's focus remained on the consolidation and expansion of his power base; in the 1830s and 1840s, the transformation of the capital received more direct attention.[25] In the 1840s, when Lewis resided in Cairo, the physical fabric of the city had not yet been transformed by the radical changes modeled on Europe's preeminent modern city, Paris, that were to take place in the 1860s under the reign of his grandson, Ismail Paşa. Parts of the city, however, were already transformed by industrial infrastructure, in particular the northwestern district of Cairo (Thackeray wrote about the new summer palaces and factories at the Quay of Bulaq, which he saw upon entering Cairo).[26] Muhammad Ali commissioned palaces and mosques that were built in a hybrid of European and Turkish styles, and he encouraged the elite to do the same. He introduced a number of mandates pertaining to domestic dwellings that transformed the appearance of homes throughout the city, reflecting European influences. These reforms included an edict in the 1840s making it illegal to add *mashrabiyah* (lattice screens) to new domestic dwellings, and in houses of the elite, rectangular windows of a European style, with iron grilles and sometimes with glass panes, replaced traditional arched apertures.[27]

The changes that Muhammad Ali ushered in are lamented throughout Thackeray's account. Thackeray was disenchanted with the "european ornaments" on the mosque that Muhammad Ali was building inside the Citadel compound; the British writer asserted that the vulgarity of this edifice was symptomatic of a degeneration in religious faith.[28] His enchantment with Lewis's exotic house contrasts with his assessment of Muhammad Ali's harem, which Thackeray described as a "comfortable white European building" when he passed it from the outside—this was as close as Thackeray got to the paşa's harem. He condemns Muhammad

Ali Paşa for his "senile extravagance," "languor," and "desperate weariness," which is attributed to a life of intoxication by hashish.[29]

Lewis's far more sympathetic portrait of Muhammad Ali is set inside the Citadel, Cairo's ancient palace stronghold that had been almost entirely rebuilt in a fusion of European and Turkish styles by Muhammad Ali during his long reign. The paşa moved into this palace for reasons of security and it was to become a key administrative center during his reign.[30] Indeed, what is interesting about Lewis's portrait of Muhammad Ali is that our vantage point on the pyramids and mosque in this painting is through such recently introduced European-style windows. These windows form a striking contrast to the mashrabiyah that gave Lewis's house such exotic resonance for Thackeray and shift us out of the realm of timeless exoticism that characterizes Western Orientalism. These architectural features, which provide an aperture onto the pyramids and the mosque of Sultan Hasan, lend an important symbolic dimension to the portrait. The paşa confidently parallels his leadership and the innovative material legacy of his rule with Cairo's prior rulers, the pharaohs and Mamluk sultans. The paşa's confidence is affirmed by his pose. Gesturing with his left arm toward the paper held in his right, he makes direct eye contact with the viewer, as if to engage in a dialogue about its contents. Muhammad Ali was famous for inviting visiting Europeans to his hall of audience in the Citadel, where he would quiz them at length about recent technological innovations and international events.[31] One wonders what he may have quizzed Lewis about during their meeting. Perhaps the British artist was another informant about recent cultural developments in Britain.

What did Lewis choose to wear to this meeting? Did he wear Ottoman dress, or were his European clothes more appropriate for the occasion? More generally, one wonders how Lewis's Orientalizing dress would have been interpreted by those Ottoman elites in Cairo on whom he modeled his Eastern masquerade. It is extremely unlikely that he would have been mistaken for one of them. No doubt, like other British citizens resident in Cairo who wore elements of traditional dress, the subtlest differences in Lewis's dress coding, his skin color, and, once he spoke, his accent would have revealed his expatriate status.[32] For his contemporary British audiences, however, there was an unquestioned assumption about his capacity to blend into elite Ottoman culture.

Throughout Lewis's lifetime the myth set in place by Thackeray's text gained force, and this view has been uncritically adopted by subsequent art historians and commentators.[33] Until recent years, Thackeray's exaggerated, playful account of the artist as a "languid lotus-eater" had been invested with veridical status by art historians and interpreted as proof of the artist's authority in relation to his favored subject matter, the harem. Following the familiar circular logic of realist Orientalism, his harem paintings are seen to confirm this claim.[34] An extract from a short monographic article on Lewis published in *The Portfolio* of 1892 succinctly articulates the enchantment of Thackeray's account for Lewis's subsequent biographers and the power of this myth of cultural cross-dressing:

> Lewis here stands before us as a living figure, in his strange metamorphosis from the Western dandy into the bearded, grave, and reverend Oriental, taking his part *au grand sérieux*, and both dressing and playing it to perfection, without the slightest tinge of the amateur ill at ease in his unwonted trappings.[35]

In this account, replaying Lewis's sartorial metamorphosis, the Occidental writer and reader become complicit with the artist: they have a shared insight into his masterful performance of cultural assimilation. Not only does this pervasive myth obscure the fact that Lewis's expatriate status in Cairo would have been self-evident to the Ottoman community, but it also occludes the fact that Lewis would have been unable to enter respectable Ottoman harems in Cairo and that in all likelihood he relied upon contemporary women travelers, who were able to gain entrance, for his knowledge of this domestic realm.

Despite Thackeray's suggestion that Lewis had completely turned his back on his former life in London during his extended time away, it is clear that professional affiliations within the British art world continued to be of great importance to him. In 1848 he sent a letter from Cairo to the secretary of the Old Watercolour Society in London expressing his allegiance to this institution and a willingness to conform to its rule requiring members to exhibit annually in order to maintain their membership. This letter was a response to the removal of his name from the Society's list of members in July 1848 because he had been in breach of this rule for some years.[36] Clearly Lewis was not willing to risk estrangement from this crucial professional body with which he had such a long-standing association. Perhaps by this time he feared losing contact with his country after such an extended period abroad. In any case, in 1850, after a nine-year absence, Lewis sent his painting *The Hhareem* to London in time for the Society's annual exhibition. This was the only harem painting he completed in Cairo. He did not return to England until spring 1851, but the overwhelming success of this painting paved the way for his reentry into the British art scene.

Thackeray's account was already well-known to the British public by the time Lewis exhibited *The Hhareem*. This painting heralded a new phase in Lewis's career, marking his emergence as an Orientalist, a designation that was given greater authority because of his decade in Cairo. Despite his long absence from England, he seemed to have astutely judged the tastes of his audience. His painting was recognized by the majority of the art critics as a technical tour de force that pushed the possibilities of the watercolor medium through a sustained attention to detail, dazzling effects of light and shadow, and the layered surface which Lewis achieved through the extensive use of bodycolor. The *Art Journal* critic pronounced it "the most extraordinary production that has ever been executed in water-colour," and *The Athenaeum* critic characterized it as "one of the most remarkable productions of this age of English Art."[37] This was his most acclaimed harem painting but by no means his last. The harem was a subject that remained a preoccupation for the rest of his career.

This enthusiastic response in 1850 is remarkable because the painting was launched into an art milieu that was coming to terms with the controversies of the Pre-Raphaelite movement. It is clear that Lewis's innovations were being judged in this context, with some critics perceiving parallels. His meticulous attention to detail in *The Hhareem* prompted *The Times* critic to see such parallels; he wrote that Lewis's painting was "the symbol of a new tendency, parallel to that of rushing back to the missal-manner, which has recently become so prevalent." This critic concluded his response by questioning whether "this sort of thing [is] likely to conduce to a progress in art."[38] *The Times* critic was not alone; John Ruskin also made the connection in the following year in his defense of the Pre-Raphaelites in a letter to *The Times*. Ruskin praised Lewis's painting, asserting that "as regards its treatment of detail, [*The Hhareem*] may be ranged in the same class with the Pre-Raphaelite pictures."[39]

Despite these perceived parallels, Lewis did not receive the same disapprobation from the critics in 1850. The previous summer was the first season in which the Pre-Raphaelites emerged onto the art scene, and in 1850 the young painters received their most vehement responses from the critics. Relentless attention to detail, jarring color, and unorthodox compositions, such as is present in John Everett Millais's *Christ in the House of His Parents* (1849–50), prompted the critics to condemn these paintings. Pre-Raphaelite painting was threatening to the critics in 1849 and 1850 precisely because it cast off accepted academic conventions of composition, lighting, and the treatment of detail, and in doing so challenged prevailing notions about pictorial order. In Lewis's painting, the profusion of details did not jar the critics. Instead, detail took on an ethnographic significance as a legible elaboration of a narrative about contemporary life in Cairo. Moreover, the composition seemed to provide a clear sense of pictorial order that set it apart from the Pre-Raphaelite experiments of the same year. *The Hhareem* initiated Lewis's particular preoccupation with the ethnographic harem, characterized by the combined traits of exoticism and veracity. It was precisely this emphasis on ethnography that articulated an acceptable harem fantasy for his British audience.

When *The Hhareem* was first displayed at Griffith's Gallery prior to the Old Watercolour Society exhibition, *The Athenaeum* critic interpreted it as a successful portrayal of a potentially problematic subject. This critic established a dichotomy between the painting's salacious subject, the Ottoman harem, and its formal attributes, which he saw as evidence of the British artist's skill and the veracity of his representation,

> the interior of a hareem, in which a Turkish gentlemen is surrounded by his wives, to whom is introduced an Egyptian slave, a recent acquisition. . . . They whose fastidiousness may reasonably be shocked by the mention of the subject, will find on inspection that their apprehensions are groundless. A sight of it at Mr Griffiths's satisfies us how completely the painter has triumphed in his treatment over his elements—how he has banished everything like grossness and sensuality. The executive skill displayed, demands unqualified praise. It combines qualities of very opposite kinds; and is wrought with a degree of fidelity in the most minute details and trivial particulars, and generally with an amount of resource, which make it almost a phenomenon of its class.[40]

This distinction between form and content articulates the ethnographic aspect, which provides an alibi for masculine fantasy. Thus, despite his purported familiarity with the harem, Lewis is distanced from the moral implications of his Eastern subject matter.

The Victorian audience was fascinated by this painting's narrative of an Abyssinian slave being introduced into the harem of a Mamluk bey in Cairo. On the right, a eunuch draws back the slave's outer cloak, unveiling her for the master as she holds on to the last piece of her drapery in modest recoil. Seated on the left, the bey for whom she is being unveiled is transfixed by this sight. Perhaps the particular appeal of this subject lay in the mixed sensations it evoked: of fascination with the exoticism of harem life and sympathy for the humiliation of the new slave. This central narrative is further elaborated by the veiled woman seated in the background, a *fellaheen*, the slave dealer's wife, who awaits the master's decision. Her presence reminds the viewer of the prohibitions that operated within Ottoman harems: the slave dealer cannot enter this space, consequently his wife is there in his place, but because she is another man's wife, she must remain veiled in front of the master of this harem. The master remains oblivious to the responses of his three wives seated next to him. The wary appraisal of the newcomer by his Georgian and Circassian wives, closest to him, betrays their apprehensions at this potential rival. Below these two, his young Greek wife looks on innocently; perhaps she too is a recent introduction to this harem. The black servants' various reactions to this unveiling add further complexity to the painting's narrative. The central eunuch relishes his role, grinning while glancing over to gauge the master's reaction to the slave he is unveiling. Meanwhile, the young Nubian servant on the right, who has entered with the *nargile* (water pipe), looks on in admiration at the older eunuch. The Abyssinian slave standing against the wall near the wives grins in detached amusement at the competition among them for the master's favors. Perhaps she is amused at the discomfort of her superiors at the prospect of their rival.

In reading this narrative, the Victorian viewer was invited to assume the position of the ethnographer by interpreting the hierarchical social relations within this elite harem in Cairo. Thus the painting promised to extend the insights of the expatriate to the gallery audience. Accordingly, the critics of the day read the modulations in skin tones and identified the various racial distinctions and the place of each in this harem hierarchy. And yet none is as specific in his attribution as Lewis was in his catalogue description of the painting in 1853, when the work was exhibited at the Scottish Royal Academy. In its precision, this text, which reads like an excerpt from Edward Lane's *An Account of the Manners and Customs of the Modern Egyptians*, further reinforces the ethnographic authority of the painting.[41]

The ethnographic aspect of the painting was the mechanism whereby the authenticity of the image was construed through the mutually reinforcing truth claims of the painting itself and the perceived authority of the painter. The precision with which every detail is elaborated works with the painting's narrative to affirm its reality effect, with even the most superfluous details announcing the veracity of this scene. In turn, the painter's authority was established intertextually through Thackeray's account, which corroborated the accuracy of the painting, reinforcing the message about the artist's unique access to the harem and his role as an eyewitness for his Victorian audience.

As well as establishing the distancing mode of ethnography, this painting solicits the viewer's intimacy with the harem. The spectator is invited to enjoy a variety of pleasures, the primary one being the spectacle of the women. The critic for the *Illustrated London News* described the central slave as possessing "exquisite symmetry, and . . . beauty," and *The Athenaeum* critic described the wives as variously "large and voluptuous in form" and "exceedingly graceful."[42] But the pleasures of this exquisite watercolor are not solely those of looking at beautiful odalisques languidly posed inside the harem; the painting sustains a fascinating elaboration of visual pleasures. Myriad details across the surface engage the viewer's attention: the tactile pleasures of the peacock feathers, the silky smooth fur of the gazelle, and the soft fall of silks in the dresses and curtains. Such visual pleasures are enumerated by the effects of light and shadow created by the mashrabiya windows. The lattice shadow falls across the fur of the gazelle and forms dappled patterns across the moiré patterned silk skirt of the Circassian. One is also entranced by the striking textual contrasts, for example, between the shiny silver base of the nargile and the soft cotton of the Nubian servant's pants. All of these pleasures are revealed through close scrutiny of the work, as the spectator momentarily disregards the narrative and moves closer to become absorbed in the pleasures of these details. The viewer is invited to entertain each small incident and then to return to the central story of the unveiling. Such details are ultimately framed by and subordinated to the narrative, which is ordered and confirmed by the painting's composition.

The painting is organized according to the logic of its central narrative, which guides the viewing process. The highly structured composition satisfied academic demands for the hierarchical ordering of the subject matter. The figures are grouped in a double pyramidal structure to create two focal points that echo the narrative. In the group on the right, the eunuch and drapery form a backdrop behind the Abyssinian slave, highlighting her as the central focus within this part of the composition, while the eunuch's amused glance diverts the spectator's attention back to the bey on the left to await his decision.[43] In turn, the bey's concentrated stare back at the new slave redirects the viewer there. The architecture of this interior constructs the orthogonals of the perspectival grid, upon which the harem narrative is played out. The receding lines of the right-hand wall and the line from the divan on the left confirm the recession of the image back to its vanishing point. This construction of horizontal depth is reiterated through the placement of the figures. Perspectivalism confirms the centrality of the viewing subject, placing the spectator at the inverse apex of this point, with all aspects of the scene appearing to unfold from this vantage point. As a consequence of this compositional structure, *The Hhareem* confirms the privilege and uniqueness of the bourgeois subject, a subject who is explicitly masculine.

The critic for the *Illustrated London News* articulated the gendered distinctions of the viewing process in his response to *The Hhareem*:

This is a marvellous picture; such as men love to linger around, but such as women, we observed, pass rapidly by. There is nothing in the picture, indeed, to offend the finest female delicacy: it is all purity of appearance; but, at the same time, it exhibits woman, to a woman's mind, in her least attractive qualities. A female slave, of exquisite symmetry, and of beauty too (in the Eastern notion of the term), is brought into the hhareem, and the heavy drapery in which she was wrapped has just been removed by a female attendant. What scene is now before her! The lord of the seraglio is seen seated, and surrounded by his women, who lie in

Eastern repose at his feet. Wherever the eye rests all is Oriental luxury and ease: flowers and fruit and rich dresses lend fresh variety and colour to the scene. How gracefully, how modestly she stands, while surveyed by the lord and ladies of the hhareem; and how unconscious she is of the laughter of the black attendants of the palace. The rich, full lazy eyes of the ladies are exquisitely caught.[44]

In this passage, the critic distinguishes several gazes: the surveying gaze of the lord of the seraglio, whose judgment of the new slave is the fulcrum of the painting's narrative; the lazy eyes of the harem wives, who scrutinize the new slave as a potential rival for their master's attentions; and the modest recoil and downcast look of the vulnerable new slave, who is not fully conscious of the dynamics within the harem she has entered. It is the gaze of the male viewer, however, which oversees and is preeminent in this passage; it is he who interprets all others, even the female gallery visitor. The critic insists that she passes by rapidly, disengaged but not offended (which does not take into account British women travelers' privileged access and sustained interest in Ottoman harems throughout the century, as is evident in their published travelogues). By contrast, according to this critic, the male spectator's eye enters and wanders through the harem, lingering on the pleasures of "Oriental luxury and ease" that are so masterfully evoked through Lewis's watercolor technique. According to the narrative logic of the work, the scene of unveiling is offered for the pleasure of the harem master, and his position of visual mastery over the harem is adopted by the male viewer, who enumerates the pleasures of this scene while also maintaining the distance of an authoritative interpreter.

The way the viewer is interpellated in Lewis's painting is comparable to the subject position in Thackeray's account of Lewis's Eastern masquerade. In Thackeray's text, Lewis becomes a surrogate for the author and his readers through his implied position as harem master; similarly, with *The Hhareem*, the viewer is offered a fictional intimacy with the Ottoman harem by identifying with the artist's point of view. A double maneuver is operative, enabling viewers to take on the imaginary guise of the master and yet also to distance themselves from this Eastern lord, casting a "disinterested" gaze, laying claim to veracity and objectivity. The formal language of the painting and its narrative construct this dual positioning. In *The Hhareem* an elaborate narrative is clearly articulated through the controlled, recessional space of monocular perspectivalism and a highly structured composition. Detail confirms the "reality effect" of the painting while also conveying the harem's pleasures. The male viewer is thus in a position of mastery, centrally positioned in a world constructed around his vantage point. These spectatorial relations were forged through a balance between part and whole, pleasure and ethnography.

The popularity of *The Hhareem* ensured a triumphal reentry into England for Lewis. This was one of the high points in his career. He was rarely to repeat this level of critical acclaim and certainly did not achieve the same accolades for any of his subsequent harem paintings. Through this painting, Lewis established a dominant model of spectatorship where the male viewer is offered a commanding view into the realm of the Ottoman harem. In some of his later paintings, this mode of apprehending the harem was significantly altered through heightened effects of entry and compositional structures that construed the harem as an enigmatic space, not fully available to the spectator. Many of these later works, such as *Indoor Gossip, Cairo* (1873) and *The Siesta* (1876), do not sustain either the strong narrative or the formal perspectival structure that so clearly privileged the viewer; consequently, these later paintings were perceived by some critics as having transgressed the parameters of acceptable representation of the subject. These later works form the focus for the following chapter, which explores these alternative harem fantasies and how they allow us to reinterpret the way spectatorship functions.

Chapter Two

 "MR LEWIS'S ORIENTAL PARADISES"

Sometime in the 1860s (the precise date is uncertain), Lewis visited a photographic studio in England. There he changed out of his street clothes into a costume which he had brought back from Cairo in the previous decade and posed for his photograph. Left hand on his hip, bending slightly, Lewis casually leaned his right arm on the back of a chair and turned his head to fix the camera with a steady gaze as the photographer set to work. The resulting image (Plate 4) shows the artist comfortably posed in his adopted dress. One imagines the weight of that scimitar held in place at a comfortable angle over his left hip by the elaborate leather strapping, the warmth of the turban that fits snugly over his hair, and the gentle pressure of the fabric tightly bound around his waist. The loose *şalvar* (pants) were probably a welcome relief from the constraints of his regular trousers. No doubt his costume still contained traces of the pungent aromas of the bazaar in which he purchased it, bringing back memories of place. Significantly, it is the turban rather than that symbol of dress reform, the fez, which Lewis has chosen to wear for this photograph, suggesting his identification with an ideal of traditional Ottoman domestic life.[1] When Lewis posed for this photograph in the 1860s, his life in Cairo was firmly part of his past, and yet he had carefully kept this costume over all those years. The experience of wearing this outfit must have been a particularly intimate way of evoking the painter's memories of his life in Cairo, experiences that were no doubt distilled and embroidered by imagination with the passage of time and the fact of distance. Such are the rehearsed pleasures of nostalgia.

The same is true of Lewis's art, which can be seen as yet another vehicle for the artist's memories and his imaginative vision of Cairo. After 1850, Lewis remained in England, living in Walton-on-Thames, Surrey, from 1854. He never returned to North Africa and yet his continuing investment in that place is evident in his painting, which remained almost exclusively focused on Orientalist themes: the desert, the bazaar, and the harem. In his studio in Surrey, Lewis's wife, Marian, posed in the sumptuous Ottoman women's costumes he had brought back. Working with these life studies, as well as the hundreds of decorative objects, sketches (including studies of his former home in Cairo), and photographs from his travels, Lewis created the harem scenes that he exhibited regularly over the next decades. Through these paintings, memory and imagination were transmuted into aesthetic pleasures. Absence from site, I would argue, necessitated new ways of sustaining an illusion of intimacy with the harem, and Lewis increasingly relied upon visual language to create such effects. Between 1857 and 1876, he undertook a series of visual experiments that were to redefine both the harem fantasy and the spectator's relationship to it. A study of the critics' responses to these paintings reveals that the audience was becoming progressively less convinced of their status as ethnographic documents of harem life. Indeed, his later paintings evidence parallels with aestheticism. With this significant shift from the ethnographic to the aestheticist harem, Lewis's later paintings introduced a different kind of harem fantasy through their unique modes of spectatorship. The viewer was no longer in the distanced and predictable position that characterized voyeurism and the perspectival model, no longer unproblematically positioned as the sovereign subject. Instead, viewers were offered a more intimate relation of proximity to the harem through an emphasis on synaesthetic and compositional effects that offered the viewer an invitation to enter into the harem.

In terms of their mode of address to the viewer, the two harem scenes that Lewis painted in 1857 and 1858 departed significantly from his grand harem narrative of 1849, the only harem painting that he actually produced in Cairo. In these later works, *Hhareem Life, Constantinople* (1857, Plate 5) and *Life in the Harem, Cairo* (1858, Plate 6), the complex multifigure composition of the master and his women of *The Hhareem* is exchanged for an intimate engagement with one or two women in quiet repose in the corner of a harem. Approximately half the size of the earlier work, the later paintings invite a more intimate viewing position, drawing the viewer in to discern their detail. Visual mastery of a large scene is replaced by immersive effects for the spectator. In *Hhareem Life, Constantinople* a narrative is suggested, but it is fragmentary. An odalisque sits on a luxurious divan, teasing her cat; she is attended by another woman standing nearby, but their relative social position and the nature of their interaction remain ambiguous.[2] The feet of a third person in the mirror suggest an imminent entry into the scene, but again this fragment offers few clues as to the purpose or identity of the figure. This narrative ambiguity contrasts with *The Hhareem*, where relative social status and the dynamics of the hierarchy are so clearly articulated. While narrative is not entirely absent from *Hhareem Life, Constantinople* (indeed, the absence of a clear story seems to compel various critics and art historians to narrate the scene),[3] its prominence as the driving force of the painting is significantly diminished. In its place, the fictional process of the viewer entering the work to become part of the scene becomes central.

The compositional contrast between this painting and *The Hhareem* is again marked. Rather than a grand vista of the harem interior, in the later work the viewer is invited to enter a small intimate setting. The mirror extends the space of the painting, inscribing the place behind the scene in view, placing the spectator within this large room. The couch opens out across the lower edge of the painting, extending beyond its limits into our space and inviting the viewer to be seated there. The women seem unconcerned by the spectator's proximity to them in this room, thus sustaining a fiction of the spectator's sanctioned entry into the harem. What is fore-grounded through the spatial construction of this painting is a shared inti-macy between the harem women and the viewer. And yet attention is as insistently drawn to the doubling and rhyming of the intricate patterning within this painting as to the figures themselves. For instance, the head and shoulders of the standing woman are doubled in the mirror behind, while the flower pattern in brilliants on the woman's headdress echoes the wall decoration behind her. These visual plays shift the focus away from the harem as a space of erotic intrigue toward a vision composed of more abstract visual pleasures. Strong angles are created by the corner of this room and the placement of the figures. These horizontals and verticals anchor the arabesque patterning of the costumes and wall, and thus visual harmony is created amid the decorative profusion by an orderly geometry. Such exotic patterned effects beguiled the critic for the *Illustrated London News*, redeeming the disruption created by a perceived ethnographic in-accuracy in the features of the seated lady. This critic wrote:

The English type of the lady's face and her want of beauty, partly de-stroy the illusion of the scene and the Oriental character which all the accessories so startlingly realise. But (whether right or wrong) the attention is soon drawn from the face and absorbed by that flashing diamond head-dress—so cunningly forced in effect by the manner in which the tone of the face is kept down. Then, with increasing aston-ishment at the illusive power, you examine successively the sheen of silk, the green and golden light of peacocks' feathers, the most gor-geous and intricate patterns of India shawls, and a great variety of other textures; till, bewildered with admiration, you allow your eye to rest on that quiet breadth of wall; when, lo! as the pupil of the eye dilates, you find it covered with the most curious and beautiful tracery imag-inable, and with a quiet gleaming of gold quite ineffable in its truth of effect.[4]

This emphasis upon the optical impact of Lewis's treatment of detail was to become a consistent theme in the critical reception of his later harem paintings.

For viewers seeking a narrative of harem intrigue, *Life in the Harem, Cairo* of 1858 seemed more promising. In this painting the woman on the couch holds a bouquet in her lap, her eyes closed, lost in reverie. Perhaps she is thinking about her lover from whom the bouquet, a love message encoded through floral symbolism, is a gift. Her solipsism is about to be disturbed by the entry of a woman and a eunuch, who stand at the threshold. Again the contrast with Lewis's first harem painting of 1849 is significant. *The Hhareem* offers an elaborate narrative of harem life observed at a discrete distance by a viewer who is the absent witness to the intrigues that unfold on the stage-like setting along which the main figures are organized. In contrast, *Life in the Harem, Cairo* directly opens up the possibility of the viewer being engaged as the subject of the narrative. As with *Hhareem Life, Constantinople*, Lewis breaks through the front edge of the frame with the couch opening out into our space, and again the combined effect of this and the mirror hanging perpendicular to the surface of the painting effectively offers viewers entry into the work, placing them in close physical proximity to the seated lover. This invitation to enter is reinforced by the woman on the right, standing at the threshold and carrying refreshments on a tray; she looks beyond the seated woman toward the spectator with a welcoming smile. In this fashion, viewers are invited to imagine that they are seated there, that they are the illicit lover, whose presence is intimated by the posy of flowers and who is about to be received in the harem. This narrative is both entertained and frustrated by the painting. Such a narrative is sustained if the woman entering is a servant, but perhaps she is an equal who will join her friend in their repast; perhaps it is she, not us, for whom the second coffee cup is intended. The ambiguous social positioning of this figure keeps both possibilities alive. Similarly, the couch in the mirror, the end of which is indicated by the break in the fabric where the armrest rises, is empty except for the peacock feather fan. Does the fan belong to the woman who is entering? And if the audience does take the place of the lover, why is their seated paramour, next to whom they are so intimately placed, so disengaged? Thus the mirror in this painting sets up a play between absence and presence. So, too, the fragments of narrative, some of which corroborate the viewer's entry, others that preclude it, invite viewers to narrate themselves into the painting. Yet that script is not absolutely fixed. The elements of this painting that seem to enigmatically refuse closure suggest that the harem is a place not entirely unveiled for the viewer, reinstating it as a provocation to desire. Perhaps this conforms to the logic of the realist harem fantasy, which is coded to suggest the real, despite a knowledge that it is not real.

Lewis's two harem paintings of 1857 and 1858 create a sense of greater intimacy between the viewer and the harem, redefining the harem fantasy and repositioning the spectator through a changed role for narrative. These detailed and quiet interiors beg comparison with the similarly realistic and intimate interiors of seventeenth-century Dutch artists.[5] These harem paintings share many of the characteristics of a mode of representation that Svetlana Alpers has termed the "art of describing" in her analysis of Dutch seventeenth-century painting. The art of describing is an exploration of space rather than of time, replacing the narrative tradition for an exploration of the "world of objects"; consequently there is often a preoccupation with still life.[6] Rather than a painting being presented as a window on the world, the art of describing emphasizes surfaces and foregrounds the craft of representation. These paintings share an emphasis on the surface of the image and a tendency to disregard the parameters of the frame. They are also characterized by a hyperreal quality that lends a tactility to the visual description of surfaces, especially of luxurious, textured fabrics within intimate interior spaces.[7] There is a static quality about these paintings to the extent that the human subject tends to become merely another object within the domestic interior. This paradigm is most pertinent to *Hhareem Life, Constantinople*, where the positioning of the lines of the women's bodies follow the architectural lines of the room so that they appear to frame the patterned wall in the center.

Lewis's compositional experiments of 1857 and 1858 are part of an ongoing process of experimentation with different ways of creating an intimate experience of the harem. While the "art of describing" is particularly appropriate as a way of characterizing these two paintings, it also provides a model by which to interpret the shift in relative emphasis within his harem paintings from this period. This change, however, is not absolute; rather, in this later period Lewis continued to vacillate between depicting intimate interior scenes and more complex harem narratives. For example, in 1869 Lewis revisited *The Hhareem* with his painting, *An Intercepted Correspondence, Cairo* (Plate 7). He reprised the interior space, articulating a different harem narrative with some of the figures in the same position as the 1849 painting. Yet despite these echoes of the earlier work there are significant compositional differences. The critics were much less enthusiastic about this later painting. This time it was claimed that profuse detail bewildered and fatigued the eye, owing to the artist's decision to place a disproportionate emphasis on such details at the expense of strong compositional unity. In my view this perception of imbalance was prompted by a change to the right side of the composition that weakens the focus on the group of figures in this section and diverts our visual interest across the canvas. With *The Hhareem*, the majority of critics were reassured that the emphasis upon detail was unified by the compositional structure of the painting. The black guardian enframes the new slave and the strong tonal contrast between the two creates a dramatic emphasis that is reinforced by the relative isolation of this pairing. *The Athenaeum* critic asserted that the dark mass of this group lent "grandeur, firmness and repose to the whole composition."[8] The central narrative, the introduction of the new slave, is dramatized visually by its prominence within the composition. This drama was not achieved in his 1869 reprisal of the scene.

In *An Intercepted Correspondence, Cairo*, the group on the left is virtually unchanged; only their master has aged and it appears he has acquired a few more women in his harem. One of these women has been caught with the evidence of an illicit romance, and the master is being alerted to this misdemeanor by the revelation of a nosegay that symbolically carries a love message. The woman who uncovers this deception reaches toward the master, proffering the bouquet as evidence while holding the arm of the transgressor. The central section of *An Intercepted Correspondence, Cairo* is much more crowded than *The Hhareem* and does not provide a strong focal point. The pose of the informant attracts our attention, but the nosegay she holds out in evidence, the centerpiece of the narrative, is obscured by the busy fabric patterning behind it.[9] At first glance there is also some confusion as to who is the guilty party, an error of attribution that *The Athenaeum* critic makes in his reading of this painting.[10] The foreground space in this work is cluttered with part objects that push into the viewer's space, in contrast to the uncluttered foreground of *The Hhareem*. In the later painting, the table is pushed up to the front at the right, jutting beyond the space of the painting; this part of the work is so busy that the woman who is reclining on the floor in the far right foreground, whose body is cut off by the edge of the painting, is easily overlooked. There are also a number of competing points of interest in the center of the work as the profusion of detail created by this crowded scene is not unified by a strong central focus. As a consequence, the narrative drama is defused. This creates a dispersal of visual interest across the canvas that prompted *The Times'* critic to question its legibility:

> Mr. J. F. Lewis, in his "Intercepted Correspondence," . . . has carried brilliancy of colour and minuteness of elaboration to a point unsurpassed by himself, and unattained by any other living painter. The picture absolutely dazzles the eye, like a variegated bed of vividly-coloured flowers under intense sunlight. It is not easy to read what is passing among the occupants of this splendid room. . . . It is impossible for pure brilliancy of colour underlight, finish or profusion of detail to be carried further than in this picture . . . its colour and intricacy bewilder and fatigue the eye. There is no repose in the picture. It is not only a *tour de force*, but a conglomeration of *tours de force*.[11]

The critic for the *Illustrated London News* shared this sentiment, praising the "microscopic minuteness of elaboration in the countless details of patterned costumes, architecture, decorations and lattice-work," but asking whether "in acknowledgement of art requirements, some subordination of parts to the whole effect should not be made."[12] What emerges here is an attitude that was to become more insistent in the critical reception of Lewis's subsequent harem paintings, a concern that an excessive emphasis on detail detracted from compositional unity. This perception of an imbalance between detail and narrative was to become even more pronounced in those harem paintings where narrative was diminished to effectively create a different focus for fantasy. With the diminution of erotic intrigue, more diffuse visual pleasures come to the fore.

The diminution of narrative is taken to its greatest extreme in Lewis's art in his harem garden paintings, *In the Bey's Garden* (1865, Plate 8) and *Lilium Auratum* (1871, Plate 9). With *In the Bey's Garden*, high narrative drama is supplanted by evocative synaesthetic effects and metaphoric resonances between the woman and the flowers that encompass her. Here a solitary woman in the enclosed, highly cultivated harem garden collects flowers for her vase. She is immersed in a profusion of flowers in the foreground such that it takes a while to notice that she is cutting white lilies with a pair of scissors. It is difficult to discern where the flowers in her vase end and the bed of flowers begins. Effects of light and color also ensure that the woman is in harmony with her surroundings. The sunlight plays on the petals of the poppies and illuminates the ermine trim of her jacket, and this same bright light bleaches the steps in the foreground. The warm sun touches her left cheek as the gentle reflected light illuminates the rest of her face. A series of color resonances are at play: her green jacket harmonizes with the green of the bower behind; the orange-red of her skirt is picked up in the poppies, and this visual parallel is reiterated by the poppies standing at the same height as the woman. Both are illuminated against a rich green background.[13] These metaphoric resonances become the subject of this painting.

In contrast to the very literal symbolism of *An Intercepted Correspondence, Cairo*, where the love missive encoded in the floral bouquet contributed to the painting's narrative, the profusion of flowers in this work conveys a more generalized metaphoric relationship between the harem woman and the flowers. In the words of the *Art Journal* critic, "The girl, a pretty plaything, is herself a flower." This critic proceeds to anthropomorphize the flowers: "Each petaled cup is brimful of light and sunshine, and each leaf enjoys the air it breathes."[14] Looking at this work one imagines the heady scents of the enclosed bower with its highly perfumed blooms. Such synaesthetic effects were not uncommon in harem paintings but usually function to augment the narrative. In works by Lewis, however, they are no longer subordinate to the painting's narrative; instead, they become its central focus. The garden with its delicate trimmed rose bush and potted plants, like the harem woman, is highly cultivated for beauty and pleasure. As such, this subject is in perfect harmony with the visual pleasures Lewis created on the canvas through the play of color and decorative effect.

While *In the Bey's Garden* admits us into a sheltered, enclosed bower of the harem garden, in *Lilium Auratum* a lady and her young attendant stand at the threshold between harem and garden. Again an immersive effect is suggested through a profusion of flowers which encompass the woman on the left. She is ensconced in heavily scented flowers, with lilies and poppies at her feet on the left and climbing roses on the wall above to her right. Even the flowers in her vase surround her; there is a large bunch of roses at the base of this arrangement and two of the tallest lilies arch over her head, with one touching her headdress. This proximity of the flowers to her head suggests that the scent would have been intoxicating. Again narrative is diminished in favor of synaesthetic effects that are offered for the viewer's pleasure, but here these immersive effects are interrupted by the curious expression of the woman's young attendant, who looks out at the spectator with a strange, disturbing, almost mocking smile. She seems to invite some kind of narrative which nothing else in the painting corroborates. *The Athenaeum* critic was disconcerted by the illegibility of this girl's look:

> We cannot understand why the younger girl is laughing; nothing in the picture suggests this expression; the idea that she is coquetting with the spectators is too subtle. This face looks, apart from the painting, like one of those dreadful "dead-and-alive" photographs, in which unhappy mortals are made to laugh.[15]

It was not just the puzzling expression of the young girl that worried the critics in 1872. *The Times* critic was among a number of writers who questioned the aesthetic merits of Lewis's recent endeavors:

> It is as if the painter had set himself the task of painting brilliant flowers in rivalry of exquisitely embroidered fabrics, and *vice versa*. There can be no question of the brightness of the positive colours, as little of the carefulness and eye-deceiving effect with which the imitation of Eastern embroidery and gold-patterned stuffs is wrought up. But, except brightness and finish, what fruit is here of all this patience and labour?[16]

Lewis's harem garden paintings most clearly express the painter's increasing tendency toward aestheticism and his shift away from the symbolic realism of the early Pre-Raphaelites. Lewis was not formally allied with the emergent aesthetic movement (as earlier he had no formal allegiances with the Pre-Raphaelites); however, there are many similarities between his later harem paintings and the work of aestheticist painters such as Albert Moore.[17] The most obvious similarities are the reduction of narrative, the integration of figure and background, the increasing prominence of effects of light and color, the incorporation of Asiatic stylistic influence, and the decorative mood of these paintings. In the 1860s and 1870s, the majority of critics for the conservative art press rejected aestheticism, which explains why they were skeptical of such tendencies in Lewis's art.[18]

To the Victorian audience of 1850, Lewis's harem painting was unique: no other painter had depicted the minutiae of Cairene interiors, harem accoutrements, and the traditional garments worn by the harem women in quite the same painstaking detail. This was a preoccupation with realism that Lewis's later paintings were to continue, and yet when many of the critics highlighted the failings of his harem paintings, most of their concerns focused in various ways on the role of detail. Detail in the early harem paintings was interpreted by John Ruskin and others as conforming to the precepts of "truth to nature," whereas the repetition of aesthetic effects in his later harem paintings denied this ethnographic function of detail. By the 1870s, Ruskin's concept of truth to nature and symbolic realism had become part of the orthodoxy of art criticism.[19] While Lewis's harem paintings of the 1850s were generally praised for their elaboration of detail that conveyed the accuracy of the image, by the 1870s a number of critics were disconcerted by their repetitiveness. They no longer seemed satisfactory as ethnographic documents. His later paintings seem to invite a realist reading but not live up to that promise. The role of detail had been redefined. It was no longer performing its role in creating the "reality effect," and in some cases the viewer becomes uncertain about the location of the scene. The mix of flowers, many of which are unlikely to have been grown in Egypt, corroborate this conclusion.[20] Responding to *In the Bey's Garden*, *The Times* critic, for example, took it upon himself to warn young painters against following Lewis's lead:

> It is important to warn young painters against being misled by Mr. Lewis's exquisite manipulation, his beautiful clear tones and brilliant hues of separate colour, and his wonderful representations of most of the textures he paints, into the belief that his is a style of painting which can ever lead to large or noble results. However wonderful and lovely in parts, his works as a whole, and except on the smaller scale, can never take rank but as miracles of handiwork.[21]

At the Royal Academy exhibition of 1874 Lewis exhibited two further harem paintings, *Indoor Gossip, Cairo* (1873, Plate 10) and *The Reception*

(1873, Plate 11), that again received a mixed response from the critics. *The Athenaeum* critic wrote:

> [*Indoor Gossip, Cairo*] shows women chattering, with the usual hareem accompaniments, dazzling effects, plump, rosy female faces and exuberant forms, with the apparently inexhaustible wardrobe of the artist's *atelier*. The effect of sunlight falling on the room, chequered by shadows of lattice, is given with the painter's usual felicity. We wonder he does not tire of painting these subjects, these hackneyed materials. His work here is but exquisitely brilliant mannerism. We enjoy the other picture [its companion, a street scene entitled, *Outdoor Gossip, Cairo*] much more heartily. It is something like a novelty to have nothing to do with the plump women of that rather tiresome hareem, the glitter of the everlasting sunlight dispersed by trellis shadows, and lying on the brocades, silks, satins, pavements, and what not, of Mr. Lewis's Oriental paradises. Here we are out of scents, away from the stupid houris.[22]

Had Lewis's audience lost patience with his obsessive preoccupation with the harem? Certainly those who were familiar with his work would have noticed his reuse of particular costumes and objects and recognized the ways he reprised compositional strategies from his earlier paintings.[23] The conclusion that his audience had entirely lost faith in his harems is contradicted by the same critic's enthusiasm for the other harem painting, *The Reception*, exhibited in the same year, and suggests that it was something distinctive about the two paintings that prompted these differing responses: "Mr. Lewis has produced a much more valuable picture than 'In-door Gossip' in the not dissimilar work, 'A Lady receiving Visitors, Cairo' [*The Reception*]. . . . The force of effect here is so great that the picture looks stereoscopic."[24] What is it that provoked such divergent reactions? It seems that *The Reception* successfully creates a new strategy for the spectator's entry into the work, while *Indoor Gossip, Cairo* blocks such an engagement.

With *Indoor Gossip, Cairo*, Lewis returned to the compositional structure that had served him well in 1857 and 1858: a quiet corner of the harem and an intimate interaction between two of its occupants. Yet the effects of entry that had enlivened the earlier paintings are not achieved in this work. Again Lewis suggests a minimal harem narrative as a pretext for his dazzling aesthetic effects. Here it is the trifling exchanges between two women as one adorns herself with jewelry while her companion holds out a necklace she has just retrieved from the jewel box on the divan. The intense coloring of the women's brocaded fabrics and the complex patterning on the wall created by the shadow of the mashrabiya lend a jewel-like quality to this small painting, an effect which is intensified by the mirror reflection of the lattice shadow and the woman's profile. Lewis imbues the scene with an element of intrigue through the inclusion of an interloper who listens to their conversation from an adjoining room, indicated by the sliver of space on the left; perhaps this eavesdropper will report their conversation to the harem master. Rather than inviting the viewer to complete the story, this signifier of intrigue enigmatically refuses closure, adding an element of mystery that increases the viewer's fascination.

This work clearly invokes a number of the features of his two earlier, more popular paintings, *Hhareem Life, Constantinople* and *Life in the Harem, Cairo*; however, the devices (the mirror and divan) that extended the work into the viewer's space and invited entry in the earlier paintings no longer operate in this manner. The divan extends beyond the edge of the frame, this time with the jewelry box half caught at the right-hand lower edge of the picture, but there is no place for the viewer on this couch as it tapers off too dramatically to the right. The mirror also offers a puzzling position for the spectator, presenting the alternate profile of the harem woman and reflecting the lattice shadow on the wall behind. This lattice reflection blocks the viewer's placement because the wall usurps it. The viewer is also more precariously positioned by *Indoor Gossip, Cairo* because the space within the painting is too shallow for imagined entry. The two women are very close to the front of the canvas, and this flatness is further emphasized by the prominent lattice shadow on the wall behind. Recession to depth is abruptly interrupted by this shadow pattern, which emphasizes the verticality of the picture plane, a marked contrast to his earlier use of the mashrabiya shadows to articulate the lines of perspectival depth in the foreground of *The Hhareem*. Depth is created in *Indoor Gossip, Cairo* through the inclusion of the adjoining room on the left, but this deep space is only summarily indicated on the painting's margin and was so insignificant as to be overlooked by all of the critics. Even the women seem to wall out the viewer as they turn away, absorbed in their mutual interaction. This contrasts with the earlier paintings in which one of the figures openly engages the spectator. In *Life in the Harem, Cairo*, the woman at the doorway advances toward the viewer, inviting us in with her welcoming smile, and in *Hhareem Life, Constantinople*, even though the seated woman's gaze is downcast, her body turns toward the viewer, suggesting an openness to our presence. Blocked from entry by *Indoor Gossip, Cairo*, *The Athenaeum* critic was disenchanted with "Mr Lewis's oriental paradises," which provided no imaginary transport to the harem in Cairo. The very subject, women dressing up, seemed only to invoke "the apparently inexhaustible wardrobe of the artist's *atelier*" in Surrey, those costume souvenirs that Lewis's wife, Marian, donned in his studio. For this critic, the harem fantasy is ruptured by a reminder about its prosaic conditions of production.

In contrast, the same critic found *The Reception* far more compelling, and the critic writing for *The Academy* also praised this painting because it "admit[s us] into the private life of the East."[25] The spectator is drawn immediately into the expansive space of this exquisite reception room in which a group of female visitors have recently entered. Positioned on the left, these visitors gesture in salutation to the senior woman of the harem, who reclines on her divan in the center. In this interior the stained-glass windows and their reflected patterns combine with the light cascading through the mashrabiya to create a jewel-like effect, flooding the space with light and bright colors and forming exquisite patterns across the divans, rugs, and the women's costumes. The glassy surface of the pond in the center reflects part of this interior with a mirrorlike clarity. This doubling within the painting contributes to the effect of the harem interior as a magical, prismatic space, a world reflected back onto itself. Intense color and pattern create a kind of hyperrealism. The dramatic orthogonals of the mosaic floor push the space of the painting out toward the spectator, clearly positioning him or her on the right side of the pool. This effect of proximity is heightened by the dramatic angle of the other side of the pool, which pulls the viewer all the more insistently into the space of the painting. The star pattern at this corner of the pool is almost anamorphic in its elongation, and the effect of the bright sunlight on the step that rises behind exacerbates the sensation that this side of the floor is slightly dropping away. Further perspectival distortion is created by the ceiling in the alcove that subtly contradicts the other lines of architectural recession, creating a sense of greater proximity, because in order to see it from this angle the viewer has to be closer underneath. The combination of these subtle spatial distortions within the composition creates a vortex effect that draws us into the painting.

Such effects prompted *The Athenaeum* critic to characterize the work as stereoscopic. This characterization of *The Reception* is apt because with stereoscopy the spectator enjoys an illusion of being inside the space of the image rather than being positioned at a distance. The stereoscope was one of a number of popular visual devices that fascinated the British public in this period. By projecting two slightly different photographs of the same scene through carefully positioned mirrors and lenses, the stereoscope creates a hallucinatory effect of three-dimensionality that exceeds monocular perspectivalism.[26] The effect was so compelling that viewers had the sensation of actually being there, as if they had just stepped into the scene.[27] Furthermore, this visual instrument created a sense of the tangibility of the objects viewed, as Jonathan Crary characterizes it: the "effect of the stereoscope was not simply likeness . . . [but] tangibility that has been transformed into a purely visual experience."[28]

Stereoscopic effects were best achieved through photographs of objects relatively close to the viewer. In *The Reception* this particular tangible three-dimensionality is most applicable to the effect created by the fountain spigot in the center of the pool and the young woman with a gazelle in the foreground on the right. Like objects in the foreground of a stereoscopic field, these elements take on a sculptural three-dimensionality, creating the sensation that the viewer could move around them to see them from another side. Furthermore, the stereoscope creates a planar effect of objects layered in space, a spatiality that is closer to wings in a theater set, rather than the smooth articulation of perspectival space. This kind of planar effect operates in *The Reception* through the combined effects of hyperrealism and the relative isolation of the figures within the tableau. There is a certain sense in which the stereoscope offered the viewer the experience of taking "possession of the object."[29] Applied to *The Reception*, this mode of visuality provided a new kind of engagement which heightened the armchair traveler's fantasy of entry into the harem.[30]

This effect of entry is in harmony with the theme of this painting: the visit. Yet one of the curious things about *The Reception* is that this heightened effect of entry into the space of the work is combined with a certain remoteness from the figures with which that space is shared. Indeed, this disengagement is affirmed by their seeming remoteness from one another. There is a pervasive stillness in this painting; very little is transpiring here. The water is absolutely calm and the figures are curiously disengaged. The visitors stand on the other side of the pool, away from the viewer but also at a discrete distance from the harem women they are visiting. They are lined up on the left following the lines of perspectival recession, bending cautiously, as if they are quarantined in this alcove on the margins of the room. Indeed, there is a separation of the two key figure groupings in this canvas created by the discrete spaces of this large room with its many alcoves, as if each group is contained within the particular part of the hall in which they are placed.[31] Most striking is the impassivity of the seated woman whom the visitors greet. Her companion has her back to the visitors, turning her head slightly in acknowledgment of their presence, but from neither woman is there a reciprocal gesture of greeting or a sense of openness to social exchange. Their apparent indifference instills a sense of their social superiority to their visitors, but the overriding effect of disengagement of this central pair is further affirmed by the blank look of the woman with the gazelle on the right.

This contrasts markedly with Henriette Browne's *Une Visite (Intérieur de Harem, Constantinople, 1860)* (1861, Plate 12), which takes up this same theme of the visit between harem women, and yet in doing so creates the opposite effect. Browne's painting emphasizes the sociability between the women who greet one another in the center of the canvas, even as it positions the spectators at a clear distance from the scene that they witness. In Lewis's painting, by contrast, there is a palpable remoteness of the figures from each other and from the viewer, and yet the work creates a compelling effect of entry into the space of the room. The pool does not block entry but creates a distance from the other people there.

We know from two extant sketches by Lewis (Plate 13) and Wild (Fig. 2) that the interior in *The Reception* is the *mandarah* (the reception room) of Lewis's former home in Cairo, a space with which the artist was intimately familiar because he lived there for so long. The presence of a harem in Lewis's Cairo home is of course fictional, additionally so because, as Emily Weeks has shown, this is a reception room in the *selamlik*, the men's quarters of the traditional Ottoman home, in which Ottoman women would not under any circumstances receive their female visitors.[32] Something of the impossibility of this vision, I would argue, is unconsciously implied

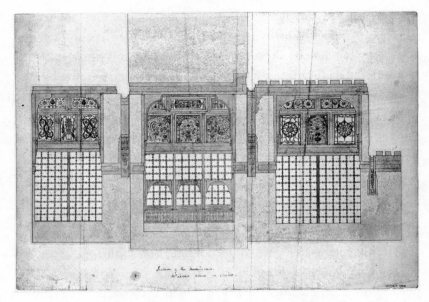

FIGURE 2. James W. Wild, *Interior of J. F. Lewis's House in Cairo*, 1842. Pencil, pen, and ink and watercolor, 31.3 x 43.8 cm. Inscribed below: "Section of the Mandarah, Mr Lewis' house in Cairo." V&A Images/Victoria and Albert Museum.

by the remoteness of the women in this painting. Indeed, the impossibility of Lewis's (and other British men's) eyewitness experience of Ottoman harems haunts his harem paintings. Even in his most ethnographic harem, *The Hhareem*, the presence of the slave dealer's wife is a reminder of the prohibitions that excluded men other than family members from this space. This is taken even further in his later works, where the repetition of costumes and the Englishness of the female faces barely disguise the fabricated nature of these harems. Yet with *The Reception*, the subtle reminders of this impossibility do not override the viewer's fantasy of entering this space that was so compellingly created by the combined effects of the painting's hyperrealism, its dazzling combinations of color and light, and its subtle perspectival distortions that pull the viewer in. In this late work, Lewis seems to have successfully redefined the harem fantasy with this new strategy of providing entry into the painted space.

The changed parameters that I have identified in a number of Lewis's later harem paintings indicate an ongoing struggle to establish an intimacy with the harem. With the diminution of narrative and the relative emphasis shifted to detail, these paintings create alternative fantasies. Different possibilities emerge that are not solely centered on erotic harem intrigues and the bodies of harem women, but instead are focused on multisensory pleasures evoked by the luxury of fabrics, textures, and the plays of light and shadow. As a consequence of these visual experiments, the viewer was no longer positioned as the distanced voyeur and was no longer unequivocally positioned as the sovereign subject of the work. While a number of Lewis's later harem paintings redefined fantasy by emphasizing proximity and intimacy and creating a compelling sense of being there, such effects sometimes reminded spectators that they did not have full access to this enigmatic space. Indeed, they seemed to foreground the very fiction upon which the British artist's representation of the harem was premised. An examination of the reception of these paintings indicates that many contemporary critics were unconvinced by Lewis's experiments because some of the features that facilitated the rearticulation of fantasy transgressed conventional aesthetic priorities. In particular, Lewis's meticulously detailed paintings seemed to create an expectation of ethnographic realism that his later paintings did not always deliver. This aligns his work more closely with an emergent aestheticism.

This shift in his art from the ethnographic to the aestheticist harem seems to be paralleled in his portraits. Thackeray's vision of Lewis as the "languid lotus-eater" that bestowed upon the artist an authority to interpret Egyptian culture has as its parallel the authoritative realism of his first and most popular harem painting, *The Hhareem*. Conversely, the nostalgic quality evoked by the image of Lewis as Oriental paşa in his London portrait photograph of the 1860s indicates a more provisional claim upon Egyptian culture that is also apparent in his later paintings. The masquerade is at the heart of Lewis's process in fabricating his harem fantasies, and his later paintings barely seemed to conceal this fiction. This is not to suggest that Thackeray's description or Lewis's *The Hhareem* is any more real than the later paintings, but by the time he returned to England, and progressively over the years, his work seems increasingly only an approximation of the real. Conviction evaporated as his aesthetic priorities shifted. His later harem paintings are particularly intriguing precisely because this struggle to establish an intimacy with the harem, through the paintings he produced after his return to England, opens them up to a multiplicity of alternative readings. This shift in his aesthetic priorities, characterized by a pleasure in synaesthetic effects, a preoccupation with detail, and a preference for intimate entry over voyeurism, has surprising parallels with the harem fantasies expressed in the travel writings of women Orientalists.

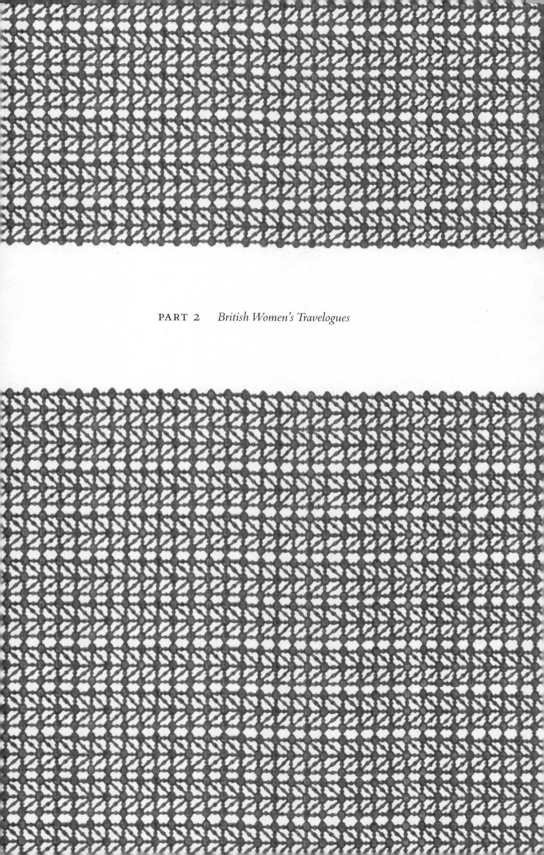

PART 2   *British Women's Travelogues*

Chapter Three

PLEASURES IN DETAIL

In gazing on the . . . sketches . . . I am tempted to believe that my hour of real enjoyment has arrived; an hour which I may prolong or multiply at my pleasure, by memories of scenes well known, and individuals vividly remembered—of beauty and of luxury, of legend and of song.

JULIA PARDOE, *THE BEAUTIES OF THE BOSPHORUS* (1838)

In 1838, two years before John Frederick Lewis visited Istanbul, Julia Pardoe collaborated with William Bartlett to publish an illustrated volume, a series of vignettes of the city and its environs, entitled *The Beauties of the Bosphorus*. While Lewis was in the early years of the journey that would keep him away from England for another decade, Pardoe was back home, reflecting upon the journey she had undertaken with her father three years earlier. For her, writing was an intensely pleasurable way of reliving her experiences of the city, and Bartlett's sketches prompted her memory and imagination. As a twenty-nine-year-old bourgeois British woman from Yorkshire, her mobility in the public spaces of Istanbul would have been constrained in ways that Lewis's was not, and yet in the private domains, the harems of the Ottoman elites, she had more privileged access than any male traveler. Like scores of other women travelers throughout the nineteenth century she was invited to visit these secluded domains from which her countrymen were prohibited. Pardoe's success as a travel writer was in large part premised upon her accounts of this private world of Ottoman women that fascinated her British audience.

Pardoe's account of the Ottoman harems she visited is but one amid an extensive body of published harem literature by women travelers that proliferated throughout the nineteenth century. While a few women travelers such as Henriette Browne and Mary Walker painted harem scenes as a result of their unique experiences, many more recorded their harem visits in their published travelogues. Travel within the Ottoman Empire had become easier in part because of changes within Ottoman culture; in the Tanzimat era of modernizing reform there was an increased openness to Western culture. These social changes impacted on the lives of elite Ottoman women in Istanbul and Cairo (many of whom were the wives and sisters of the Ottoman and Ottoman-Egyptian reformers) and resulted in their increased willingness to invite foreign women into their homes. British women visited the Ottoman Empire for a range of reasons, and their familiarity with Ottoman culture varied enormously. Some of them were tourists on short holidays for whom it was a novelty to include a harem visit in their travel itinerary; others, such as the wives of embassy and military personnel, were long-term residents, some of whom developed sustained friendships with Ottoman women. The differing levels of these travelers' familiarity with the private world of Ottoman women and their distinctive motivations for travel ensured the diversity of this body of literature. Yet together, these texts constitute a genre of harem literature that forms a sustained feminine response to prevailing Western fantasies about the exotic harem.

This genre of women's harem literature was initiated by Lady Mary Wortley Montagu's famous *Turkish Embassy Letters* in the eighteenth century but took on an ethnographic inflection in the nineteenth century in the hands of bourgeois British women.[1] Sophia Poole's travelogue, *The Englishwoman in Egypt*, is the archetypal example of this ethnographic approach. She was encouraged by her brother, the eminent Arabic scholar

Edward Lane, to write about the customs of harem life in Cairo because he was unable to enter the women's quarters of Islamic households; thus her text was seen as a supplement to his own book, *An Account of the Manners and Customs of the Modern Egyptians*.

In recent years feminist scholars have prompted a reassessment of the harem genre by drawing into the debate the paintings and travel writings of European women Orientalists. The debate has focused on the ways European women's harem representations challenged male fantasies of harem life because of their unique access to these secluded domains. As Billie Melman and Reina Lewis have argued, this ethnographic perspective, whereby the harem was interpreted as a familial and social space, constituted a profound challenge to prevailing masculine fantasies of the harem.[2] I move beyond this interpretation, arguing that these texts not only convey an ethnographic interpretation of the harem, but also disclose alternative feminine fantasies premised on both their unique proximity and their selective appropriation of masculine fantasies. Through a sustained analysis of women's travelogues in this second part of the book, I uncover a feminine fantasy of the harem that selectively appropriates and disrupts the more familiar masculine harem fantasy. Examining these travelogues enables me to intervene in debates about gendered spectatorship. Written texts may seem a surprising place to investigate questions of spectatorship, but it is here that we find the most sustained articulation of these perceptual processes. In turn, my analysis of women's travelogues enables me to extend a reading of Lewis's later harem paintings.

In this chapter I explore the ways women travel writers adapted and transformed more familiar masculine harem fantasies by establishing themselves as an eyewitness and participant within the harems they visited. The more extravagant harem fantasies of their countrymen were dismissed by these writers; however, we see evidence of a continuing investment in the harem as a place of mystery and intrigue. I first explore women travelers' narratives of harem intrigues in which they were protagonists. These feminine fantasies encompassed all the mystique of harems as conveyed in the *Arabian Nights* tales. The very fact of being inside these secluded Ottoman households prompted the British women to invent these exotic narratives, and the harem interiors and accoutrements were deployed as the mise-en-scène for their tales. In these texts we also discover intimate visual pleasures of the exotic that are enhanced by multisensory experiences. I then explore the ways these sensory experiences inside harems became a prompt for fantasy for women travelers. In turn, these intimate pleasures provide a model for feminine spectatorship. Lewis's later harem paintings, such as *The Siesta* (1876, Plate 16), are intriguing when considered alongside women's travelogues because those features that distinguish his work from other harem paintings (and which disquieted some of his critics), such as his preoccupation with detail, have resonances with women's harem fantasies. One of the remarkable qualities of Lewis's style of painting was its capacity to suggest a range of sensory experiences not solely based on the visual. It is precisely such sensory experiences that were the catalyst for feminine fantasy in the travelogues. In examining the women's travelogues, it becomes clear that a particular kind of harem prompted these fantasies, that is, the traditional harem that conformed to Western ideals of the exotic.

Women travel writers persistently dismissed the more lurid masculine sexual fantasies of the harem while emphasizing it instead as a respectable domestic space to which they alone had access.[3] In these texts the British women often assume the position of the ethnographic participant-observer, extensively recording the "manners and customs," kinship structures, and domestic routines in the Islamic households they visited.[4] These texts contain a plethora of descriptive detail that functioned to convince their readers that these were real harems rather than imaginary places. The accounts are also inflected with the middle-class values and prejudices of their authors. Their notions of bourgeois domesticity became the normative measure for their harem visits; it was often a moral framework for a critique of the cultural differences they encountered in harems.[5] In some cases, however, bourgeois etiquette also provided a code of behavior whereby they felt their visit should be mutually entertaining. For instance, in E. Baillie's diary of 1873, bourgeois etiquette was instrumental in shifting relations from a distanced observation to intimate domesticity. Baillie offered to sing "a simple English air" to the Turkish ladies she visited and recounted that "a few musical notes [broke] the ice; they saw that we had come not merely to look at them, but were willing to give pleasure in our turn; and they grew quite at home with us."[6]

Although these texts appear to preclude fantasy by persistently dismissing Western preconceptions of the sexualized harem and replacing it with the more prosaic pleasures of bourgeois visiting etiquette, they by no means dispensed with fantasy. Instead, they appropriated aspects of harem fantasy, particularly the popular trope of the *Arabian Nights* that enabled transformation of their experience in the harems into the "imaginary Orient."[7] This transformation is evident in Mary Herbert's diary when she concludes the account of her harem visit:

> The *soirée* lasted till two o'clock in the morning, when the royalty withdrew; and the English ladies returned home, feeling the whole time as if they had been seeing a play acted from a scene in the "Arabian Nights," so difficult was it to realise that such a kind of existence was possible in the present century.[8]

Travel writers such as Herbert could assume their audience's familiarity with the *Arabian Nights* because of its enormous popularity in Britain throughout the eighteenth and nineteenth centuries. To the Victorian audience, the *Arabian Nights* signified a timeless world of exotic adventure. Within this imaginary scenography of the East, harems were exotic, sumptuous places of limitless enchantments and intrigues, and the women who inhabited them were either beautiful tragic victims or scheming femmes fatales. Popular with both adults and children, the *Arabian Nights* conjured up a dreamlike world "of wonder and wish-fulfilment."[9] For the Romantics, whose approach to the tales was very influential in the early decades of the nineteenth century, the *Arabian Nights* provided the opportunity for imaginary identification with their dramatis personae.[10] Read by the Victorian audience as a complex mix of fact and fantasy, the tales were persistently interpreted as a record of the manners and customs of the East as well as a fictitious account of magic and the supernatural, an approach that was encouraged by Edward Lane's ethnographically annotated translation of 1838–41.[11] Given this ethnographic reading, it is not surprising that the *Arabian Nights* tales were to color travelers' descriptions of Eastern life, and these preconceptions were to influence the way harems were represented by women travelers.[12]

As a case in point, Emilia Hornby's entire visit to the harem of Riza Paşa in 1856 was framed by reference to the *Arabian Nights*, thus facilitating the transformation of her experience into fantasy. Characterizing her experience inside the harem, Hornby exclaimed that she "could hardly believe . . . [it] to be real: 'It is so like an Arabian Night!'" She concluded her account with the reflection, "It seemed as if we had had a dream." These references to the *Arabian Nights* enable Hornby's entry into this fantasy and to imagine herself and her companions as protagonists in adventures in the harem. In her text, domestic and exotic narratives are intermingled, creating a complex negotiation between fantasy and "reality." She entered the harem of Riza Paşa with two friends, Mrs. Brown and Madame la Vicomtesse de Fitte de Soucy. Having lived in Istanbul for six months (she was there with her husband, who was negotiating a British loan with the Ottoman government), Hornby was familiar with visiting etiquette in elite Ottoman harems. Her two friends, however, were recent arrivals in Istanbul and novices in the matter of harem visitation, and she took great delight in initiating them into the harem. The difficulties of communicating with the women they met was cause for trepidation on the part of Hornby's companions, while for Hornby herself it enabled playful, erotic speculation:

> the slaves laughed and clapped their hands, and two or three of the principal ones rushed out of the room. We could not think what they were about, and poor Madame de Souci became very nervous. "I hope to goodness they won't undress us," said she, colouring up, and every ringlet shaking with fright; "I was told that perhaps they would." "Never mind if they do," said I, laughing; "the room is very warm, and it would not hurt us. We must look out though that they do not divide our garments among them, and that they turn out these black men." Just at this moment, unluckily for the fears of poor Madame de Souci, our hostess made a sign to be allowed to look at her dress, which she pronounced to be *"chok ghuzel"* — "very pretty"; the fair Circassian then quietly lifted up Mrs. Brown's dress to look at her petticoats. Poor Madame de Souci certainly thought that the dreaded moment had arrived. "But they are such pretty creatures," said I, jesting; "it will be like being undressed by fairies."[13]

For Hornby this encounter with the harem women is the catalyst for a sapphic fantasy.[14] There is an important role here for the joke. Due to

Hornby's prior knowledge, humor transformed the harem visit into a game. Through playful euphemism she could enjoy the fantasy of being undressed by the harem "fairies," the imaginary transgression of Victorian proprietorial taboos, precisely because she knew that there was no possibility of its happening during their visit.

Hornby extended her erotic speculations further, when the harem servants entered with large shawls, by playfully asking, "Which of us was to be rolled up in them when stript of our decent European garments?" When the shawls were thrown over the heads of the harem women rather than the British, a new twist to her imaginings was instigated: speculation that the paşa may be about to enter with the intention of bidding for them as his new harem acquisitions. Instead of recoiling at the prospect of becoming the object of the paşa's desire, this possibility prompts Hornby's question, "I wonder if he is good-looking?" A certain narrative tension is developed at the prospect of a male entering the harem:

All the young and pretty slaves had now disappeared, as silently and swiftly as so many mice, behind one of the hangings, and only the old and plain ones remained. Two huge black men entered, and stood, like sentinels, mute and upright, by a little white fountain in the recess. "What dangerous person is coming?" said we: "with no cashmeres to protect us, how are we to stand such a blaze of manly beauty?" We could not help laughing, in spite of ourselves, when again the curtain was lifted, and, guarded by another Black, entered the meek, white-whiskered little beau of seventy-five, our kind escort M. Robolli.[15]

This scene is described as if it were a piece of exotic theater, and as such is the prompt for Hornby's supposition of an erotic intrigue. Once their Armenian guide has entered there is renewed speculation; this time Hornby playfully entertains the idea that an intrigue is about to develop between him and one of the older women of the harem. Hornby's text is surprisingly sexual in its attitudes to the Oriental men she meets (or hopes to meet) inside the harem. Evidently the experience of being in this exotic place liberated feminine desire, allowing the Englishwoman to imagine herself as a participant in and witness to forbidden adventures. This feminine version of Orientalist eroticism is, however, embedded in a prosaic narrative of the harem as a social realm. After this speculative interlude, conversation with her hosts resumes, and the interchange returns to a discussion of domestic matters, in particular exchanging stories about their children. At this point there is a return to a perception of the harem as a familial and social structure in which some form of mutual exchange between women is emphasized. This shift in register from fantasy to domestic narrative is characteristic of these texts, in which the women travelers' experience of the harem visit is intermingled with fantasy.

Hornby's indulgence in these fantasies was encouraged by the luxurious surroundings of the harem and her knowledge of the harem tradition associated with the *Arabian Nights* tales. Through her playful engagement with harem fantasy, she can be both in the respectable harem and part of the *Arabian Nights* exotic fantasy: the mise-en-scène of the former is a catalyst for imagining the latter. This is also evident in Annie Jane Harvey's diary, where she describes the audience hall and apartments in the harem of the daughter of Ali Agha. The exotic decor of this place enabled her to imagine she had stepped into the *Arabian Nights* and escaped to the realm of childhood memory:

> The great height of these rooms, the brilliancy of the colouring, the lavish decoration, the shaded light, the sweet scent of the flowers, and the soft splashing of the fountains, make one feel on entering as if suddenly transported into the scenes of the old stories of childhood. As the fairy palaces of the Arabian Nights' are real, so must be their fairy owners. Good Genii or beneficent Perizades could alone be meant to dwell in such quaint Oriental magnificence; and it seemed but right that the ugly old lamp in the corner, should be the identical one by which Aladdin summoned his faithful slave; and then how we should have rubbed it, to have been able to carry away so pleasant an abode![16]

For other diarists, participating in the rituals of the visit enabled them to playfully imagine their entry into the harem fantasy. It was precisely this fantasy of becoming part of the exotic harem that appealed to Theresa Grey when she and the Princess of Wales (with whom she was traveling as her lady in waiting on their royal tour) were dressed in the veil in the harem of the viceroy of Egypt. Entering into the spirit of the fantasy, she was amused when their hosts encouraged Princess Alexandra to return to her husband, the Prince of Wales, dressed in this fashion and with this disguise to pretend that "his Princess has been kept, and a slave sent instead!"[17] Again the possibility of a romantic intrigue with the master of the harem is intimated. Perhaps these harem games were a welcome relief from the formalities of a royal tour. Just as their unique proximity to the harem enabled these writers to assert authority over their countrymen in relation to the ethnographic claim, it also enabled a unique articulation of fantasy. The very fact of being there and being involved heightened the fantasy, and traditional harem accoutrements were deployed to stress the women's involvement in this fantasy.

In these travelogues feminine fantasy is not just premised on the writer narrating herself into the harem; it also has a strong visual and multisensory aspect that lends the fantasy a unique tangibility. Just as there is a feminine narrative equivalent to imaginary male adventures in harems in these travel diaries, there is also an indulgence in scopic pleasures which is evident in the numerous lengthy descriptions of the beauty of the harem women. While the masculine harem fantasy often emphasized a superabundance of female beauty, the nineteenth-century women diarists insisted that beauty was rare, thus requiring a search by the persistent female visitor. This notion of the search constituted another strategy for privileging the British woman's point of view due to her ability to enter the harem and arbitrate. These writers provided lengthy ethnographic portraits of the appearance and costume of the women they met. When they discovered a woman whom they judged beautiful, their descriptions display an exuberance and undisguised fascination. Annie Harvey, for example, wrote:

Nothing could be more decorous than the appearance and manners of every woman there present, but in one respect we were disappointed. There was a remarkable want of beauty. With the exception of the pretty Georgian, there was scarcely a good-looking woman in the room. The handsomest were, beyond all question, some coal-black Nubian slaves. One of them had the most beautiful figure we had ever seen. Tall, lithe, and supple, her small head exquisitely poised on a throat round and shapely as that of a statue, she moved about with the undulating grace of some wild animal. Coal-black though she was, her features had none of the unseemly coarseness and grotesqueness of the negro; on the contrary, the nose was delicately cut, while her mouth, though full, had the waving lines of beauty, only seen in the Egyptian sphinx.[18]

Similarly, Emilia Hornby provides her readers with a sensuous description of the paşa's second wife, a Circassian woman. Earlier in her visit she had endeavored to converse with her hosts, but here she objectifies these women:

She was very tall; but it is impossible to describe her winning beauty, or the exquisite grace of her movements. We were all three instantly charmed with her, and no longer regretted their not understanding English; it was such a pleasure to exclaim every now and then, "Oh you pretty creature!" "Did you ever see such a figure?" "Do look at the shape of her head and throat." "What a lovely mouth! and just listen to her voice." "There's a plait of glossy hair! quite down to her feet it must be when unbound!" This pretty creature . . . we instantly named "the fair Circassian." . . . I must now tell you her dress. Her trousers, and the robe which twists round the feet, and trails behind, were of the most brilliant blue, edged with a little embroidery of white. Her cashmere jacket was of pale lilac (like the double primroses), lined with a gold-coloured fur. A delicate lilac gauze handkerchief was twined round her head; among the fringe of which, diamond heartseases, of the natural size, glittered on golden stalks which trembled at the slightest movement. Lilac slippers, embroidered with seed-pearls, completed her toilette. No, I must not forget the shining plaits of black hair which escaped from the handkerchief and hung down behind, and a diamond of enormous size and great beauty, which glittered on one of her white fingers. We decided that this must be a present from the Sultan, and that it must also be one of the stones spoken of in Eastern fairy lore as "lighting the chamber," etc.[19]

In Hornby's account of the "fair Circassian" there is a blending of ethnographic realism (an exhaustive account of her clothing and demeanor) and delight at these visual pleasures. Several pages later she resumes her description of this woman, enchanted by what seems to conform very closely to Western pictorial stereotypes:

The beautiful Circassian seemed to feel cold, and half sat, half knelt by the enormous *mangale* (a kind of brazen tripod, filled with charcoal) in the centre of the room. I thought I had never seen anything more lovely and graceful, as she dreamily smoked her chibouque, and her great diamond flashed on her white hand, and she lifted up her head now and then to join in the conversation of the other two, or to laugh in the low, musical tone which had charmed us so much at first. Our visit seemed very like a tale of the Arabian Nights, especially when the slaves entered with tambourines, and, sitting down cross-legged at the further end of the apartment, entertained us with a concert of "music."[20]

The scene Hornby describes conforms to the formulaic Western picture of the exotic harem woman, albeit more like John Frederick Lewis's clothed exotic beauties than French nudes. Yet for Hornby this living picture is exciting because it has a purchase in reality and is grounded in a scene she has actually experienced. Hornby's use of descriptive detail both corroborates the ethnographic authority of her text by creating the "reality effect" and heightens the fantasy for the British woman by making it more vivid.[21] The ethnographic detail plays an important role in signifying that a real place, to which European women uniquely had access, was the catalyst for this feminine fantasy.

Given these pleasures, it is worth considering what these women's attitudes were to painters' harem representations. Very few of these travel writers made the direct connection between their harem experiences and the imaginary harem scenes that appeared so regularly at the art exhibitions in London and Paris throughout the same period. For those few who did, each felt empowered to arbitrate on the painter's work because of her own experiences. For Alicia Blackwood, disenchantment with the costumes of the harem women that she met in the district of Scutari in Istanbul prompted her to dismiss the fanciful representations of painters.[22] Over a century earlier Lady Montagu had taken quite another approach, humorously offering advice to improve the art of one of her contemporaries, the painter Charles Jervas. Taking great delight in seeing so many nude harem women in the baths of Adrianople and describing this scene at great length in her letter of April 1, 1717, she was reminded of nudes by Jervas, cheekily suggesting, "To tell you the truth, I had wickedness enough to wish secretly that Mr. Jervas could have been there invisible. I fancy it would have very much improved his art to see so many fine women naked in different postures."[23] Through this playful reference, Montagu inserts herself as a privileged intermediary between the painter and his subject (a role that her collected letters continued to play for artists and writers, most famously for Ingres's many Turkish bath scenes in the nineteenth century). Reminding the reader that she could go where Jervas could not and enjoying the spectacle of these naked harem women, she underscored her interpretive privilege while having a jibe at the painter's shortcomings.

In Julia Pardoe's account, first published in 1838, we find yet another approach to the art of her countrymen. In this case, the sketches of Istanbul by William Bartlett, for which her text is the accompaniment, are a catalyst for tangible memories of place. When considered specifically in relation to women travelers' unique experiences inside harems, this notion of tangible memory, and the role of the visual image as a catalyst for such memories, provides an alternative model of spectatorship for harem paintings.

In the introduction to the book, *Beauties of the Bosphorus*, Pardoe writes about the three stages of travel and their distinct pleasures, delineating a triadic process that can be usefully transferred as a model of spectatorship. The first stage, anticipation, is characterized by limitless imagination:

> I had nourished visions as bright and as impalpable as the rainbow. I anticipated I knew not what—adventures as numerous and as romantic as those of the "Thousand and One Nights"; and I dreamt dreams impossible of accomplishment . . . content to inhabit my cloud-land castle, and to look down from the unstable edifice in all the luxury growing out of my self-created images.

The second stage, conditioned by the tangible experiences of travel, is characterized as a reality preferable to anticipation. Pardoe noted that her travels were

> favoured by circumstances which seemed to shape themselves to my wishes in a manner to make me doubt whether the spells of fairy-land were indeed all broken, I was enabled to penetrate to the very centre of Turkish society, and to domesticate myself both with princes and peasants, I found that the fallacies which had evaporated, would have been but a sorry exchange for the reality that remained; and I gave the advantage of the fact over the anticipation.

It is the third stage, however, which she found the most pleasurable, when in the comfort of her home, upon returning to England, she relived those tangible experiences as intensely pleasurable memories:

that brief period of delight—conjured back, as if by magic, in gazing on the extraordinarily faithful and admirable sketches which lie upon my table in "merrie England," from the pencil of Mr. Bartlett,—I am tempted to believe that my hour of real enjoyment has arrived; an hour which I may prolong or multiply at my pleasure, by memories of scenes well known, and individuals vividly remembered—of beauty and of luxury, of legend and of song. I look back upon my residence at Constantinople and its environs as upon a bright vision, which I am glad to have an opportunity of calling up once more, and investing with tangibility: and thus I feel that I am now, perhaps, enjoying the true and enduring privilege of the traveler, as I turn from one graphic sketch to another, and recall the circumstances and incidents which have tended to impress each spot upon my memory; while I am compelled to doubt if the romance of anticipation, or the fatigue and risk of positive residence, indeed outweighed the quiet memories which throng about me to-day, and people my cheerful apartment with by-gone brilliant shapes, and scenes never to be forgotten.[24]

The pleasures of recollection are evocatively characterized here, and Bartlett's sketches have an important role as a prompt to Pardoe's vivid memory. This particularly eloquent articulation of the romance of travel is fascinating when considered in relation to the subject of the Ottoman harem. The way gender conditions this experience for the European traveler is highlighted in the contrast between Bartlett's sketch of a Turkish domestic interior with its museumlike stasis and Pardoe's animated text about harem life drawn from her experiences inside them. Yet what is significant is that what seems to us a rather prosaic sketch could actually become the inspiration for Pardoe's animated recollections.

Bartlett's sketch of "A Turkish Apartment in the Fanar" (Plate 14) is empty of furniture and devoid of signs of habitation, except for the three figures who drift through, rather than inhabit, this space. The dramatic light highlighting the alcove in the midground has the effect of underscoring the emptiness of this part of the room, as if to announce that this is where the harem would have been. There is a marked contrast between text and image here: Pardoe's text confidently declares her intimacy with Ottoman domestic life, whereas Bartlett's interior seems only to underscore his inability to enter harems in Istanbul. To my surprise, Pardoe does not dismiss the artist's sketch that seems to be so much less animated than her recollections; instead, she uses it as a prompt to her lengthy disquisition about harem life. Lending some specificity to her observations about this interior (and thereby affirming her expertise), she notes that the presence of the hearth in this illustration indicates that the apartment was once inhabited by a Greek prince because this is "an accessory never found in an apartment originally designed by a Turk," and yet, Pardoe reassures her reader, "in every other respect it is precisely the description of [a] room common to every handsome harem."[25] The stiltedness of the sketch is no impediment to Pardoe, who loquaciously peoples the space with the customary bathing practices and prayer rituals within Ottoman harems and characterizes the carefree life of Ottoman women by drawing from her intimate experiences.

Bringing her experiences to bear enables Pardoe to animate the visual image. For her, Bartlett's engraving functions as a catalytic fragment, invested with a capacity to conjure concrete sensory memories of physical encounters. Due to the specificity of personal memory, this was neither random fantasy imagining, nor was it rigidly dictated by the image. In this model, memory differs significantly from the disembodied dreaming which characterized the initial stage, primarily because of the multisensory, sometimes corporeal experience that lent it tangibility. Considering Pardoe's triadic structure in relation to harem representations, "tangible memory" was the privilege of women travelers because they were able to transform their imaginings through the experience of entering harems, whereas male travelers had only the imaginary first stage. Many of the harem diaries invoke this concrete fantasy through elaborate descriptions of traditional costumes, objects, and harem interiors or by reference to multisensory experiences. Through this they conjured a tangible sense of being there for their female readers.

We find evidence of this in descriptions of the scented flower gardens that were part of the harem enclave. In Theresa Grey's diary, for instance, the garden fragrances were part of her experience of entry to the harem. Activating her olfactory senses, the garden evokes the pleasurable scene that she is about to encounter inside:

We passed first through a large courtyard, where five or six gazelles, and some beautiful large wild ducks, were walking about; and then came to a lovely garden full of high trees of roses and jessamine, oranges, etc.; the smell was most delicious as we walked through it. It was an immense garden, and given up entirely to flowers.[26]

Such sensory pleasures bring to mind Lewis's harem garden paintings, such as *In the Bey's Garden*. There the flowers are so palpable, so present in the front of the canvas, crowding into our space, that the viewer can imagine their aroma. Read in relation to the diaries one can well imagine that these harem garden paintings may have evoked a tangible memory experience, akin to that recorded by Grey.

Sartorial display was another important touchstone for tangible memory in these travelogues. The display of clothes was one of the rituals of entertainment in the harem visit that enabled the British visitors to establish a rapport with the women they met there. In recounting this ritual, the diarists wrote lengthy descriptions of fabric textures, colors, and styles. For Annie Harvey, it was not just the stunning beauty of the Ottoman women's clothes that she was shown inside the harem in a paşa's Bosporus palace that delighted her, but also the sensuous appeal of wearing the *yaşmak*:

Upon our expressing a wish to know how the "yashmak," or veil, was arranged, Nadèje immediately had one put on, to show how it ought to be folded and pinned; and as by this time we had become great friends, it was good-naturedly proposed that we should try the effects of yashmak and "feredje," and the most beautiful dresses were brought, in which we were to be arrayed. Further acquaintance with the yashmak increases our admiration for it. The filmy delicacy of the muslin makes it like a vapour, and the exquisite softness of its texture causes it to fall into the most graceful folds. Some of the feredjes, or cloaks, were magnificent garments. One was made of the richest purple satin, with a broad border of embroidered flowers; another of brocade, so thick that it stood alone; another of blue satin worked with seed pearls. The jacket, "enterrees," &c. &c., were brought in piled upon trays and in numbers that seemed countless. A Parisian's wardrobe would be as nothing compared with the multitude and magnificence of the toilettes spread before us.[27]

More than anything else, Harvey emphasizes a proximity through tactile corporeal experience, and here touch becomes a key indicator of a contiguous relationship to the harem. Although she is recounting the familiar scenario of the Westerner transforming her appearance through cultural cross-dressing, she deploys it in an unusual way. She does not present the narrative that the cross-dressing facilitates but instead emphasizes an embodied sensuous fantasy through the touch of abundant luxurious fabrics. This aspect of the diaries is analogous to Lewis's meticulous treatment of fabrics and his tendency to eschew narrative in many of his later harem paintings. The sheen of the cushion which the seated odalisque touches in *Life in the Harem, Cairo*, for example, is so carefully recorded as to invoke a sensation of its softness to the touch. Similarly, with the brocaded dress fabrics in *Indoor Gossip, Cairo*, one can imagine the tactile sensation produced by the uneven texture of the embroidered satins. In Lewis's harem paintings the feminine body is luxuriously clothed rather than nude. This does not preclude erotic fascination, and yet narratives of sexual adventure were displaced in favor of a fantasy prompted by detail. This emphasis constituted a new model of pleasure, which, read in conjunction with the diaries, we might call feminine, although it was not necessarily, nor exclusively, so.

A further instance of corporeal involvement is evident in accounts of smoking the nargile. In harem paintings the pipe was a potent symbol, often suggesting the harem woman's opium-induced state and her sexual abandon; in the diaries it was part of the visiting etiquette in which British women were encouraged to participate. The diarists most often refused the pipe; some of those brave enough to attempt to smoke were embarrassed by their failure. Nonetheless, the offer to smoke signaled the novelty and intimate inclusiveness of their harem visits. For those few who delighted in the experience, their involvement in the ritual provided an opportunity to signal their implication in the harem fantasy. Mary Rogers wrote about the nargile in an evocative passage which shifts from the visual pleasures of the magnificent jeweled water pipe to the delightful olfactory experience of its aroma, which culminates with the experience of inhaling and tasting the delicious flavors of the tobacco:

A very beautiful nargile was prepared especially for me. It was at least half a yard high. The glass vase or bottle was clear as crystal, and well cut. It was filled with water, in which rose-leaves were floating. At the top of the long-necked vase was a well-chased solid silver bowl, holding the burning charcoal and Persian tumbac. The pliable snake-like tube or hose connected with it, was covered with red velvet and bound with gold wire; it was about four yards long. The mouthpiece was of amber, set with rubies and turquoise. The smoke passed through the water, bubbling and disturbing the red-rose leaves, and then travelled up the long tube. Thus the fragrant fumes of the tumbac were cooled and purified before they reached my lips.[28]

Felicia Skene also enjoyed the fragrant smells and taste sensations of the pipe, even though her consent to smoke was prompted by a somewhat reluctant concession to harem etiquette. Skene's text is particularly fascinating because the experience of smoking the nargile plays with the humorous notion of the British traveler momentarily being implicated in the harem fantasy:

I was determined . . . to omit nothing that should give them a high idea of my "savoir vivre," according to their own notions, and began by once more gravely accepting a pipe. At the pasha's, I had managed merely to hold it in my hand, occasionally touching it with my lips, without really using it; but I soon saw that, with some twenty pairs of eyes fixed jealously upon me, I must smoke here—positively and actually smoke—or be considered a violator of all the laws of good breeding. The tobacco was so mild and fragrant, that the penance was not so great as might have been expected; but I could scarcely help laughing at the ludicrous position I was placed in, seated in state on a large square cushion, smoking a long pipe, the other end of which was supported by a kneeling slave, and bowing solemnly to the sultana between almost every whiff.[29]

The daring of this activity, and the fun for Skene, were derived from racial and gender transgressions given the stereotypical association of the pipe with the sexual abandon of the harem women and prevailing attitudes toward smoking among the British bourgeoisie. In her own culture, codes of etiquette and social conduct, including the sartorial rituals of smoking jacket and cap, reinforced that this was a masculine activity, whereas in the harem, Skene was challenged to conform to another set of customs, in which it would be positively rude for her not to smoke. By following the customs of another culture she is allowed to transgress the codes of propriety of her own.

Synaesthetic effects associated with smoking are a familiar trope in harem paintings, as is evident, for example, in Lecomte de Noüy's *l'Esclave blanche* (1888, Plate 15), where the viewer is tantalized by the curl of smoke that wafts from the white slave's lips. One can imagine its pungent aroma, while the food and wine are also set enticingly close, inviting us to imagine their taste and providing a metaphor for the availability of the white slave for the viewer's pleasure. But Skene's diary takes such synaesthetic effects in a different direction, enabling an immersive effect for a British woman who momentarily and playfully identifies herself with the position of the harem woman.

For Hornby, Rogers, and Skene, tangible experience prompted their intensified fantasy of the harem. Tactile sense experience was important in reconfiguring their subject-position inside the harem by emphasizing their proximity and physical presence as their own bodies became implicated in their harem experiences. Recounting such experiences in their published travelogues was an intensely pleasurable way of reliving them and provided a point of identification for their female readership. Such a phenomenological engagement is distinct from the more familiar voyeuristic fantasy of the harem. With voyeurism, the subject who looks is physically separate from the object viewed, whereas touch involves proximity and the potential permeation of boundaries, opening up the potential for shifting points of identification.

Lewis's *The Siesta* most powerfully suggests the idea of a tangible fantasy which closely approximates the corporeal effects that one discovers in women's travelogues; like Skene's text, it creates the potential for an imagined identification with the harem woman to experience her pleasures. In this painting, the sleeping woman's supine pose, the curve of her body and seductive open bodice affirm a reading of this beautiful woman as a passive object for specular consumption, a reading that is reinforced by the symbolism of the poppies that hint to us that her sleep is an opium-induced oblivion. Another reading, however, is also possible. The spectator is also offered a pleasurable tactile experience through the temporary identification with the harem woman. This painting is highly evocative of tactile sensation. The diaphanous green curtain, such a prominent part of the painting, has been cleverly painted to evoke the interaction between sunlight and a gentle breeze. Lewis has cleverly studied the folds of the curtain, and the distorted lattice shadow on the fabric suggests the gentle movement of the breeze in an otherwise motionless scene. The subtlety of this kinesthesia is underscored when it is compared with another harem interior, *A New Light in the Harem* (1884, Plate 17), by Lewis's contemporary Frederick Goodall. In this painting, the unmodulated, even light behind the window does not cast a distorted shadow on the diaphanous curtain. As a consequence, the curtain fabric has the static quality of classical drapery that is also evident in the reclining odalisque's costume. What animates the scene in Goodall's painting is the game between the seated slave and the baby in the foreground, and our attention is also drawn to the body of the odalisque, who is curiously distant from her child's play, drawing back and conveniently displaying herself for the viewer. In *The Siesta*, by contrast, because the woman is positioned beneath the moving curtain, one imagines that the breeze which stirs that fabric also caresses her face. This is an instance of Merleau-Ponty's "inscription of the touching in the visible" because through the visual lexicon of this work, the viewer can imagine the pleasurable sensation of the warm breeze on the cheek of the reclining woman and the warmth of the sun which touches her right arm that gently cushions her face.[30] This tactile experience is achieved through momentary identification with the position of the woman.[31] One can imagine Lewis's wife, Marian, the model for this painting, experiencing such delights, and she provides a compelling point of identification for subsequent female viewers.

Like a number of Lewis's later harem paintings, *The Siesta* creates an effect that prompts an alternative interpretation of harem spectatorship to the more familiar disembodied gaze of the voyeur, instead emphasizing diffuse, multisensory pleasures analogous to those in the contemporaneous women's travel diaries. Both displace a preoccupation with the spectacle of the female body and narratives of sexual adventure for a multisensory fantasy prompted by detail. Although these are not exclusively feminine pleasures, such multisensory effects would have had a gender-differentiated effect for the Victorian audience. For the male spectator such an effect offered compensation for lack of access to harems. The diaries, however, indicate that for female travelers it could function to confirm an experience vividly remembered, with lived experience as the touchstone for this fantasy. The diarists articulated a fantasy premised upon their exclusive access to harems: the insistent "I was there" claim that also established their authority to represent the harem. When we consider Pardoe's triadic structure as a model for spectatorship, we can see that in relation to the harem, this structure privileged European women travelers because they were able to transform their imaginings through the experience of entering harems. In contrast to this tangible memory, for male travelers the visual image instead played a compensatory role because they were prohibited from the harem.

Although these British women clearly entered harems on the understanding that their experiences would live up to, or exceed, their fantasies, there was no guarantee that what they encountered would satisfy these expectations. Ethnography and fantasy were co-implicated only when they encountered harems that conformed to preconceived Western stereotypes. The traditional clothing, Ottoman interiors, and familiar harem accoutrements that prompted such fantasies were being selectively supplanted in many of the harems of the Ottoman elites in Cairo and Istanbul. Although these changes were not universally adopted, ironically they seem to have been most prevalent among those Ottoman women who were likely to invite foreign female visitors because of their own curiosity about Western culture. The potential for disenchantment in these modernized harems of Istanbul is succinctly expressed by an anonymous woman traveler quoted in Murray's guide book of 1854:

> The most remarkable harems are of two kinds—those where European notions and manners have been engrafted on Asiatic splendour, and those which retain with religious scrupulousness all the ancient customs of the Turks. In the former no Arabian Nights reminiscences will be called up, and disappointment will probably be felt when a spurious imitation of our own drawing-rooms will alone be found behind those trelliced screens and lattice-work, which were supposed to conceal a whole world of a novel fashion.[32]

The distinction this writer is making indicates the author's desire for the traditional harem that could conjure up fantasy. The British women were particularly offended by what they interpreted as mimicry of Western fashion, especially the tendency of the harem women to misappropriate elements of bourgeois dress. Fanny Blunt complained when she was visited by a group of harem women dressed in scarlet harem trousers, because the "beauty and grace" of this garment "was lost in the expansion caused by a monstrous cage crinoline introduced within it, which gave the otherwise sylph-like figures of the wearers the appearance of a shapeless balloon supported on large pairs of gentlemen's patent-leather boots."[33] In this instance, there is a conflict between what the British woman observed and what she desired to see. As a consequence, those same harem spaces that prompted women travelers' unique harem fantasies in this period also potentially threatened those cherished fantasies. Yet women travelers could also turn the harem women's curiosity about their culture to their own advantage. The curiosity of Ottoman women about European manners and customs enabled a reconfiguration of the gaze as European women inscribed themselves in the harem through a process of both seeing and being seen.

Chapter Four

 BEING SEEN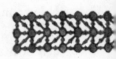

In Lucinda Darby Griffith's diary of 1845 there is a most unusual lithograph entitled "The Interior of the Hharee'm of Mochtah Bey" (Fig. 3). Despite the awkwardness of the amateur artist's work, this sketch conveys the exoticism of the Cairene interior, with its mashrabiyah screens, cooling fountain, and sumptuously cushioned interior peopled by exotically attired Ottoman women. As such, this illustration conforms to the European stereotype of the harem. There is, however, one significant incongruity, namely, the inclusion of Griffith in bonnet and crinoline seated on a chair at the right. All eyes are directed toward this newcomer to the harem whose difference is so marked by her attire. The very fact that it is so jarring to see a respectable Victorian woman inside an Ottoman harem indicates the pervasiveness of a stereotype that asserts the distance and difference between these women. As Lisa Tickner has observed, according to the logic of Victorian domestic ideology, the bourgeois woman was compromised by the eroticism intrinsic to the Orientalist harem fantasy.[1] Yet like so many other Victorian women, Griffith was a ready and willing harem visitor who was enthusiastic to communicate through her diary what she saw inside the harem of Mochtah Bey in Cairo and how she was perceived by the women who lived there.[2]

This lithograph emphasizes the formalities of that visit. Griffith is being approached by a servant bearing coffee; her hosts, Mochtah Bey's wife and her mother, are both rather grandly seated on cushions, each smoking a *çubuk* (pipe), while the more junior members of this household, the Georgian and Circassian slaves (one of whom is the wet nurse holding the lady of the house's adopted child), stand at the back of the room watching the proceedings unfold. Griffith's written account, by contrast, suggests a more robust interaction between the harem women and their British visitor. Griffith was assailed by a string of questions about her personal circumstances and English customs. For their part, the harem women showed her their home and explained their family circumstances, which were undergoing considerable change with the recent death of Mochtah Bey and his widow's imminent remarriage. In the sketch there is a discreet distance between these women and their English visitor, whereas during the visit no such reserved distance was observed. Griffith recounts a minute, rather intimate inspection of her clothing; her rings were scrutinized and her hands examined. From there the harem women proceeded to a rather intrusive inspection of her face:

> All the slaves, one by one, were allowed to peep into my face: one, in particular, a tall, bony-looking Nubian, the most hideous creature I ever saw, who had acted as wet-nurse to my pretty hostess, and was consequently a great favourite, never having seen an European lady before, was so much astonished at me, that after having touched all my clothes, and stared well into my bonnet, she could scarcely be persuaded to move away, and, when she did, seated herself . . . in the corner of the room, fixing her eyes upon me, with a broad grin on her countenance during the whole time I remained.[3]

This lithograph, and even more its accompanying text, strikingly foreground the fact that upon entering the harem, the British traveler was an object of scrutiny as much as she herself was able to look.

FIGURE 3. George Darby Griffith, "The Interior of the Hharee'm of Mochtah Bey," frontispiece to Lucinda Darby Griffith, *A Journey across the Desert, from Ceylon to Marseilles: Comprising Sketches of Aden, the Red Sea, Lower Egypt, Malta, Sicily and Italy*, vol. 1 of 2 vols. (London: Henry Colburn, 1845). 10 × 14.5 cm. Collection of the British Library, London (1426.c.7). By permission of the British Library.

While painters and writers produced voyeuristic images of the harem that emphasized the Western viewer's fantasy of looking without being observed, the experience of being inside the harem as an invited guest precluded such anonymity. Yet many of these travel writers turned such curiosity to their advantage, which resulted in a profound transformation of viewing relations. Such transformation is initially apparent in these diaries, where the British women wrote about their fears upon entering the harem of an unlocatable gaze. By crossing the veiled threshold they were no longer in the protective company of the men with whom they were traveling. As a consequence, some were anxious and feared losing control in this labyrinthine space. An unsettling sense of being watched provoked a profound fear in these women because they had entered to look, and yet, once inside, they found themselves under the gaze of another. This experience inside the harem threatened to destabilize the European traveler rather than confirm her prerogative to look. Lacan's theory of the gaze enables us to explore the implications of this conflation of spectator and spectacle. To allay these initial fears and to establish their interpretive privilege, the women travelers invoked a range of different strategies. One of the ways they asserted their privileged proximity was through a reciprocal process of observing the harem women and being seen by them. Through this transaction the British woman surrendered unequivocal control as the viewing subject. Yet she also negotiated a new relationship to the harem and demonstrated to her readers her privileged proximity to these secluded spaces by occupying a vacillating position between being both the subject who looked and the object that was viewed.

For many women travelers, entry to the harem provoked mixed feelings. While they were excited because this was an experience uniquely available to them, the actual experience of entering the secluded realm of an Ottoman harem was approached with considerable trepidation. Despite what they may have known in advance about Ottoman domestic life, the harem myth, with its associations of feminine enslavement and despotic power, must have played on their minds as they left their male traveling companions behind in order to enter these secluded domains. For many of these travelers, their entry into the harem was initially tinged with fear about surrendering themselves to the unknown by entering a place over which they had no command. Sophia Poole, for example, noted her trepidation when at the harem threshold it was announced from within, "'The lady must enter alone.'" She remarked, "I did not quite like to lose my conductor, but I could not draw back, and could only hope that my excursion through nearly the whole range of that extensive palace might not end in adventure. The door was very slowly and cautiously opened."[4]

The diarists expressed fears about their physical vulnerability and misgivings about the pleasure palace becoming a prison or an inescapable labyrinth.[5] In Britain rumors abounded of European women being invited into harems under false pretenses or being stolen into slavery and thereby sequestered in an Oriental harem. Emmeline Lott, the English governess who resided in the Egyptian khedive's harem in 1863, recounts rumors of a scam whereby young British and French women were entrapped under the false pretenses of an appointment as a governess and were instead sold into the harems of Egyptian princes.[6] This was also a popular subject in nineteenth-century pornographic texts such as *The Lustful Turk* and has been a continuing theme in Orientalist literature.[7] It even forms the motivating theme of the popular Hollywood film *Harem*, released in 1986 and starring Nastassja Kinski and Ben Kingsley, which begins with the central protagonist, a young professional woman living in Manhattan, being drugged and taken to the harem of Prince Selim.[8] The opening scenes are particularly menacing because the eye of the man who is stalking the young American woman is aligned with the look of the camera; the reverse shot, which should establish her pursuer's identity, is withheld, and thus he remains unknown.

For the nineteenth-century diarists, the incipient fears associated with entering the space of the harem, coupled with the potentially dislocating experience of travel to a foreign country, provided the conditions by which the British woman was confronted with an experience of radical alterity.[9] This feared loss of control was often encapsulated in a description of an unlocatable gaze in the harem, indicating that entry to the harem could be a profoundly dislocating experience, one of being out of place.[10] This phenomenon can be explored in reference to the Lacanian gaze. Rather than the harem being a manageable space that confirmed the subject, this experience threatened its destabilization. A key aspect of this experience was the notion of a power vested elsewhere, its precise source unlocatable and its manifestation unclear, which is akin to Lacan's concept of the gaze. The Lacanian double dihedron schema, which diagrams the relation between the eye and the gaze, challenges the perspectival system of vision that is premised upon the illusion of an alignment between the two and is applicable to the harem diary scenario. Lacan's model demonstrates the radical rupture of the eye by the gaze. Constituting the subject via the opaque screen, the gaze is both radically exterior and simultaneously its internal blind spot. As Lacan states:

> What determines me, at the most profound level, in the visible, is the gaze that is outside. It is through the gaze that I enter light and it is from the gaze that I receive its effects. Hence it comes about that the gaze is the instrument through which light is embodied and through which . . . I am *photo-graphed*.[11]

This concept is a profound challenge to the fictive mastery implied by the perspectival model of visuality, which is familiar to us as the implied position of the masculine spectator in harem paintings such as John Frederick Lewis's *The Hhareem* of 1849. In this painting the clear geometry of the orthogonals, marked out by the architecture and furnishings of the interior, are reiterated by the lines of lattice shadow across the foreground, and they corroborate the position of the spectator, ensuring that the entire scene is organized around his vantage point. Within this model of spectatorship the male viewer's look commands the visual field, ensuring an alliance between the perspectival model of vision and Orientalist power relations. Lacan's theory of the gaze shows such mastery to be a fragile illusion. For Lacan the unlocatable gaze is chiasmically related to the subject's look: the inverse of the perspectival triangle, it is both the source of authority and a form of disruption to the subject. The gaze functions to institute split subjectivity because the subject is caught between the illusion of mastery at the apex of the perspectival triangle and the suspicion that there is something beyond that field of vision. The women's harem diaries are significant in this respect because they recount an unsettling sense of being watched, which provoked a profound fear because the woman who had entered to look was herself under the eye of another. As with Lacan's theory of the gaze, what is at stake in this aspect of the diaries is the conflation of spectator and spectacle, rather than their reassuring split into subject and object.

Lacan's theorization of the relation between eye and gaze, however, also stresses the mediatory function of visual representations and texts. The relationship between gaze and subject is mediated by the screen, to which the subject must conform. As Kaja Silverman has argued, the screen can be defined as the "culturally generated image or repertoire of images" which differentially constitute the subject according to race, class, sex, and age.[12] This notion of textual mediation can be used to clarify the relation between fear and pleasure in the harem diaries by explicating how the gaze is tamed or defeated by some process or object, what Lacan has termed the *dompte-regard* function.[13] In Lacan's "Seminar XI," the gaze is not necessarily aligned with the physical eye; therefore, no subject inherently possesses it. This is a significant reconceptualization of the problem of the look from that of his earlier work, which has been mobilized by many feminist film theorists, most notably Laura Mulvey, who asserted that the eye and gaze were uniformly aligned with masculine privilege under Western patriarchal modes of visuality.[14] Severing the gaze from the male subject opens up the possibility of theorizing a feminine version of the look. In other words, the Lacanian gaze as *objet a*, and the strategies for its taming, enable the proposition of a feminine agency. In the context of the diaries, the Lacanian notion of the dompte-regard (which emphasizes the mediatory role of texts in taming the gaze) can be usefully mobilized to explain the function of the diaries in manipulating the gaze in favor of the British woman. Women travel writers invoked a range of different strategies in order to negotiate a relationship to the harem that allayed their initial fears through instances where they were simultaneously subject and object of the look.

The process of writing their diaries was one strategy through which the British travelers managed this crisis, by reenacting it at a safe distance, eliciting a frisson of fear for their readership, and benignly producing unique pleasures associated with the harem for the British woman.[15] Another strategy for asserting the British woman's privilege in the harem was by incorporating the harem woman's look; for the British woman this was a process of acknowledging herself as simultaneously both subject and object. The British women travelers were persistently aware that upon entry into the harem they were not only looking, but were being looked at; in fact, they became curious spectacles. Laura Starr wrote in her account of 1898, "We went to interview them; but my impression is that we were as much interviewed as they were."[16] Similarly in 1860, Lucy Cubley wrote about being subjected to an extremely thorough inspection by the harem women, who were interested in her dress shape, boots, arms, and even a small mole on her neck.[17]

For the female travelers, being an object of curiosity was not limited to their harem visits. British women attracted a good deal of attention, sometimes a crowd of curious onlookers, when they moved around the streets of the Eastern cities that they visited. Anne Elwood experienced this when visiting the Cairo slave markets:

> In the slave-market, a sort of piazza, or square, were several negroes seated on a mat, who seemed very much gratified with some money C—— threw to them. Some Nubian girls then came out, their hair greased and frizzed in the latest and most approved Nubian fashion, but whilst I was considering whether it were right and delicate to

annoy their feelings by gazing at them, the tables were turned completely upon me, for they fell to laughing, and grinning, and quizzing, and pointing at *me*; my English riding-habit seeming far more *outré* to them, than their curiously-plaited hair did to us.[18]

Like Elwood's experience in the slave market, the British women who visited harems were often surprised and sometimes affronted at the uninhibited curiosity of the women there. The active look of the harem women invoked by the diarists is markedly different from the visual stereotype in harem paintings, where the women depicted are most often oblivious to the spectator's gaze. In the rare instances when the odalisque appears to look at the viewer, it is usually a passive, inviting look rather than an interrogative stare, such as is evident in the woman on the left in Delacroix's *Femmes d'Alger dans leur intérieur* (1849, Plate 18).[19] Although she alone looks out toward the viewer, the relative passivity of this woman's gaze and posture creates only the subtlest distinction between this and the self-absorption of the others. They seem to share a level of ennui that is reinforced by the contrast with the relative exertions of the black servant who steps across to the right, sweeping the curtain aside to facilitate a view of the seated odalisques. This servant's position at the harem threshold, stepping into the picture plane, mediates between our space and theirs, underscoring our active looking in contrast to the relative passive receptivity of Delacroix's harem women of Algiers. An extremely different dynamic operates in women's travelogues. By recording the often confronting experience of being investigated by the harem women, these writers register a far more robust engagement between the harem women and their guests. In doing so the British writers reinforced that their entry was sanctioned, in contrast to the illicit "stolen glances" that characterized the male voyeurs' keyhole view.

Often the women travelers were delighted when the traditional relations of Orientalism were inverted—when they became the object of the Eastern woman's inquiry instead of, or as well as, the reverse. The Englishwomen wrote that their harem hosts were particularly curious about their bonnets, gloves, and corsets. Upon entering the harem, the process of removing their outer garments—the voluminous traveling coat and sometimes a veil—created an opportunity for the harem women to examine the elements of their dress that they found particularly strange. Whereas these outer garments conventionally functioned to interiorize notions of respectability for the bourgeois British woman and to exhibit a woman's respectability to others, these instances of reinterpretation in the harem defamiliarized these signifiers—and they became visible in new and novel ways.

In her diary of 1846, Isabella Romer wrote that she was amused by the harem women's interest in her gloves, which, being light tan in color, were taken as her own skin. Taking them off, she passed them around, providing an impromptu game:

> They all leaned forward to examine first my hands and then the gloves, it is evident they imagined I had been St. Bartholomewising myself in their honour. I put the gloves on and off several times to please my entertainers, at which they laughed with all the glee of children; and had I had an interpreter at hand I should certainly have told them that having been afflicted by nature with a white skin, I had adopted that darker covering for my hands to assimilate them to their own more beautiful complexions.[20]

The gloves, signifiers of Romer's middle-class respectability, were defamiliarized by the harem women, and in response Romer transformed this experience into a game. Fascinated by the women's curiosity, she accommodated herself to their misinterpretations and was delighted to be able to entertain her hosts. By transforming her own outer garments into objects in the game Romer was playing with the screen in the Lacanian sense—playing with that culturally inherited set of defining images that both positioned her as the spectacle of bourgeois femininity and placed her at a distance from the masculine harem stereotype as distinct and distanced from the harem women. This form of identity is premised upon the subject's recognition of the split between "being" and "semblance"; it imputes a form of agency to the subject which is not a form of self-presence.[21] In Romer's diary it was precisely by integrating the harem woman's look that the priority of the British woman could be asserted and pleasures produced.

Lady Mary Wortley Montagu may be said to have established the trope of the British woman as harem spectacle when she wrote of her encounter with the harem women in the public baths in Adrianople in April 1717.

This is the famous incident where the women in the bath encouraged Montagu to open her skirts and show them her corsetry. Montagu concluded that the harem women interpreted her stays as a cage in which her husband imprisoned her.[22] It is my contention that Montagu set in place a tradition of a unique relation to the Ottoman harem that was a form of female narcissism.

Like Montagu, many of the nineteenth-century diarists also wrote about the harem women's fascination with the shape of the English woman's body created by her corset. In 1849, Isabella Romer wrote that her corseted body elicited a surprised reaction; she described a scene of her dramatic unveiling in front of the harem women:

> In rising to make my adieu, my shawl fell off, and the three wives, in astonishment at the shape of my dress, so unlike their own, which leaves the waist quite unconfined, and everything else —
>
> To rise and fall as Heaven pleases, spanned me round with their hands, and inquired how I could have got into my gown![23]

In noting their interest in her corset and tight-fitting bodice, Romer established an interpretive comparison between different body shapes. However, in this diary the comparison was noted only as a curious difference, whereas the harem woman's uncorseted figure in visual images conventionally signaled a moralizing or lascivious interest in her sexualized body. What is of primary significance is Romer's surprise and interest in being a spectacle for the harem women. Similarly, in 1881 Alicia Blackwood was flattered by the harem women expressing a preference for her English fashion above their own.[24] By stressing the British woman's fascination with the harem women's interest in her (thereby staging herself as object), these texts supplemented the voyeuristic or ethnographic look with female narcissism — a strategy by which the British woman reaffirmed her priority as subject. However, in these instances neither the harem nor British woman was exclusively an active subject or a passive object.

This type of narcissism is akin to Sigmund Freud's concept of secondary narcissism in being premised upon affirmation from another source. In the travel diaries, however, it was the harem women who fulfilled this function for the British woman. The uniqueness of this narcissism in the nineteenth-century context becomes particularly clear when compared to the more stereotypical role for female narcissism in harem paintings, which conventionally signaled masculine desire. Freud's argument that narcissistic women "have the greatest fascination for men" is exemplified by Lord Frederic Leighton's painting, *The Light of the Harem* (Plate 19), exhibited in 1880.[25] Here a porcelain-skinned odalisque is frozen in a moment of self-absorbed contemplation. Beholding herself in the mirror, she is poised in the act of wrapping her richly brocaded head scarf so as to augment her radiant beauty. This woman's self-absorption is matched by the adoring look of her young attendant, who holds up the mirror, transfixed by her mistress, but this circuit is not closed. The oblique angle of the mistress and her servant to the front of the picture plane opens up a space for the viewer to admire this harem beauty. With her left foot positioned slightly forward and her left arm lifted, she opens out to us as her right hand holds her scarf up as if to enclose us within this circle. What is visible in the frame of the mirror is invisible to the viewer, but her absorption in it and the fascination of her assistant both anticipate the Victorian viewer's fascination for this woman who is alluringly presented for him. This image of female narcissism provokes, and is directed toward, a masculine fantasy of the harem.

The importance of the type of female narcissism evident in the travel diaries, as distinct from its function in Leighton's painting, is that it referred to the female subject's desire without primarily being directed toward masculine fantasy. In the travelogues, the harem woman's gaze functioned as an indirect means of self-reflection for the British travelers. When the harem women presented their opinions about the British woman's body shape and clothing, they offered to her a distorting mirror in which her self-image was reflected back in a fragmented, novel form. The consistency with which these travel writers recorded such investigatory games leads one to suspect that they were not just passively being investigated but were self-consciously exhibiting themselves in order to solicit their hosts' curiosity. What occurs here is a reversal of viewing relations that signals the British woman's visibility inside the harem and inscribes her corporeally and sartorially "in the picture."[26] As distinct from the unlocatable gaze that provoked fear in the British women, the look of the harem women solicited through exhibitionism functions in many of these diaries to confirm the British women's presence. This interaction enabled the British woman to see herself in the harem by being seen.

This trope of the British woman as harem spectacle is a testimony to the inventiveness of these women travelers. Surprised by the curiosity of their harem hosts, they turned such a situation to their advantage. In these texts the British writers incorporated the harem women's look in order to establish their own priority within the harem, and in doing so they experienced self-affirming narcissistic pleasures. These travelogues are particularly significant because they displace the authority of the more familiar masculine voyeuristic model of vision and map the contours of another kind of Orientalist fantasy.

Chapter Five

SARTORIAL ADVENTURES
AND SATIRIC NARRATIVES

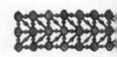

Opening to the title page of Emmeline Lott's travelogue of 1866, the reader is assailed by the image of a woman fully enclosed in the *habarah*, her head entirely obscured by the wrapping of her head scarf, except for her eyes, which fix us with a resolute stare (Fig. 4). This woman's gaze is intensified by her concealment because it underscores her power to see from behind the veil. Swathes of luxuriously embroidered fabric are visible in the gap in the front of her cloak, and one wonders what luxurious Ottoman costume is worn beneath this plain covering that was the conventional street wear for a Cairene woman of the period. Were it not for the caption underneath, signaling that this is Emmeline Lott, the author of these memoirs, one would assume that this was one of the Ottoman women in whose harem Lott resided in 1863. Not so, for this is an Englishwoman, *The Governess in Egypt*, who, as the title page promises, will tell her readers about *Harem Life in Egypt and Constantinople*, disclosing insights gleaned in her role as *Governess to his Highness the Grand Pacha, Ibrahim, Son of his Highness Ismael Pacha, Viceroy of Egypt*. This title page and the accompanying portrait of the veiled Lott succinctly assert her authority based on her privileged insight into these secluded domains. They are a declaration that she, unlike us, went behind the veil.

Lott's unusual portrait falls within the rubric of Orientalist cultural cross-dressing, whereby the authority of the Western traveler was established through a practice of sartorial assimilation which signaled to those back home a deep affinity for and mastery over the cultures among which they traveled. British women travelers in the nineteenth century generally refrained from this practice of cultural cross-dressing. It is more commonly associated with male travelers such as Richard Burton, whose disguise as a Parthan doctor enabled him to venture into the sacred cities of Mecca and Medina in 1853. While it was popular to adopt elements of Ottoman women's luxurious and decorative indoor costumes for masquerade balls back in England, there seemed little strategic advantage for women travelers to do so while abroad.[1] The veil, however, was different. It was a potent symbol of the harem, and adopting this disguise underscored these women's unique access to these secluded domains. Lott's self-presentation in the veil, like the examples I explored in the previous chapter of women travelers turning the harem women's curiosity to their own advantage, is a strategic declaration of her privileged relationship to the Ottoman harem. In this instance, however, it is not by being seen that Lott establishes her privilege, but by adopting a position where she, like the women of the harem themselves, is able to see without being seen.

Women travelers were intrigued by the role of the veil in Islamic cultures because it was such a potent symbol in the West. The veil was an insistent reminder of the differing codes of propriety governing women's appearance in public and private spaces in Islamic cultures. Orientalist street scenes including veiled women inevitably alluded to the private space of the harem in which those veils could be removed and from which all men except the master of the household were excluded. As Malek Alloula and others have characterized it, the veil was like a mobile extension of the harem.[2] Orientalist painters repeatedly deployed the veil to underscore the prohibitions of the harem and heighten the spectator's

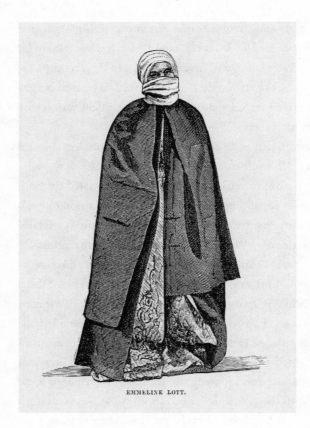

EMMELINE LOTT.

FIGURE 4. Emmeline Lott, frontispiece, *The English Governess in Egypt: Harem Life in Eygpt and Constantinople* (London: R. Bentley, 1866). Photograph by Jenni Carter.

desire to look. This dynamic is evident in Edward Armitage's painting *Souvenir at Scutari* of 1857 (Plate 20), where the processes of veiling and revealing invite the male spectator's look while construing it as transgressive. In this painting, Armitage depicts Ottomans at leisure in the public gardens on the Asian shore of the Bosporus, one of many popular excursion sites in nineteenth-century Istanbul.[3] In the middle distance, a group of Ottoman women are fully veiled because they are in a particularly public part of this park, whereas nearer to us there is a group of women who are situated in a part of the grounds that is secluded enough for them to let down their guard a little. Within the privacy of their secluded circle, the seated woman on the left pulls down her face veil slightly in preparation to eat from the bowl that is being offered to her. Next to her, the woman seated with her back to us has loosened her yellow *ferace* (coat), revealing the pretty patterned fabric of her top beneath, while the young woman on the far right is confident enough to remove her head scarf completely. Her black servant, however, cautiously shields her mistress, ensuring that she remains screened from the view of men, such as the one on the left, who is leading his oxen along the roadway below. This young woman is protected from his view while remaining oblivious to the spectators' gaze. In this way the viewer is admitted into the intimacy of their circle. Such a gesture of veiling and revealing heightens the spectators' curiosity and inscribes their viewing as illicit, a gesture that heightens the transgressions of the woman in the center of this painting, who is so obviously coquetting with the viewer through her translucent veil. With her head coyly tilted, one hand out to the side, the other propping her parasol over her shoulder, her blue ferace almost slips off her right arm. With her coat open at the front, her diaphanous face veil covers but does not hide her curvaceous chest and tiny waist that is cinched with a pink scarf. This flirtatious engagement is all the more enticing because of the relative closure and the lack of self-consciousness of the women around her. The play of prohibition and transgression that is set up across this painting heightens the viewer's fascination with looking at these Ottoman women who have been temporarily released from their harem cloister.

This Western obsession with seeing behind the veil is transmuted into a desire for transgressive touching of the veiled woman in Holman Hunt's *A Street Scene in Cairo. The Lantern Maker's Courtship* (1854, Plate 21). The subject of this unusual painting is a scenario that Holman Hunt claimed to have witnessed, in which the lantern maker is exploring the veiled face of his prospective bride. Tradition required that he not see her face before their wedding ceremony. The lantern maker's compulsion to touch the veiled face of his betrothed heightens the viewer's fascination for this woman.

Male painters repeatedly staged the viewer's transgression of the prohibitions instituted by the veil, ensuring their imagined entry to the harem. Women travelers, by contrast, were more preoccupied with the particular advantages and freedoms that veiling facilitated for the women who wore them. They became intrigued with it as a form of disguise, and some even playfully adopted the veil. Lady Montagu created a precedent for nineteenth-century travel writers when she emphasized the freedoms, pleasures, and intrigues that the harem women experienced when wearing the veil in public. She wrote:

> 'Tis very easy to see they [the women of Constantinople] have more liberty than we have, no woman of what rank soever being permitted to go in the streets without two muslins, one that covers her face all but her eyes and another that hides the whole dress of her head and hangs half-way down her back; and their shapes are wholly concealed by a thing they call a *ferigée*. . . . You may guess how effectually this disguises them . . . there is no distinguishing the great lady from her slave, and 'tis impossible for the most jealous husband to know his wife when he meets her, and no man dare either touch or follow a woman in the street. This perpetual masquerade gives them entire liberty of following their inclinations without danger of discovery.[4]

Similarly, over a century later Anne Elwood wrote about the advantages that the anonymity of the veil facilitated when she met the women, whom she had previously visited in their harem, completely veiled in the street. In a striking reversal, she emphasizes their intrusive curiosity about the men in her company:

> They were so carefully veiled, that I had some difficulty . . . [recognizing] my friends of the Haram again, but they affectionately seized my hand, and caressingly invited me to return with them to their apartments. All the gentlemen were with me, and I cannot help thinking that the Arab ladies prolonged their interview purposely, in order to have a better view of the Fringee Cowasjees, my companions.[5]

Other travelers noted that harem women used their veils to taunt men. Emilia Hornby, for instance, recounted the story of a Turkish piano teacher who was harassed by his pupils. Necessarily veiled in the presence of their instructor, these young women delighted in terrifying him by exposing their faces at any clandestine opportunity. His response was terror rather than delight, because he so feared the consequences of being caught. Hornby evidently enjoyed recounting this story because it is such a surprising reversal of expectations, wherein the harem women have playfully turned the tables on this hapless man.[6] In each of these tales the woman who is veiled occupies a privileged position.

Inside the harem, the mashrabiyah which screened the apertures within the women's quarters operated like the veil to enable the women who looked through them to see what was going on outside without themselves being visible. British women travelers were fascinated with these screens because of this vantage point. Anne Elwood was surprised to discover that the realm of the harem that she assumed was cut off from the public spaces of the city instead offered her a particularly unique view of them: "Zaccara [took] my hand with a very caressing air, invited me to accompany her, and she showed me all over the house. . . . I saw a number of small rooms, with loopholes and windows in every direction, where they could see without being seen." Elwood noted that from this vantage point she could see the bazaar, the mosque where important public ceremonies took place, and even the ship on which she herself had arrived. Transferred to the space of the harem, this form of veiled looking served to emphasize the British women's proximity to the harem and created an inversion of the viewing relations that positioned the harem as the object of the gaze. Looking through these harem lattices, Elwood was surprised and delighted to see her husband "walking in the streets, with one of his servants holding an umbrella over his head."[7] She amused her harem hosts by pointing him out to them and was startled by how strangely out of place he appeared in his English clothes and hat in this context.

The viewer is reminded of a similar vantage point onto the streets of Cairo through the mashrabiyah screen that occupies a prominent position in John Frederick Lewis's *Street Scene in Cairo Near the Bab-el-Luk* of 1855 (Plate 22). The human interest of this painting takes place at street level, at a public thoroughfare where we see Bedouins with their camels, merchants in the doorways of their shops, and numerous other citizens of Cairo engaged in social interactions. Above the central archway, a few pigeons flutter and dart upward toward the mashrabiyah screens, animating this part of the painting and reminding us of the life within this secluded domestic space that the screens mark out. The openings of three small windows built into this mashrabiyah screen are apertures enabling an unimpeded view of the life in the street below. Clearly, the small openings on either side have been deliberately pushed open. Can we see a shadowy presence behind the small central opening in this mashrabiyah? We cannot be certain, but the possibility is there.

A similar potential is present in Lewis's *The Midday Meal, Cairo* of 1875 (Plate 23). This time the mashrabiyah is prominent within a domestic courtyard. The activity within this scene takes place in the second-floor covered balcony, the space in the traditional Cairene home reserved for men's dining in summer months. In the foreground a group of men seated on cushions around a low table enjoy their repast of ripe peaches, melons, figs, and grapes. One of the cushions has been pulled back, signaling that someone has recently departed from their circle, opening up a space taken temporarily by a bold pigeon; this anecdote animates the picturesque scene. The painting is bisected by the stone columns and balustrades. Below them we see men conversing and tending to their horses in the open courtyard that is the entry and exit point for this home. Only men are visible in these semipublic domestic spaces, and yet above the open courtyard the intricate lattice screen marks out the harem, reminding the viewer that the women therein may be watching. The emergence of servants carrying dishes of food from the doorway at the end of the balcony to the left also reminds us of the life within the hidden recesses of this domestic realm, where this meal has been prepared. With his intimate knowledge of the structure of the traditional Ottoman home in Cairo, as a result of living in one, Lewis would have been well aware that the mashrabiyah screens, which often faced onto the courtyards as well as the interior rooms of the selamlik or men's quarters of the home, provided something like a panoptic view of the goings-on within these public spaces of the house. The compositional prominence of the mashrabiyah screens in both of these paintings marks out this other vantage point, emphasizing the view from, rather than of, the harem. This was a vantage point that women travelers were introduced to by their harem hosts.

These examples suggest that, as a result of their experiences inside Ottoman harems, many nineteenth-century women travelers became aware of the complex relationship between processes of looking, veiling practices, and the gendering of space within Islamic cultures. Furthermore, they were able to turn such insights to their own advantage. In doing so, they provide us with quite a different attitude to the more familiar Western interpretations of the veil as a provocation to masculine desire or as a symbol of women's oppression.[8] Not that these women's more nuanced understanding necessarily led to a more empathic relationship with the women they met inside these harems; indeed, it emerges instead as a way of establishing their own privilege within Orientalist discourse.

Emmeline Lott is exemplary in this respect. Her account was based on her experiences as a governess to Ibrahim, the son of Ismail Paşa and his second wife. In 1861 Lott negotiated a contract with Ismail's agents to undertake this post in Cairo. By imaging herself in the veil in the frontispiece to the travelogue that she subsequently published in 1866, she declared her authority to write about the harem for her readers.[9] Embracing the more familiar gesture of the Western desire to unveil the harem, she articulates her task in writing her memoirs of harem life as "uplifting that impenetrable veil, to accomplish [that] which had hitherto baffled all the exertions of . . . travellers." Indeed, she explicitly sees her achievement as analogous to that of Richard Burton's pilgrimage to Mecca. There is no suggestion of Lott's identification with the khedive's harem women in her text. She remains resolutely, often indignantly English as the eyewitness to the elite harems in Cairo. In fact, the solitary pleasures of writing her diary become a refuge from and compensation for the rigors of life as a harem governess.[10] Lott explicitly maintains her status as an English lady. Her difference is demonstrated in her text through the rituals associated with her dress and is further underscored by the harem women's curiosity about her clothing.

Given the way she frames her own project in writing about the harem, it is surprising that we should also find within its pages a story that explicitly satirizes men such as Burton who had transgressed Islamic sanctions. She does so by recounting a story about two European men whose desire to enter the harem was exploited by the sultan's eunuchs. The eunuchs staged an elaborate harem charade, disguising themselves as odalisques to profit from the travelers' gullibility. This story inverts and displaces the privilege of the European male traveler by enlisting cross-dressing for the purposes of parody. This tale of Ottoman cross-dressing emerges as a means of establishing the English writer's authority over her countrymen in relation to the Ottoman harem, but it is also an Ottoman response to Western cultural intrusion. As a result, the practice of sartorial metamorphosis emerges not only as a powerful strategy by which European women staked a privileged status in relation to the Ottoman harem, but as one that was strategically engaged by Ottomans in the nineteenth century.

The English harem governess recounts this tale told to her by the itinerant storyteller, the Mohaddetyn Yusef, inside the harem of Ismail Paşa, the viceroy of Egypt. The story is at least third-hand. Yusef had been told it at the Ottoman court by Hassan Ali, the sultan's grand eunuch, who himself heard it from the story's central protagonist, Kaleb, one of the eunuchs in his charge.[11] Although the story bears some remarkable similarities to Adolphus Slade's travelogue, its truth is difficult to ascertain.[12] I am, however, less interested in confirming the veracity of this account than in exploring it as a form of mythic recasting of the power relations in the harem fantasy through the strategy of cross-dressing.

The tale involved two travelers, the Duke of Oporto and Sir Robert Cotton, whose desire to enter the Ottoman sultan's harem was exploited by the harem eunuchs. These two "renowned adventurers" approached Kaleb, requesting access to the harem women in his charge in exchange for a vast sum of money. Capitalizing on the gullibility of the English travelers, Kaleb colluded with the young eunuchs in his charge and Barbab Ali to stage an elaborate harem charade. The eunuchs masqueraded as odalisques to "entertain" their Western guests. Those who masterminded this theater conceived it not only as a way of profiting from the fools, but also as retaliation against Western men who had transgressed Islamic religious sanctions through cultural cross-dressing. Their retributive sentiment was focused in particular on Richard Burton.[13]

We are told that Kaleb thought long and hard about how to carry out his deception and thereby "clutch the *paras* [money] of the *Frenks* [Europeans], and then laugh in their beards, without committing any real indiscretion, or bringing himself within the pale of the Moslem law." To negotiate these considerations, a clear distinction is made between the site of the real harem of the reigning sultan and the sham. The chosen venue was the rococo kiosk "in the now wild and neglected grounds of the old Seraglio," well away from the sultan's harem it purported to represent. To further secure the distance between the sultan's harem and its simulation, the reader is informed that at the time the deception was enacted the sultan and his harem were at his summer kiosk in Ismid.[14]

The exuberant descriptions of the rehearsals of this performance evince the anticipatory pleasures for the participants, and our narrators (Yusuf and Lott) also enjoy rehearsing it for their respective audiences. Costume and makeup were crucial, so they procured "all the most magnificent dresses, shawls, and kerchiefs, all the most costly jewels, all the prettiest embroidered slippers, all the gaudiest artificial flowers, and all the choicest cosmetics." Much time and effort were exerted transforming the young, mostly dark-skinned eunuchs into fair and feminine odalisques. The alchemy of this transformation is described as follows:

> [They used] marvellous cosmetics, by the power of which it was possible to make black, white. Eastern washes and dyes, however, are truly wonderful. . . . The countenances of the dusky eunuchs became as white as alabaster; the tint of roses rested on their cheeks, their lips were ruby bright, and their hands and arms were suffused with a pink shade as beautiful as that which adorns the loveliest damsels of the icy-cold West.[15]

The rituals that conformed to the Western stereotype of the harem were enacted: smoking the çubuk, indulging in confectionery, and drinking coffee served in exquisite jeweled *fincans* (cups) and filigree *zarfs* (holders). The crowning glory of the charade was the presentation of bouquets of flowers by Sorab Ali and Yaneh to the two "duped Englishmen." This action received great praise as evidence of the thespian skills of the "improvised ladies," and the reader is assured that there is no trace of the caricature in the elegant performance of these eunuchs. Here we find a satiric counterpart to the finesse that Burton had stressed in his narrative of cultural cross-dressing, which functioned as evidence of his cultural immersion. This is just one example of the way Burton's prose, as Edward Said has argued, "radiates a sense of assertion and domination over all the complexities of Oriental life."[16] In contrast to the assertion of Orientalist mastery in Burton's account of his disguise, Lott's reader is encouraged to enjoy the lampoon at the expense of the Western men. Throughout the rehearsals, the hilarity of the charade and its enjoyment by the participants are repeatedly emphasized. The room was decorated to perfection and the spectacle described as follows:

> The whole scene was, indeed, one to charm the eyes and stimulate the senses of the infatuated intruders on the sacred precincts. No enchanted palace of the Peris could have more enraptured the gazers. . . . The masquerading houris had been so admirably got up, that the delusion was complete.[17]

An important feature of this room was a trapdoor, on which the two Englishmen were seated, giving Kaleb the power to facilitate their speedy departure. At the commencement of the rendezvous the duke and Sir Robert apprehended the scene before them "in a paroxysm of delight." Refreshments were duly served and the planned entertainments proceeded without difficulties until the two "simulated stars of loveliness" presented their posies of flowers.

> As fate would have it, as they were in the very act of making their last salutation, their headdresses became unfastened, fell, and displayed to view two shaven skulls. The two Giaours [foreigners] who were on the point of taking the proffered flowers with outstretched hands, rose from their *kursis* in evident amazement and bewilderment at this unexpected sight.

At this point the trapdoor was activated and the foreigners were disposed down its chute into the Bosporus, while the performers dissolved into fits of laughter, shouting, "*Mashallah! Mashallah! Janum! Janum!* We now can laugh in the beards of the *Franks*." The men who retrieved the Englishmen from the Bosporus reported their response:

> Gradually they called to mind, that, a short time before, they had been feasting their eyes on a bevy of lovely Peris. Then the strange incident of the falling head-dresses crossed their minds, and began to excite grave doubts as to the nature of the spectacle for which they had paid so dearly. Whether they really comprehended thoroughly how far the Moslems had laughed in their beards must ever remain a mystery. At the time, they felt only too thankful at having escaped a fearful death, or a disaster almost more fearful still.[18]

The tale is concluded with an account of their speedy departure from port.

Like so many harem paintings, in Lott's story, the harem is staged for the British men, organized around their vantage point; it is enticingly close and excites all their sensory pleasures. This tale also, however, places the reader behind the scenes to witness the delight of those who are performing this harem theater. The British gentlemen have the illusion of control, but it is the eunuch Kaleb who orchestrates the show, terminating it at whim. The gap between performer and performance is crucial. In Kaleb's tale, great pleasure is derived from the effectiveness of deceiving the unsuspecting Englishmen and the conspiratorial knowledge of a distinction between the eunuchs and their cross-gender masquerade. The revelation of this discrepancy at the moment of narrative climax, when the eunuchs' wigs slip to reveal their bald heads, ensures an appropriately humiliating revenge for the two Englishmen. It ensures that they are ejected from their fantasy of mastery and disposed down the notorious chute into the Bosporus, thus suffering the fate of the degraded odalisque. All the while the Ottoman harem is dissimulated from this sham performance. What remains is doubt and uncertainty for these men; the prospect of having escaped death or castration is their only consolation. In contrast to the confirmation of identity offered by the harem paintings, this story profoundly disturbs the positioning of the European male subject.

Lott effectively deploys this tale to imply authority over her countrymen in relation to the Ottoman harem. In effect, she also unveils masculine fantasy by making untenable the claim to combine ethnography and fantasy in men's harem representations. This dislocation is achieved by surfacing the impossibility of an eyewitness experience. Through this storytelling we find a surprising point of identification for the author, that is, with the position of the Mohaddetyn, the eunuch.[19] Elsewhere in her extensive writings, her attitude to the senior harem eunuchs vacillates between disgust and awe at their power as intermediaries between the harem women in their charge and the world beyond the harem's confines. Their power is in counterpoint to her own constrained position within a domain in which she is the newcomer. Yet the process of publishing her diary gave her a position of power as an intermediary, analogous to that of the eunuch, who is intimate with the community of women inside the harem while not being of their number.

There are, however, other subject-positions to consider, other storytellers. Lott's tale of the harem masquerade is Kaleb's and Yusef's tale as well. Before its retelling in Lott's travelogue published in London, the story circulated within the elite harems of Istanbul and Cairo. In this context it is placed within a tradition of storytelling in Ottoman culture, where tales circulated and were reiterated and modified. In this context its retelling enhances the symbolic triumph of the Ottomans over the arrogant and intrusive Western men. Perhaps this Ottoman storyteller was capitalizing on Lott's interest to ensure that this satire of Western cultural intrusion upon Islamic mores would reach a British audience. The reader is made aware of the Ottoman's sophisticated knowledge of Western culture, including recent travel literature and social trends. The tale not only satirizes the ignorance of the British gentlemen through the sham harem performance, but also dissimulates the tale from the real harem, enabling a number of stereotypes of Ottoman culture to be revised. The story presents an alternative image of the sultan as a learned man and worthy inheritor of a noble lineage. Before entering the sham harem, the two travelers are shown the sultan's huge library, a genealogical tree of the sultans' portraits, and the magnificent throne room.[20] For the reader, the Ottoman palace emerges as a place of learning and religious reverence, "in full keeping with that exalted sanctity investing the great Deity of Islam."[21]

In Lott's tale, identity is articulated on both sides of the cultural divide through a parodic response to the Western masculine fantasy of the seraglio. Lott's travelogue establishes her authority as intermediary for her British readers, proposing a mutable subject-position for the Englishwoman that has numerous points of identification. She capriciously stages her power and privilege over both harem women and Western men. At one point, the eunuch's power as the go-between is transmuted into the authoritative position of the travel writer as storyteller and ethnographer. At another point, Lott adopts the veil of the Ottoman women in an assertion of her privileged insider status, but this text also restages the eunuch's symbolic revenge, shared with his harem audience.

This tale brings into focus the role of the British woman traveler and the eunuchs who mediated the harem for a Western audience and the way they distinguished between the erotic fantasies of male Orientalists and the respectable domesticity of the Ottoman harem. There is a striking contrast between the eunuchs as witty satirists in Lott's travelogue and the more familiar trope of the eunuch as brutish harem guard who is so prominent in the foreground of Jean-Léon Gérôme's painting, *Le Harem dans le kiosque* (c. 1875–80, Plate 24). Yet what is similar is the role they play in physically intervening between the harem and the Western viewer. Gérôme's formidable guard, who is spectacularly armed, leans on the sandstone parapet in the foreground of the painting, alert and ready to act should anyone transgress and come too close to the harem women in his charge. His presence is all the more forbidding because of the deep shadow in which he is cast. As an intermediary between the viewer and the veiled women in this kiosk on the Bosporus, he reminds us of the interdictions of the harem for male travelers such as Gérôme when they visited Ottoman culture. Yet that interdiction is transgressed in Gérôme's numerous bath scenes and harem paintings, where the viewer is admitted as a voyeur into the imagined private rituals of harem life. In relation to the logic of the voyeur's harem fantasy, Gérôme's *Le Harem dans le kiosque* functions as a prelude to those scenes by inciting the desire to see, to un-veil. The implication in this scenario is that the guard will ultimately be powerless to prevent the intrusion of this desiring male gaze.

Yet another possibility suggests itself. The oblique angle of the parapet in the foreground of this painting that connects with the walkway to the kiosk establishes a zigzag that leads the eye back to the harem women, and yet at each stage a blockage prevents the viewer from accessing them. The guard at the front is the most immediate impediment, but his interdiction is reinforced by the two eunuchs on the walkway behind. The veils of the women themselves impede our view, but above all it is their indifference to us that walls the viewer out. Drawing closer to examine these women in the kiosk, we see that some are self-absorbed, others are happily chatting or attending to their children, while the three veiled women on the right are completely turned away from us. They strain outward, waving their white kerchiefs in the direction of the *kayık* that glides across the Bospo-rus some distance away. Although this kayık is only sketchily suggested, its grandeur is indicated by its size and the sheltered central section, the part of the boat in which wealthy Ottoman harem women traveled. Gérôme has highlighted the exchange between this floating harem and the Otto-man women on shore by placing the waving women at the very center of the painting and by ensuring that the kayık is the only vessel in what was, and still is, an extremely busy waterway. As a consequence, this paint-ing emphasizes the social exchange between women not only within one harem but also between harems, and we are reminded of a social world in which the viewer is not a participant.

Gérôme's painting establishes a clear distinction between the shadowy foreground, which we occupy along with the eunuch who peers warily out at us, and the space behind, occupied by the fashionable harem women in their brightly colored feraces. These cloaking garments playfully harmonize with the opalescent purples and blues of the summery sky and the waterway, and their white yaşmaks rhyme with the brilliant white of the houses on the nearby shoreline.[22] This contrast between the space occupied by the viewer and the realm beyond serves to further reinforce the distinction between the prohibited looking of the Western male and the cheerful sociability of these harem women of Istanbul. In all these ways the visual language of this painting bespeaks the unassailable distance between Gérôme and the Ottoman harem.

In Gérôme's painting the women's veils do not promise revelation for the intrusive viewer; instead, the work foregrounds the harem women's capacity to look while retaining their anonymity (unless they should choose to identify themselves, as do those who gesture toward the passing kayık). The privilege of their vantage point is underscored by the very prominence of their viewing platform, which displays Istanbul's beautiful waterway to such spectacular advantage. One wonders how women travelers who had visited harems might have approached Gérôme's painting, which grafts the complexities of veiled looking onto the picturesque view without conferring to the Western viewer all the authority to look. Given their privilege to cross the veiled threshold of the harem, to adopt the vantage point of seeing the public spaces of the city from within that secluded domain, and to playfully adopt the veil as a disguise, one assumes that these women travelers would have recognized the constraints imposed upon the outsider by Ottoman veiling conventions as articulated in Gérôme's painting, but they would not necessarily have seen them as applicable to themselves. Their texts disclose the scopic privilege they could accrue by playing with the veil as a means of seeing without being seen. Nonetheless, their capacity to see inside the harem was constrained by the levels of access that they were permitted by an extremely hierarchical Ottoman social institution. The women of the harem themselves could interdict their viewing, even if they had little control over the texts that they published back in Europe. Nowhere is this power more evident than in the portrait sittings where elite Ottoman women commissioned European women artists to represent them.

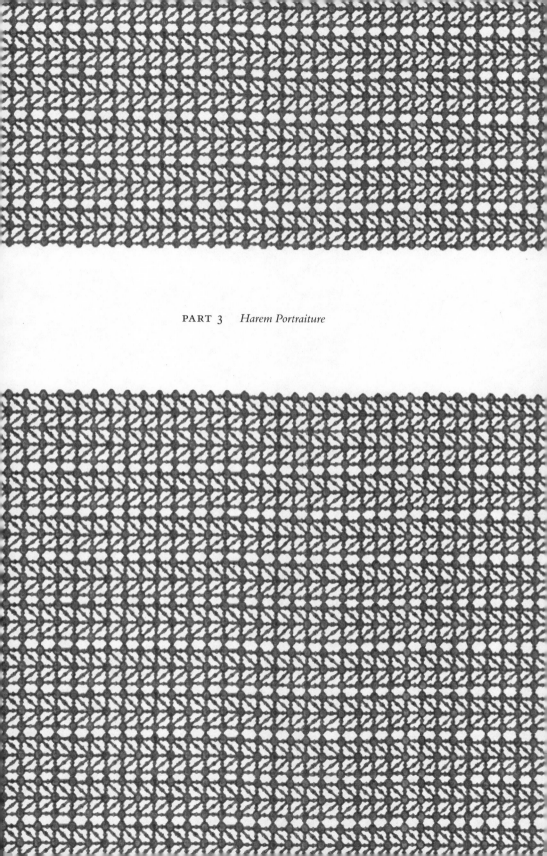

PART 3   *Harem Portraiture*

Chapter Six

 ## THE POLITICS OF PORTRAITURE
BEHIND THE VEIL

On a warm summer's day in Istanbul in the late
1850s, Princess Fatma Sultan, the esteemed
daughter of Sultan Abdülmecit, invited the British
artist Mary Adelaide Walker to meet with her in the
sumptuous rooms of her summer palace in Baltalimanı
on the Bosporus. The imperial princess kept the artist
waiting for a considerable length of time in one of the
many sitting rooms of her magnificent palace. With
the assistance of her interpreter, the artist wiled away
the time chatting with some of the many palace min-
ions and enjoying the view of the Bosporus afforded by
this palace that was (and still is) so prominent on the
beautiful waterway (Fig. 5). The inconvenience of this
delay was obviated by the British artist's enchantment
at being inside one of the largest palace harems in the
Ottoman capital, where so few foreign women were
ever invited. Eventually Walker was summoned into
Fatma Sultan's sumptuous upper rooms. Seated in a

FIGURE 5. Sergis Balyan, *Mustafa Reşit Paşa Yalı*, Baltalimanı. Photograph by Mary Roberts.

large armchair beside one of the lattice windows, dressed in a magnificent green silk *entari* (dress), the princess addressed her visitor courteously and conducted their exchange with a level of formality befitting an imperial princess interviewing someone whom she was about to engage to render a service. By the time Walker departed from the palace an agreement had been reached that she would embark upon a most unusual commission: a portrait of this imperial princess.[1]

Fatma Sultan was a young woman in her late teenage years at the time of her first meeting with the British artist, and Walker was impressed by her intelligence and forthright manner. Fatma was educated and knowledgeable about contemporary politics within the Ottoman Empire and abroad. She was an avid reader of newspapers. During her father's lifetime she reputedly exercised considerable influence over the affairs of state. She presided over a harem where more than a hundred women lived. Although smaller in scale than the sultan's harem at the Dolmabahçe Palace, it was organized according to a similar hierarchical structure, except in this household Fatma Sultan was more powerful than her husband, Ali Galib Paşa, because of her good relations with her father. Their short-lived marriage, an alliance of political convenience arranged by the sultan himself, was, by all accounts, a loveless union in which the princess exerted considerable authority.[2] The Baltalımanı Palace was a wedding gift to the princess from the sultan, and Ali Galib Paşa's quarters, the selamlik, were considerably smaller than Fatma's harem. Fatma Sultan made many of the key decisions within this household, including the choice to commission her portrait. She arranged for one of the harem rooms to be vacated to accommodate the artist's temporary studio for the duration of the sittings, which lasted almost six months. Thus began an association between the expatriate artist and her Ottoman patron that was to last for many years.

For her part, Walker was delighted to receive this portrait commission. This was in the early years of her thirty-year residence in the Ottoman capital and it was a great opportunity for her. Although it was not her first harem portrait commission, having this very senior member of the Ottoman royal dynasty as her patron was beneficial to her career, leading to further commissions from Ottoman elites. As an amateur artist and expatriate who was unknown in professional artistic circles in Britain and completely absent from subsequent art historical accounts of British Orientalism, it was important for her to have such recognition among the Ottoman elites in her chosen city of residence. By 1867, the regard for her within Ottoman palace circles was such that she was invited to paint Sultan Abdülaziz's portrait for the Ottoman pavilion at the Exposition Universelle in Paris.[3] This was a prestigious commission because the exhibition was attended by Abdülaziz himself and was the first visit of an Ottoman sultan to Europe.

Almost thirty years after her first meeting with Fatma Sultan, when Walker came to publish her memoirs, she recorded in great detail the negotiations that occurred between herself and the princess during her harem portrait sittings, preserving the anonymity of her patron by invoking the pseudonym Zëineb.[4] The artist knew that this and her other harem portrait commissions would be fascinating to her British readers. Representations of the secluded women of the harem commissioned by the women themselves would no doubt have come as a surprise to an audience who knew about the Ottoman custom of feminine seclusion and Islamic prohibitions against figural representation.

This chapter addresses a body of work that is absent.[5] Mary Walker's harem portraits either no longer exist or are as yet untraced in private collections. It seems appropriate that these portraits should elude our gaze, given that they were never intended to be seen by audiences outside of the Ottoman harems in which they were created. In lieu of the portraits, we have the artist's forthright account that discloses something that the finished paintings could not: the negotiations that occurred during their production. Walker's travelogue is a unique document because for the first time it enables us to address the role of elite Ottoman women in the patronage of Western painting. What comes to light are the tastes and cultural values of her Ottoman sitters and their forthright interventions in fashioning their portraits. These alternative harem representations, which remained within the secluded realm of the Ottoman family, bring to light a very different visual economy from the familiar Western paintings of the seraglio.

Fatma Sultan spent a long time deliberating over the dress and pose for her portrait. Much to Walker's chagrin, she changed her mind several times, requiring the painter to rework the large figure study until she was satisfied with the results. The princess finally settled on a very formal portrait. Her outfit in white French silk was a hybrid of European and traditional Ottoman dress, a style which was the height of fashion among women of the Ottoman elites of the period. The bodice was structured in the style of a European evening gown and was accompanied by the traditional Ottoman entari and şalvar (baggy trousers). She adorned her costume with many of her most costly jewels. Fatma Sultan's jewelry signaled the prestige of her status as the sultan's daughter. Amid the array of magnificent diamond-encrusted jewels that were a reminder of her own immense personal wealth, she wore a medal that had been conferred by the sultan along with a miniature portrait of him; both were a measure of the Ottoman leader's esteem for his daughter and signifiers of her loyalty to him. By far the most magnificent of her adornments was her girdle, a wedding gift from the sultan. The clasp of this enormous belt, covered in diamonds, had formerly been used to fasten his cloak of ceremony.[6] Such a magnificent present was in line with the extravagant official ceremony held to celebrate her marriage in 1854. Custom dictated that the sultan and his male heirs did not marry; consequently the marriage of the sultan's daughter was one of the great occasions of state, an opportunity for celebrating the prestige of the sultanate and thereby to reflect the magnificence of the empire.[7] The prominence of this significant gift in her portrait signals the recent change in Fatma Sultan's social position resulting from her marriage.

With all its indicators of rank and status, Fatma Sultan's portrait is akin to the official state portraits of Sultan Abdülmecit such as that painted by Rubens Manasie a few years earlier in 1857 (Plate 25). In this full-length portrait, the sultan, a man of dignified bearing, fixes us with a direct look. With his right foot slightly forward and his ceremonial sword held so as to display its magnificent jeweled handle to full advantage, his upright posture bespeaks a slightly stiff formality. Instead of the traditional turban and caftan, for this portrait, as with so many of his others, the sultan chose the ceremonial uniform of trousers, dress coat, cape, and fez. This was a relatively new dress uniform adapted from European costume that was introduced during the reign of his father, Sultan Mahmut II. As in his daughter's portrait, Abdülmecit's rank and standing are signaled by the choice of jeweled adornments for his costume. The sultan's traditional aigrette on his fez and the two decorations worn on his neck and chest as well as the ceremonial sword signify his position. The image that his costume projects of a modernizing sultan is reinforced by the choice of setting, both the neoclassical balustrade (in all likelihood this is the balcony of the old Çirağan Palace built during his father's reign) and behind that the Mecidiye mosque, commissioned by the sultan himself.[8] The prominence of the dome and minaret of this mosque, a stylistic fusion of imported European styles and traditional Islamic structure, projects an image of this sultan as the religious leader, the caliph, and the modernizing reformer of his empire.

Both Fatma Sultan's and her father's portraits are part of a long-standing tradition of portraiture within the Ottoman court. In these privileged realms, the Islamic injunction against figural representation, so strictly applied in the public realm, was not rigorously observed.[9] By the nineteenth century the tradition of commissioning portraits of the sultans from visiting European artists was several centuries old. Sultan Mehmet II initiated this practice when he invited Gentile Bellini to paint his portrait when resident in Istanbul between 1479 and 1481.[10] The practice proliferated in the nineteenth century, when the Ottoman rulers had their portraits painted by local Ottoman painters as well as numerous visiting Orientalist artists, such as David Wilkie, Charles Fuller, Stanislaw Chlebowski, and Pierre Désiré Guillemet.

While the portraits of Fatma Sultan and her father project the regal prestige of the sitter and indicate an openness to Western cultural influence, they differ in one crucial respect: the conditions under which they were displayed. Manasie's portrait of the sultan was sent to Stockholm as a gift to the Swedish queen, imbuing it with a very public, diplomatic function, whereas under no circumstances was Fatma Sultan's portrait to be seen outside the harem in which it was commissioned. In this period, portraits of the reigning sultans were to have an increasingly important role in the public sphere, in both their diplomatic and honorific functions.[11] In the early nineteenth century, Sultan Selim III was the first to participate in the European practice of gifting portraits as a symbol of his authority. In this diplomatic role, the sultans' portraits, such as this one by Manasie, were presented to foreign courts as a gesture of goodwill between nations. During the 1830s, the early years of the period of Westernizing reform, Sultan Mahmut II further broke with convention by publicly exhibiting his portrait in official buildings within the empire, thus capitalizing on the honorific function of portraiture to signal the authority and reaffirm the dynastic legitimacy of the Ottoman ruler to the empire's citizens.[12] Many of these portraits hung in official buildings, introducing the iconography of the balcony portrait into the repertoire of Ottoman imperial portraiture.[13] This iconographic convention, again an adaptation from European portraiture, is reiterated in Abdülmecit's portrait by Manasie.

Walker's portrait commissions emerged as part of this increasingly public role for the sultans' visual representation, and yet her paintings of imperial and elite Ottoman women were distinctly different: unlike the portraits of men, they had no public function beyond elite female and family networks. Portraits of Ottoman women from this period are rare, and those that existed were discretely housed in the Dolmabahçe, Yıldız, and other Ottoman palaces or within the homes of the Ottoman elites in Istanbul. These paintings were for restricted viewing within the harem, being selectively shown only to family members and other elite Ottoman women. Those few portraits that remain have been on public display only since the demise of the sultanate in the twentieth century, when their palaces were transformed into museums.

PLATE 1.   John Frederick Lewis, *The Hhareem*, 1849. Watercolor and bodycolor, 88.6 × 133 cm. Private Collection, Osaka.

PLATE 2.   John Frederick Lewis, *Portrait of Mehemet Ali Pasha*, 1844. Watercolor, 37.5 × 33 in. V&A Images/
Victoria and Albert Museum.

PLATE 3.   David Wilkie, *Mehemet Ali*, 1841. Oil on board, 61 × 50.8 cm. Tate Gallery. © Tate, London, 2005.

PLATE 4. *John Frederick Lewis in Oriental Dress*. Albumen print by an unidentified photographer, 14 × 10.8 cm. Collection of Cyril Fry. Photograph: BMS.

PLATE 5.   John Frederick Lewis, *Hhareem Life, Constantinople*, 1857. Watercolor and bodycolor, 62.3 × 47.6 cm. Laing Art Gallery (Tyne and Wear Museums).

PLATE 6.   John Frederick Lewis, *Life in the Harem, Cairo*, 1858. Watercolor, 60.7 × 47.7 cm. V&A Images/
Victoria and Albert Museum.

PLATE 7.   John Frederick Lewis, *An Intercepted Correspondence, Cairo*, 1869. Oil on panel, 51.4 × 89 cm. Whereabouts unknown. Photograph by Jenni Carter.

PLATE 8. John Frederick Lewis, *In the Bey's Garden*, 1865. Oil on panel, 106.6 × 68.6 cm. © Harris Museum and Art Gallery, Preston, Lancashire. Photograph courtesy of The Bridgeman Art Library.

PLATE 9.   John Frederick Lewis, *Lilium Auratum*, 1871. Oil on canvas, 137.2 × 87.7 cm. Birmingham Museums and Art Gallery.

PLATE 10. John Frederick Lewis, *Indoor Gossip, Cairo*, 1873. Oil on panel, 30.5 × 20.3 cm. The Whitworth Art Gallery, The University of Manchester.

PLATE 11.   John Frederick Lewis, *The Reception*, 1873. Oil on panel, 63.5 × 76.2 cm. Paul Mellon Collection. © Yale Center for British Art, Paul Mellon Collection. Photograph courtesy of The Bridgeman Art Library.

PLATE 12. Henriette Browne, *Une Visite (Intérieur de Harem, Constantinople, 1860)*, 1861. Oil on canvas, 86 × 114 cm. Private Collection. © Christie's Images, Ltd.

PLATE 13.   John Frederick Lewis, *Mendurah in My House in Cairo*. V&A Images/Victoria and Albert Museum.

PLATE 14. William Bartlett, "A Turkish Apartment in the Fanar," in Julia Pardoe, *The Beauties of the Bosphorus: Illustrated in a Series of Views of Constantinople and its Environs from original drawings by W. H. Bartlett* (London: George Virtue, 1838), plate opposite page 125. Photograph courtesy of Rare Books and Special Collections Library, University of Sydney.

PLATE 15.   Jean Jules Antoine Lecomte de Noüy, *l'Esclave blanche*, 1888. Oil on canvas, 146 × 118 cm. Musée des Beaux-Arts, Nantes. Photograph courtesy of RMN/© Gérard Blot.

PLATE 16.   John Frederick Lewis, *The Siesta*, 1876. Oil on panel, 88.6 × 111.1 cm. Tate Gallery. © Tate, London, 2005.

PLATE 17.   Frederick Goodall, *A New Light in the Harem*, R.A. 1884. Oil on canvas, 122 × 81 cm. © National
Museums Liverpool (Walker Art Gallery).

PLATE 18.   Eugène Delacroix, *Femmes d'Alger dans leur intérieur*, 1849. Oil on canvas, 89 × 112 cm. Musée Fabre, Montpellier. Photograph courtesy of RMN/© Philippe Bernard.

PLATE 19.   Frederic Leighton, *The Light of the Harem*, exhibited R.A. 1880. Oil on canvas, 122 × 81 cm. Private Collection. Photograph courtesy of Julian Hartnoll.

PLATE 20.   Edward Armitage, *Souvenir at Scutari*, 1857. Oil on canvas, 183 × 122 cm. Laing Art Gallery (Tyne and Wear Museums).

PLATE 21.   William Holman Hunt, *A Street Scene in Cairo. The Lantern Maker's Courtship*, 1854. Oil on panel, 29.4 × 18.8 cm. © Manchester Art Gallery.

PLATE 22.   John Frederick Lewis, *Street Scene in Cairo Near the Bab-el-Luk*, 1855. Oil on panel, 56 × 44.7 cm. Private Collection, England. Photograph courtesy of The Fine Art Society, London.

PLATE 23.   John Frederick Lewis, *The Midday Meal, Cairo*, 1875. Oil on canvas, 87.6 × 115.6 cm. Private Collection. © Christie's Images, Ltd.

PLATE 24. Jean-Léon Gérôme, *Le Harem dans le kiosque*, c. 1875–80. Oil on canvas, 76.2 × 115 cm. Najd Collection. Photograph courtesy of Mathaf Gallery, London.

PLATE 29.   P. Sébah, *Princess Nazlı Hanım*, n.d. Carte de visite. Private Collection, Denmark.

PLATE 30.   Elisabeth Jerichau-Baumann, *The Princess Nazili Hanum*, 1875. Oil on canvas, 132 × 158 cm. Private Collection. Photograph by Jenni Carter.

PLATE 31.   Photographer unknown, *Princess Nazlı Hanım*, n.d. Courtesy of the Staffordshire Record Office, ref: D593/P/24/7/15.

PLATE 32.   Elisabeth Jerichau-Baumann, *An Egyptian Pottery Seller Near Gizeh*, 1876–78. Oil on canvas, 92 × 114 cm. Private Collection. Photograph by Jenni Carter.

Underscoring the uniqueness of her endeavor, Walker noted that for elite Ottoman women of the harem, visiting a painter's studio would be "contrary to the rules of orthodox Mussulman society."[14] As a consequence, she was instructed to execute her paintings entirely within the harem, including the varnishing and framing. These were precautionary measures to ensure that the portraits were not seen outside the harems in which they were commissioned. Even within the harem the visibility of these portraits was regulated to ensure that only sanctioned individuals viewed them. For instance, Walker's large portrait of Fatma Sultan was hung in a sitting room of her summer palace in Baltalimanı veiled by a curtain of white silk. Explaining the rationale for this as an extension of Islamic veiling practices, Walker wrote, "As the features of women are veiled, so also, according to orthodox custom, must a female portrait be hidden from the gaze even of the men who perform the rough work of the house."[15]

In the same period, portrait photography was introduced into elite Ottoman harems, and it too was rigorously controlled. The English governess Ellen Chennells wrote about the difficult process of producing photographs of Princess Zeyneb, daughter of Khedive Ismail in Cairo. The challenge was to control this infinitely reproducible medium in order to maintain the conventions of feminine seclusion. Initially a female photographer was commissioned, but, because she was unskilled, the results were unsatisfactory. A decision was made to engage a male photographer, but, as Chennells states, it could not be a European, who "might sell her likeness, or send it to Europe for sale, [which] would violate all ideas of oriental propriety. . . . So it was decided that an Arab photographer . . . should be introduced, and he being an Egyptian subject, could not possibly either sell or show the portraits to other persons."[16] The photography session took place in the harem gardens because this man could not be admitted into the harem itself. Through the lens of these British women's diaries we gain insight into the ways elite Ottoman women in Istanbul and Cairo adopted and adapted visual technologies imported from Europe within their local cultural context.

It was not only the restricted visibility of Walker's portraits that reflected Islamic cultural influences, but also the conventions of pictorial representation derived from the miniature tradition. When Walker painted a portrait of a woman whom she refers to only as "a handsome Circassian" she employed the conventions of chiaroscuro to convey the solidity of the figure and was affronted when her sitter insisted that such tonal contrasts be reduced. Walker was forced to concede to what she determined was an unreasonable demand: "The softening tones were gradually reduced to imbecile weakness; in short, I yielded, spoilt my work, and contented my model."[17] This was not an isolated incident.[18] Her sitters' tastes were influenced by the linear two-dimensionality of the Ottoman miniature tradition and in turn governed her own painting process.

What expresses most strikingly the agency of the Ottoman women in Walker's account are the disagreements she records over costume and pose. The sartorial disputes bring to the fore a mismatch between the Ottoman women who were embracing change and Walker's continuing investment in a fantasy of the exotic harem. Walker preferred to paint Fatma Sultan in her traditional Ottoman dress, whereas Fatma was interested in recording her modernity by being painted in the latest Parisian fashion. Walker wrote, "Such was the appearance of my imperial model: the ease, the grace, the dazzling magnificence of the East lost and dimmed by a painful striving after Western fashions." When Walker objected to Fatma's requirements, the response was an ultimatum that the "portrait must be done according to her wishes, or —not at all." Walker conceded, with the recognition that she "could not risk the 'not at all'" and consoled herself about this compromise to her work with the thought that "the picture when finished would rarely, if ever, be seen by persons competent to judge the merits of a painting."[19] Despite her condescension one gets a clear sense from her account that it is her wealthy sitters' preferences that determine the outcome. In the production of these harem paintings, it is the harem woman who exercises control, in contrast to the pervasive European stereotype of the passive odalisque.

Walker's Western preconceptions about the exotic harem were repeatedly foiled by her various sitters' tastes for Western dress. When commissioned to paint the portrait of Eminé Hanım, the only wife of an officer of high rank in the Turkish army, Walker noted that Eminé was up half the night manufacturing a "Frank" dress copied from a French fashion magazine which she describes as "a handsome crimson velvet bodice trimmed with white lace, shapely and stiff with whalebone. Ah! how much more fascinating would be the easy flowing cotton 'guidjélik,' in which she usually indulges, than this ungraceful buckram attire! But it is 'à la frança.' I sigh and submit."[20]

Similarly, when she revisited Fatma Sultan at her winter palace in the center of Istanbul some years after painting her portrait, Walker was affronted by a request to update this work by repainting the dress so that it reflected new trends from a fashion book recently received from Paris.[21] The artist was offended at her painting being subjected to the whims of fashion. While harnessing the skills of the British painter, Fatma refused to conform to her preconceptions of the exotic harem. The Western Orientalist's desire for the fixity of the subject under the exoticizing gaze was frustrated as her sitter embraced changes in fashion in order to be up to date and modern. Indeed, upon this return visit, Walker was disconcerted that the entirety of Fatma Sultan's harem had been transformed. Instead of what she had earlier interpreted as a living embodiment of the *Thousand and One Nights* fantasy, she was confronted with the women dressed in "skirts hideously distended over crinoline" and a harem interior decorated with Brussels carpeting, chests of drawers, and vases of French artificial flowers.[22] In what seemed to her an ironic encapsulation of these changes, Walker noted that one of these modernized harem women had taken an interest in literature and insisted upon reading to her from *The Thousand and One Nights*.

The period in which these portraits were executed was one of considerable transition in upper-class women's fashion. Walker's sitters exemplify the increasing interest in adopting European fashions for indoor wear among elite Ottoman women. This trend was to become even more popular after the visit of Empress Eugénie to Istanbul in 1869. French fashion magazines circulated within the elite harems and the latest Western fashions were ordered directly from Paris or commissioned from dressmakers in Pera, the European quarter.[23] In this transitional period, elements of Western dress were selectively adopted and combined with elements of traditional dress. For Walker, these hybrid fashions could only be disruptive to her preconceived ideas of the exotic harem and were distinctly unpictorial, whereas in the hands of the Ottoman painter Osman Hamdi Bey these fashion innovations are envisioned as elegant and picturesque.

Osman Hamdi Bey represents the spectrum of fashions worn by Ottoman women in the public spaces of Istanbul in his painting *Feraceli Kadınlar* (1887, Plate 26). In front of the wall of a mosque courtyard, an elegant group of fashionable Ottoman women stroll past a group of street vendors. The woman in the center of this painting wears the *çarşaf* (skirt and cape) favored by traditionalists, whereas all the others are clothed in the fashionable transparent *yaşmak* (veil) and *ferace* (coat) and sport modish parasols in matching or complementary colors.[24] The contours of their feraces indicate that most of them are wearing European bustle dresses underneath. In some cases, the tucks and pleats of their dresses are visible because the matching feraces are open at the front. Such a move to adapt the ferace to simulate the European-style coat reflects a very recent fashion trend in Istanbul.[25] Across this painting Ottoman women are wearing a mix of traditional Ottoman and imported European fashions, and there is an ease and grace about them in their colorful hybrid costumes. These are clearly women of considerable social position and their relative prosperity is measurable in the contrast between their luxurious outfits and the clothes of the humble street vendors to the left. In this painting, it is the women's clothing that locates the scene unequivocally in the cosmopolitan capital of the Ottoman Empire, and these fashions are celebrated by Hamdi Bey as a picturesque symbol of cultural change. European Orientalists rarely painted such Ottoman fashions, preferring instead stereotypical street scenes in which any trace of Western presence or influence is absent.[26]

Hamdi Bey's painting depicts the sociability of Ottoman women and their easy congress in the public sphere, a point he also emphasizes in the text for the Ottoman costume book of 1873, published on the occasion of the International Exhibition in Vienna. Within the conventional costume book format he took the opportunity to refute a number of erroneous Western assumptions about his culture. A distinctly different worldview is promulgated in this costume book from the more familiar exoticist surveys of Eastern dress. Not only does the project as a whole, which celebrates the cultural diversity of the Ottoman Empire, express Ottomanist sentiments, but its text takes to task erroneous European assumptions about Ottoman culture, thereby using the very public forum of the International Exhibition to present a revisionary view. The text accompanying the photograph of a Turkish schoolboy, for instance, refutes a European prejudice about poor educational standards with an assertion about Turkey's impressive achievements in literacy. Similarly, the section on women's costume in Istanbul provides the occasion to refute Western assumptions about the cloistering of Ottoman women within the private sphere:

In the West much is said about the iniquitous system of seclusion that systematically confines Turkish women to their homes. Nothing could be further from the truth. All it takes to convince oneself of the truth is to spend a few hours on the bridge between the main part of the city of Constantinople, commonly known as Stamboul or Islambol (the city of faith), and its European quarter, contained within Galata and Pera, home to the foreign ambassadors and a floating population. In fact, standing on this bridge, for every 100 women that crossed, you would see that no less than 80 or 90 of the women passing from one shore to the other would be dressed in a yachmak and feradje, compared with 10 to 20 wearing dresses and hats. Furthermore, it is notable that whereas the European ladies, and those who present themselves as such, are generally accompanied by a husband, brother or some other friend or relative who takes them under their protection by offering their arm, the Turkish ladies come and go with utter freedom, completely alone.[27]

Hamdi Bey's street scene, where veiled women congregate unchaperoned in the public sphere, can also be seen to articulate this sentiment about the relative liberty of women. The viewer is close enough to witness their amiable social interaction but maintains a polite distance. Some of these women look out of the painting, but they do not engage us. The differing levels of veiled concealment bespeak differing codes of social propriety within a respectable elite group. This is distinct from the erotic charge that is so familiar in Western Orientalist street scenes such as Edward Armitage's *Souvenir at Scutari*, where varied levels of unveiling are staged across the painting, thus heightening the sexual promise of the central woman, who boldly flirts with the viewer. Hamdi Bey's revision of an Orientalist stereotype articulated within the language of the picturesque is characteristic of the Ottoman painter's subtle and persistent revisionary realist representations of his culture.[28]

Instead of eroticism, Hamdi Bey provides a vision of social harmony and, in doing so, clearly signals his commitment to modernization. Women's costume in this painting stands as a symbol of the profound changes sweeping through elite culture in the Ottoman capital and forms a marked contrast to the traditional costume of the lower social strata of Ottoman society represented on the left in this work. Yet Hamdi Bey accommodates these differences within a harmonious scene where color unites by creating an ordered rhythm within difference. Like the patterned ironwork inserts in the stone wall behind, differences across the front of this painting are ordered by a structured repetition. The green of the vendors' umbrella harmonizes with the woman's costume of the same color, and they are part of a repeated sequence from right to left of black, red, and green. Such harmonies and repetitions are played out against the shared sandy creams and whites of the dusty ground and carved stone wall. In these ways color creates an ordered rhythm across the scene, and Hamdi Bey subtly deploys a picturesque aesthetic to present a harmonious social order. Clearly because of his commitment to modernization, Osman Hamdi Bey can accommodate contemporary Ottoman fashions within this picturesque vision of his own culture.

In this respect Hamdi Bey's painting forms a contrast to Walker's account, where she finds the hybrid Ottoman fashions disjunctive and distinctly unpictorial. This sensibility is evident in her description of her first portrait of the young Circassian. Walker evokes the appearance of her sitter to give us a vivid word-picture:

> I can recall every line and curve of that first portrait; I see the oval face, the soft, dark, almond-shaped eyes, the delicate aquiline nose and well-formed mouth of the handsome, imperious-looking Eastern lady. Her dark hair was cut nearly short, according to the fashion then in favour, and a small gold cap, bordered with a wreath in gold filigree work, was placed on one side, a massive tassel drooping on the shoulder; her dress, a deep rose-coloured satin embroidered in gold. Out of such materials a graceful picture ought surely to have been produced, but nothing could persuade my model to fall into an easy attitude. The gold-embroidered costume, which, comprising a trailing skirt and very ample "schalwars," hung in exquisite folds as she sat with one foot raised upon the sofa, had been fashioned in the upper part into an imitation of a "Frank" bodice. This was (at that time) a daring innovation on the usual style of Turkish dress; the hanum was consequently very proud of her stiff, unbending waist, and insisted on being represented as sitting perfectly upright, and with her elbows squared to the utmost, in order that each side of that objectionable waist might be clearly defined. The drooping hand, exquisitely formed by nature, which would have slightly modified the outline, was twisted into a constrained front

view for the purpose of exhibiting the full splendours of a monstrous diamond ring disfiguring the little finger.[29]

What is so intriguing about this passage is the way Walker's desire for the exotic odalisque of Western fantasy is both elicited and frustrated by the appearance of her sitter. The beauty of the Circassian woman's face, her "almond-shaped eyes," "delicate aquiline nose," and "well-formed mouth," conform to Walker's expectations, as does the luxuriousness of the gold-embroidered fabric of her costume and the exquisite draping of her skirt and pants, which are shown to great effect by the casual pose of one foot raised upon the sofa. And yet there is a profound disjunction between the upper and lower parts of this woman's costume that is jarring to the artist's sensibilities because the upper body has been disciplined by the European bodice into an upright posture associated with contemporary Western bourgeois dress. As a consequence, the angularity of her pose contradicts the vision of the languid odalisque that Walker upholds as her model for representing the Eastern woman. This bodily transformation through hybrid fashion is confronting for Mary Walker because it dispels the picturesque fantasy image of the Ottoman woman as odalisque and brings the disruptive temporality of Western fashion into collision with Western notions of atemporal Eastern costume.

Many Ottomans in the same period also expressed a distinct preference for traditional clothing, although they did so for vastly different reasons from Walker's Orientalist exoticism. Adherence to tradition was advocated by some to ensure the maintenance of Ottoman society in the face of the pressures exerted by the influx of European culture and Ottoman reform policies. Changes to Islamic women's fashion occurred in the context of official policies of modernization in nineteenth-century Ottoman society. From 1839 onward, successive sultans adopted a series of economic and sociopolitical reforms based on Western models. The Ottoman leaders faced the challenge of European economic superiority and sought to strategically adopt Western technological advances while preserving Islamic religious and cultural values. Within Ottoman culture, opinions were divided about the cultural impact of such policies.[30] Many of the Ottoman elites embraced Western cultural influences and did not view these selectively adopted elements as incompatible with the integrity of a changing Ottoman identity. This view was resisted by traditionalists.

Changes to clothing were entangled in these debates. In 1829, Sultan Mahmut II introduced legislation for men's dress, making the fez, Western jacket, and trousers mandatory for civilian men, thus extending the clothing reforms introduced into the Ottoman military the previous year.[31] Changes in women's dress were less strictly decreed; Western dress was avidly adopted by some elite women, although such changes were not uniformly embraced. Traditionalists and those who could not afford these fashions continued to wear and to advocate Islamic styles of dress. As Nora Şeni's research has brought to light, these debates between modernists and traditionalists are evident in satirical cartoons printed in the Ottoman press of the period.[32] Women's outdoor dress became a particular focus for debate around questions of moral probity and the social implications of modernization. In one cartoon we see a woman in a çarşaf facing a woman in a dress showing European influence (Fig. 6). They challenge one another about cultural pride in a period of change. The woman in the çarşaf voices the traditional view: "Girl, what sort of clothes are those? Have you no shame?" The woman in European–influenced attire admonishes her with the words "In this century of progress, you are the one who should be ashamed!" Other cartoons satirize Western codes of bourgeois dress propriety (an amusing reversal of the Western Orientalist's gaze). In one, the caption points out the apparent absurdities inherent in a European dress code that implied the shamefulness of revealing one's ankles while a more décolleté fashion prevailed in evening dress. These cartoons can be construed as evidence that a lively dialogue about women's dress codes was taking place in Istanbul in this period, and the changing codes were playing a role in defining a new self-image for the Ottoman Empire. Seen in conjunction with Walker's portrait dialogue and Hamdi Bey's painting, we can see how these debates were brought to bear in issues surrounding artistic production at the time.

The harem women Walker painted were clearly aligned with the modernists. Fatma Sultan's husband, Ali Galib Bey, was the son of Mustafa Reşit Paşa, one of the founders of the Tanzimat reform movement and a former ambassador to Paris and London, but she herself was also keenly interested in European culture.[33] She had grown up in a palace environment that was open to and engaged with European culture. At her father's insistence, Fatma and her brother Murat received a modern education, including tu-

FIGURE 6. Cartoon caption: "Girl, what sort of clothes are those? Have you no shame?" "In this century of progress, you are the one who should be ashamed!" Reproduced in Nora Şeni, "Fashion and Women's Clothing in the Satirical Press of Istanbul at the End of the Nineteenth Century," in Şiren Tekeli, ed., *Women in Turkish Society: A Reader* (London: Zed Books, 1995), 37. Photograph by Jenni Carter.

ition in French.[34] Riza Paşa, another of Walker's patrons, was appointed to various senior military and administrative positions throughout Sultan Abdülmecit's reign. During the Crimean War he was commander in chief of the army, a factor that is likely to have been particularly significant because this was a period of close contact between the Turkish army and their allies, the French and British diplomats and military corps, which ushered in an increased openness to Western cultural influences.

From Walker's account we get the sense that her harem portraits had a certain novelty value for some of her sitters, while, for others, their function in the private realm of the Ottoman family was honorific and commemorative. For instance, her portraits of Eminé Hanım and her two children were executed at the request of Eminé in order that her husband, a senior officer in the Turkish army based at Schumla, "should possess some visible reminders of the family ties left behind in Stamboul."[35] Despite her patrons' willingness to engage with Western portraiture, in their conditions of production and reception they are distinctly different. Walker's portraits, governed by a strategy of concealment that ensured they were visible only to her patrons' familial and female cultural networks, could not be further from the ubiquitous staged paintings and photographs of harem women produced for the Western tourist market, which, as Malek Alloula has noted, merely serviced the West's collective phantasm of the harem.[36]

It becomes apparent in the disputes between Walker and her harem patrons that the artist attempted, unsuccessfully, to impose conventions of the Western harem genre instead of the conventions of honorific portraiture. As a consequence, painting these portraits seems to have been a particularly unrewarding task for Walker because she had little control over pose, costume, mode of pictorial representation, and circulation of the finished work. So why did she persist? It seems that she persevered with these portraits because they provided her with the opportunity to access harems for extended periods of time, thus enabling her to claim a privileged position as an ethnographic participant-observer of harem life through her published diary, while also allowing her to undertake sketches of the women for her own harem paintings.

Walker noted that residing in the harem for several months during the production of her portraits gave her access to the daily life of Fatma Sultan's immense palace. She was able to enter the classrooms, "where the most effective, because unconscious, 'subjects' [for an artist] were to be found." She also facilitated Henriette Browne's entry into these music and dancing classes and noted, "We sat for some time watching the groups so fascinating to an artist, and soon afterwards the art exhibitions of Paris and London were graced by the works of her delicate brush, chiefly inspired by the thoughtful studies made in this seraï on the Bosphorus." Walker underscored the uniqueness of their access to this palace harem, which was unlike the experience of most other Western female visitors, who were constrained by the formality of a ceremonial visit. In the harem of Fatma Sultan Walker compiled her own sketchbook of preliminary drawings of the harem women in their traditional dress. She admired their chaste beauty and the poetic way their traditional costume made the women appear to glide across the room, their long trains "sweep[ing] majestically behind them." She also praised the effect created by the dress of the sultana's attendants, who were required to tuck up this train which sometimes "took the classical outline and folds of old Greek statuary."[37]

This too became a source of conflict between Walker and her harem host. The artist was summoned to surrender her sketch book, which was returned with

> one of the most cherished sketches of the "classical draperies" scored all over with pencil marks and nearly torn away, and a polite message from the Sultana, who begs that I will not do any more pictures of her women in their morning dresses, "with their robes all twisted about them; it is ugly, and the Franks will think her harem very ill-dressed." I may, if I please, draw them in their best clothes—meaning plenty of starch and crinoline. The proposal does not tempt me to further efforts.[38]

Again, it is the conflicting determinations of what is suitably pictorial that is at issue. For Fatma Sultan, it was formal attire rather than informal clothing in daily use that was appropriate for memorializing in the visual medium, whereas for Walker, traditional costume worn on informal occasions accorded more closely with her preferences (informed by preexisting stereotypes of the harem) than these hybrid fashions.

Inside Fatma Sultan's harem the princess's will prevailed. Walker, however, proceeded to represent the type of harem attire which she preferred in her illustrations for Emilia Hornby's diary of 1863.[39] There are striking differences between Walker's anonymous harem illustrations for Hornby's diary and her descriptions of her harem portraits. Instead of the formal pose adopted in a portrait sitting, Plate 27 is a genre scene depicting the ritual of daily ablutions as a senior harem woman is attended by two junior members of the harem. One attendant kneels to pour water from the *tombak* (ewer) into the bowl balanced precariously on her knee while the other distractedly waits to dry her mistress's hands with a cloth. In another illustration for the same book (Plate 28), the feminine rituals of dressing for congress outdoors are carefully described. A young girl holds up a mirror so that the senior harem woman who is being clad can supervise the fastening of her yaşmak by one of her attendants. Another holds open the ferace in preparation for its placement over the indoor garments. Cultural difference is foregrounded through this display of veiling, and the unique privilege of the female traveler to witness this preparatory scene is underscored. In these illustrations there are no signs of the popular hybrid fashions, but only what Walker determined as more picturesque, that is, traditional dress. In short, in these images there is a reassertion of the Western female artist's point of view and with it the Western fantasy of the harem—albeit one that is a restrained fantasy of bourgeois British women, rather than the eroticized masculine tradition.

In her diary Walker is at times condescending, censorious, and disapproving and at other times respectful of her patrons. But ultimately, in the production of their portraits she is a servant to their wishes. Through the frank recollection of these disputes, her diary discloses their divergent priorities. The will of her sitters is clearly registered and their active intervention in fashioning their own representations dispels a notion of the silence or passivity of Ottoman women. The results of this collaboration, the "fashionable" portraits, tell us much about the specific place and time of their production in the cosmopolitan capital of the Ottoman Empire in the Tanzimat reform period. The issue of sartorial modernization which manifests itself in Walker's portraits resolutely resists the Western stereotype of a frozen traditional culture. Neither is it simply a Francophile's imitation. More complex processes of cultural transmission are at work in these portraits. Parisian fashions are adopted in a context in which Islamic cultural conventions are observed through the restricted visibility of the finished paintings. These harem paintings circulated within elite Ottoman familial and female networks. The seclusion of these representations within the private sphere of Ottoman women of powerful social standing indicates a refusal to participate in the prevailing economy of Orientalist visual culture with its insatiable desire to uncover the secret of the harem. By ensuring that their portraits remained within a restricted environment, they were soliciting the skills of the British painter yet detaching their self-representations from a Western economy of visibility—a powerful gesture for a harem woman to undertake.

Walker's account not only enables a reassessment of gender politics in the relations between Ottoman and British cultures, but also provides insights into the changing and contested identity of Ottoman women within their own culture in the late nineteenth century. This narrative of harem portraiture enables us to examine the role of visual culture in the shifting contours of Ottoman women's identity. The representations they created contested Walker's preconceptions of the harem genre as well as refuting traditionalists within their own culture. In doing so, these women were forcefully intervening in local debates about Ottoman women's identity in a period of enormous social change.

Chapter Seven

ORIENTAL DREAMS

In 1869, the Egyptian princess Nazlı Hanım, a member of one of the best-known of the Ottoman families in Istanbul, received word from Madame d'Ehrenhoff, the wife of the Swedish ambassador, that the Danish painter Elisabeth Jerichau-Baumann had recently arrived in the city and wished to meet with her. Princess Nazlı was curious to meet this artist, who had a considerable reputation as a royal painter to the Danish court and who had been recommended by her friend Princess Alexandra, the Princess of Wales.[1] An invitation was promptly issued, and on November 18 the first of a series of meetings transpired between the painter and the princess in Nazlı's apartments inside her father's harem in Istanbul. Three portraits of the Egyptian princess resulted from these visits.

Although there are obvious similarities between this encounter and Fatma Sultan's commission from Mary Walker a decade prior, there are also significant differences in circumstance and outcome. In Fatma Sultan's patronal relationship with Walker, Fatma effectively governed the outcomes of her sittings, sequestering her portrait within the harem, controlling its aesthetic parameters, and thereby dashing Walker's harem fantasies. For Princess Nazlı and Elisabeth Jerichau-Baumann, however, the encounter was a mutually beneficial and yet ambivalent cross-cultural exchange. For the young Princess Nazlı the interaction that prompted her interest in painting was a catalyst for the later development of her own career as a painter, whereas for Jerichau-Baumann the encounter with Nazlı inspired her exotic harem fantasy. In contrast to Fatma Sultan's portrait that was kept inside the harem in which it was painted, only one of Nazlı's three portraits remained in her possession. The other two were taken back to London and, unbeknown to the Ottoman princess, exhibited at the New Bond Street Gallery. In this chapter I examine the distinctive itinerary of these portraits and their shifting meanings as they moved across cultural boundaries, from the seclusion of the harem in Istanbul to public display in London. In doing so, I address both the Ottoman and European contexts for their reception.

At the time of Elisabeth Jerichau-Baumann's first visit, Princess Nazlı was only fifteen years old, not yet married, and still living in her father's household. She was part of the powerful Muhammad Ali dynasty; her father, Mustafa Fazil Paşa, was the disaffected brother of Khedive Ismail.[2] During his exile in Istanbul, Mustafa Fazil Paşa was one of the most prominent members of the social elite, colloquially known as "the Egyptians," who were renowned for their openness to Western culture. Like a number of the men of the ruling Egyptian family, he had studied in France as a young man and was a vocal proponent of modernization. In the Tanzimat period of restructuring the Ottoman state, Nazlı's father was a prominent advocate of Western-style political reform as a solution to the Ottoman Empire's beleaguered situation. His commitment to reform was most famously evident in his letter addressed to Sultan Abdülaziz, published in 1867 while he was resident in Paris, in which he advocated a constitutional government for the empire.[3] Mustafa Fazil Paşa's political liberalism was matched by his social liberalism. The paşa's home became well-known for its political and literary meetings as well as its garden parties and masked balls, to which were invited the aristocratic elites and foreign dignitaries and their wives.[4] He also entertained the Prince and Princess of Wales during their visit in 1869 and was friends with Napoleon III.

His liberal views extended to his family life. Two of his daughters, Nazlı and Azize, had European governesses, spoke French and English fluently, and were given an unusual degree of liberty for Muslim women of their era.[5] Although not the most powerful woman in her father's harem, Nazlı had her own domain within his immense home. The entire second story was designated for her use. She regularly received prominent foreign and local women within her apartments. She had fifteen female slaves at her command and regularly entertained in her vast suite of rooms, which included a reception room, a great library, and a concert hall elegantly appointed in a European style with crystal chandeliers, carved chairs, a barrel organ, and an Erhard piano. When Jerichau-Baumann first visited Nazlı she was already becoming known for her soirées, at which the highest levels of elite local and foreign women were entertained. In 1869, Princess Nazlı had entertained Princess Alexandra and Empress Eugénie of France and held a concert in honor of the visit of an Italian countess.

For her part, Jerichau-Baumann was completely enchanted by the young Egyptian princess and immediately resolved to paint her portrait. The artist visited quite a number of harems in Cairo and Istanbul, but of all the women she encountered it was Princess Nazlı who held a special significance. In her letter to her husband and children on November 19, 1869, she wrote, "Yesterday I . . . fell in love with a beautiful Turkish princess Mustafa Fazil Pashah's daughter, niece of the viceking of Egypt."[6]

Before she embarked upon her trip, the East must have seemed particularly promising for Jerichau-Baumann because she had a letter of introduction from her patron, Princess Alexandra, which she anticipated would facilitate portrait commissions inside the wealthiest Ottoman harems.[7] While excited at this prospect, what she encountered often presented a profound challenge to the exotic stereotype of these forbidden realms. She witnessed harems in a process of profound social change resulting from Western influence, and many of the women she met made demands upon her that were contrary to her expectations. In this respect her encounter with Princess Nazlı was exceptional because it both sustained her fantasy of the harem and in the process significantly reconfigured the character of it. Nazlı became the cynosure for Jerichau-Baumann's fantasy of Oriental beauty. Describing her first encounter in her travelogue, she wrote:

> [When the door to the reception room opened] there appeared the star of my Oriental dreams. It was Nazili Hanum, the Khedive's niece, who rose with calm dignity from a richly appointed Turkish ottoman. . . . The expensive floor carpet was thick, soft and springy as forest moss. On a low, richly-inlaid table, stood one of the most valuable Sèvres vases I have ever seen — again a blend of Oriental and Parisian luxury. The same was true of the Princess's attire. Nazili Hanum was then fifteen years old, yet utterly grown up. She was an extraordinary mixture of European and Oriental influences. Thus it was that her movements were well balanced, soft, slow, elastic, though at the same time lithe and powerful like a panther's. Her almond-shaped, black-lashed eyes were light blue, *languissante* and wild, with exceptionally large dark pupils, and the same eyes could flash and burn while she listened to what I was telling her. . . . In Nazili Hanum's dress, the influence of Parisian fashion was also clearly traced; a black dress in silk grenadine, embroidered with coloured silk flowers that only just hid the wide harem pantaloons that had apparently modified the Paris cut of her dress. Her tasteful, light turban, was ornamented with three yellow feathers and her long, black, silk gauze veil was sewn through with gold and multi-coloured silks, and fringes of the same hung loosely about her fine face. This face was framed by beautifully cared-for hazelnut-blonde hair, which, let down, cascaded over her shoulders and surrounded her delicate velvet cheeks, unspoiled by any cosmetics; her mouth was unusually small. . . . In the course of this, my first visit, I formed an extremely favourable impression of this interesting young creature, with such amiable grace, feminine dignity and Oriental "prestige." . . . This, combined with a meticulous European upbringing, was however not enough to utterly overshadow the Turkish side of the girl and made her into a divine, bewitching presence. This being, so pure and at the same time so fervent, was brought up in a harem.[8]

This remarkably sensual description of Nazlı is evidence of Jerichau-Baumann's investment in a harem fantasy and an example of the citational nature of Orientalism: what she sees and experiences upon meeting Nazlı is recognized through preexisting Western ideals of the odalisque. Yet there is also a transformation of the fantasy. For Jerichau-Baumann, Nazlı's appeal resides in a combination of seemingly contradictory attributes: she is both languishing, wild, pantherlike, enchanting in appearance and yet dignified, graceful, and genteel in her manners. For Jerichau-Baumann, Nazlı is an ideal synthesis of European and Oriental influence in both dress and upbringing.[9]

In Jerichau-Baumann's text, a discourse of desire is enmeshed within a discourse of social progress. The artist's perception of Nazlı as her harem ideal is premised on a set of distinctions between this Egyptian princess and the other women of Mustafa Fazil Paşa's harem and ultimately a condemnation of the harem system for stifling the young princess. Jerichau-Baumann's derisive account of Nazlı's mother, Bukana Hanım, operates as a foil highlighting Nazlı as the exemplary modern harem woman. The artist's account of Bukana Hanım's rudeness during their first meeting forms a striking contrast to Jerichau-Baumann's first impressions of Nazlı's gentility: "[Bukana Hanım] examined our attire, smoked cigarettes, and made remarks about us in Turkish that shocked those who could understand them."[10] Nazlı's fluency in several European languages and her fascination with European culture is contrasted with her mother's illiteracy in her own language, her misguided efforts to speak a few words of English, and her adherence to so-called traditional superstitions. These differences in education and attitude toward European culture can be understood in terms of generational differences in Ottoman harems in a period of momentous change.[11] For Jerichau-Baumann, however, such distinctions are apprehended through the prejudicial filter of her Orientalist values in which Ottoman traditions are equated with superstition and prejudice. This strategy of contrasts serves to highlight Nazlı as an ideal.

Jerichau-Baumann's feminine fantasy is premised on a notion of the pure beauty of Nazlı, and again this is established by negative reference to the crudeness of her mother and the immorality of the harem system. The opinionated artist was left speechless when Bukana Hanım drew her attention to the "eunuch character" of her cat, whom she called her "favourite." She was similarly offended by what she construed as an indelicate song about a Persian painter that was sung in her honor, which was not suitable for polite ears. . . . It is easy to see that the ways of the harem would not suit modest maidens. Nazili Hanum, however, has escaped so pure and unsullied by these surroundings, that one might regard her as one who, given favourable circumstances in the future, could regenerate the unfortunate position of Oriental women.[12]

In Jerichau-Baumann's text, Nazlı emerges as a victim of circumstance, constrained by the weight of tradition within the harem system. Nazlı's European education, which, according to Jerichau-Baumann, raised her expectations for liberty, assumes a tragic cast because of her continuing entrapment within the harem. Yet despite her faith in Nazlı as a very model of social progress, Jerichau-Baumann stops short of endorsing other advocates for social reform whom she met inside the harems of Istanbul.[13] Neither is Jerichau-Baumann's view consistent with feminist Orientalism of the same period, in which the Eastern seraglio is often invoked as a pretext for critiquing domestic relations at home.[14] Reflecting an attitude that is consistent with her distaste for feminism in Europe, Jerichau-Baumann dismisses aspirations for reform as entirely misguided. She does not reconcile her praise for Nazlı with a call for general social reform; instead, her individualism, which colors her attitude to harem life, is channeled toward her artistic aspirations. In Jerichau-Baumann's reinterpretation of a familiar Orientalist theme of claustration, Nazlı emerges as the perfect hybrid of European education and Oriental beauty, a pure beauty heightened by the tragic circumstance of her entrapment in her gilt cage—an ideal subject for Jerichau-Baumann's art.

From this very first meeting, Jerichau-Baumann was determined to persuade Nazlı's parents to grant her permission to paint their daughter's portrait. The artist proceeded with characteristic determination, undeterred by the unusual nature of her request.[15] This motivation lay behind the artist's unprecedented step of bringing with her into the harem a range of her portraits and subject paintings and displaying them before Nazlı and the senior women of the harem. The painter approached this improvised harem exhibition with a mix of fascination and anxious anticipation. Much hinged on the response of the harem princesses whose imprimatur she was seeking. Inside the harem, these senior women had the authority to grant or deny what the artist most desired: the harem portrait sitting. At this moment of intimate encounter inside the harem, the authority of the Western Orientalist was provisional and her achievements were as yet uncertain. Jerichau-Baumann recorded this encounter in her travelogue, published a little over a decade after the portraits had been painted, and it is retrospectively cast in such a way as to suggest the entanglements of the Western Orientalist's gaze and the alternative priorities of the harem princesses:

> I had promised Nazili Hanum that I would show her [my] pictures. . . . It was an exhibition of a quite singular nature. Each of the rolled-up pictures was held up by four slave women, often the prettiest, while the smaller works were all in frames. I do believe that this method of exhibition would have caused a sensation in art-surfeited Paris. There the living easels might have aroused more interest than the pictures themselves—but, above all, the public would have completely disregarded the pictures in favour of the beautiful harem princesses who admired them. Here, however, the situation was reversed: here it was the very first time that the phenomenon of a human being's artistic likeness of a human face had appeared before these beautiful harem eyes. The admiration that greeted my works was so naive, so utterly primitive and so unprejudiced. One of the ladies . . . tried to touch a painted piece of gold jewellery, and another the silk gown in the portrait of the Princess of Wales, which was of serious interest to all of them, especially those who had had the opportunity to see her during her stay in Constantinople. Next it was the pictures of my three blonde daughters which enchanted them. These charming children's fair heads and a little Amager girl in red and white finery with smiling mouth and pale blue eyes went from hand to hand and mouth to mouth and were cosseted and kissed. The last named picture became a favourite of the harem, as did the one of an Italian mother breastfeeding her child.[16]

Humorously recounting the unusual conditions of display of her art inside the harem, Jerichau-Baumann positions herself as a proxy for her Parisian audience, anticipating their fascination with the harem princesses whose beauty was so dazzling that it even eclipsed a fascination for the slave girls who acted as "human easels." Jerichau-Baumann's authorial priority is established by this invocation of her imagined Parisian audience: the artist is intermediary, fascinated and enchanted, turning the harem women into an exotic spectacle for her reader's delight. And yet her text also registers another set of priorities, those of the harem women, and it was their judgment upon which she was dependent for permission to paint Princess Nazlı.

Considering the relatively liberal views of Mustafa Fazil Paşa, it is not surprising that he should consent to his daughter's portrait being painted, but permission to paint was also premised upon gaining the trust of the senior women of the harem. In Ottoman harems, especially those of the elites, considerable power was vested in senior female members; matriarchal elders had authority over both young men and women in the family.[17] In Jerichau-Baumann's travelogue, the exercise of matriarchal authority is registered as a barrier to the artist's desire to paint the young princess, and Nazlı is portrayed as her co-conspirator in a shared mission to achieve the sittings. After a careful process of negotiation permission was eventually granted. Jerichau-Baumann characterized the successful conclusion to her negotiations with Nazlı's mother, Bukana Hanım, by stating, "The plan succeeded, the fortress was capitulated."[18]

As the sittings proceeded Nazlı was fascinated with the process of painting, often sitting next to the painter, watching her at work, whereas her mother remained wary of these portraits of her daughter. Jerichau-Baumann wrote that Bukana Hanım was quite frightened by the result of her work and reported to the other Turkish women, "The foreigner has stolen my daughter's eyes and her soul."[19] This contrast between Nazlı's fascination with easel painting and her mother's grave reservations is indicative of the differing beliefs in the power of the figurative image within Ottoman culture in this period. This interchange suggests that liberal views were not uniformly held in the households of the Islamic elites open to Western influence. Nazlı and Bukana Hanım's differences of opinion over the propriety of image making is indicative of the debates between modernists and traditionalists, such as was evident in the dress reform debates discussed in the previous chapter. Yet the Western Orientalist painter shows very little insight into the complex responses to these social changes within Ottoman society, curtly dismissing Bukana Hanım's reservations as resulting from ignorance and superstition.

Of the three portraits of Nazlı produced from these sittings, the first represented her as Jerichau-Baumann had first encountered her, in her hybrid mix of French and Ottoman clothing. This painting was gifted to the Princess of Wales (Jerichau-Baumann's patron and Nazlı's friend). The second portrait of the Egyptian princess, depicting her, as Jerichau-Baumann characterized it, in her "true harem costume," the artist was permitted to keep. This gift seems fitting, given Jerichau-Baumann's preference for re-iterating exotic dress in her later harem fantasy paintings, produced once she returned to Europe. The third portrait, "with her hair down her back and eyes looking upwards, like those of an angel," was presented to Nazlı.[20] Another painting exchanged hands in the harem; a miniature of the Princess of Wales was presented as a gift to Nazlı. At this stage, or perhaps during her second visit in 1874–75, Jerichau-Baumann was given a carte de visite of Nazlı which remains in the collection of the artist's family in Denmark (Plate 29). This is a striking photograph of an elegant, worldly young woman; like many other Ottoman women of her elite social standing in Istanbul, Nazlı wears the latest Parisian fashions.

The two portrait paintings of Princess Nazlı that Jerichau-Baumann took with her from the harem were exhibited at the New Bond Street Gallery in 1871. They were hung alongside her Norse mythological paintings, sentimental depictions of children, and canvases from recent travels to Greece, Turkey, and Egypt (including a portrait of the queen of Greece). This was an eclectic exhibition of the painter's work that was characterized as ranging from the "epic" to the "ethnological."[21] How were the portraits of Nazlı interpreted in this new context? Given that these paintings conformed to the codes of honorific portraiture that emphasize the individual character of the sitter, it is possible that they challenged the viewers to the London gallery. The notion of the timeless, exotic odalisque was also potentially dispelled by one of the portraits, in which Nazlı was represented in her hybrid mix of French and Ottoman costume. The response of the *Art Journal* critic registers a challenge to prevailing fantasies of the odalisque, affirming the veracity of the artist's unique eyewitness view of harem life. The paintings are, however, interpreted as anonymous ethnographic types rather than honorific portraits. A critic for the *Art Journal* wrote:

> "The Favourite of the Hareem," an oil-picture, declares itself at once a veritable study from Oriental life. All attempts at the improvisation of Hareem beauty by painters and poets have been very wide of the

truth, as we learn from this and all other genuine representations of so-called eastern beauty. There are several pictures of eastern women: what is most valuable in them is their indisputable nationality, which is brought forward without any modification or dalliance with conventional prettiness of feature.[22]

In this instance the shift in context for the portraits entails a loss of connection to the individual subject, a wrenching of signifiers from honorific portraiture (with its implications about the sitter's subjectivity) to an anonymous racial type.

The display of these portraits in the London gallery also raises an ethical issue. Given the strictures against the visibility of Ottoman women and their representations, it is likely that their exhibition to the London audience was a betrayal of Nazlı's trust. The portraits were presented as private gifts to Nazlı's two friends, the artist and the Princess of Wales, rather than as objects intended for public presentation. Although we have no record of Nazlı's response to their exhibition (or indeed, whether she was cognizant of it), evidence from other accounts suggests that the visibility of her portraits at the New Bond Street Gallery would have been a profound violation of Islamic cultural mores. As we saw in the previous chapter, even in those more liberal harems open to experimentation with Western modes of visual representation, extreme measures were taken to ensure that these representations of Islamic women were not publicly visible.

Given these circumstances, Bukana Hanım's initial caution about Jerichau-Baumann's portrait of her daughter turns out to be fully justified. Accordingly, Jerichau-Baumann's declaration that the harem "fortress" had "capitulated" takes on the more troubling implications of Orientalist conquest when we become aware of the epistemic violence inherent in the portraits' public display in London. Inside the harem in Istanbul, the permission to paint was the result of a collaboration with Nazlı; in London, Nazlı is reduced to an object of fascination for a Western audience.

Jerichau-Baumann's visit to Nazlı Hanım not only resulted in these harem portraits, it also inspired a number of other fantasy paintings that are extremely unusual for a woman artist of her era, for example, *The Princess Nazili Hanum* (1875, Plate 30). Languidly reclining in traditional harem costume with her black servant crouched mysteriously among the curtains in the background, this white odalisque strokes the head of her pet monkey, offering herself to the viewer and actively inviting a game of erotic seduction.[23] This painting stages a familiar Western fantasy of the harem in which the odalisque is an alluring object of desire, while at the same time her desire is directed toward captivating the Western viewer. The surprising and radical aspect of this work lies in the fact that a Western female artist should orchestrate this circuit of desire.

Jerichau-Baumann's odalisque paintings were clearly aimed to satisfy the expectations of her European audience. She was undeniably an ambitious painter with a strategic eye for the various requirements of the differing art markets in which she aimed to sell her work. Throughout her career she traveled regularly to the key European capitals to promote her practice by exhibiting at the major salons and academies and to solicit portrait commissions from various European royal households.[24] The impetus to establish an international profile was prompted by the financial necessity to support her large family and the fact that her work was only slowly accepted in her adopted hometown, Copenhagen. Throughout this period the Danish art world was riven with clear divisions between the Nationals (referred to colloquially as "the blonds") and the Europeans (dubbed "the brunettes"). In this context, Jerichau-Baumann's fortunes were hampered by her status as a foreigner (she was born in Warsaw) who had trained in Düsseldorf and painted in a style that clearly allied her with the less favored international tendency.[25] The fact that she did not have an assured local market for her work (at least in the early stages of her career) meant that she became highly attuned to the requirements of her various audiences. It has also resulted in her work being scattered throughout a range of European collections. This and the fact that her art is not clearly allied with any national school have resulted in her marginal position in the art historical record, despite her concerted efforts throughout her lifetime. Nonetheless, upon returning to Europe from Constantinople, Jerichau-Baumann was buoyed by the prospect of enhancing her artistic reputation with her exotic subject matter. She would have been well aware of the marketability of her images of the harem, particularly because her fantasy paintings were endowed with the additional cachet of the artist's eyewitness experience of elite Ottoman harems.

It seems, however, that her investment in these fantasy paintings was not solely market-driven. There is abundant evidence in her letters to her

husband and children and in her published travelogue of her own pleasures in a harem fantasy. In contrast to the veiled eroticism of other female
harem painters and travel writers, Jerichau-Baumann's desire to unveil the
harem and her captivation with Nazlı in particular is undisguised. Nazlı
became the focus for the artist's harem fantasy; surprisingly this did not
preclude a continuing friendship between the two women. Yet the artist's respect for the Egyptian princess didn't eclipse her sense of cultural
superiority or her apparent obliviousness to her transgression of Islamic
cultural decorum.

Jerichau-Baumann's Orientalism redefines and reaffirms Orientalist
categories. In her travelogue, paintings, portraits, and letters, a complex
range of attitudes toward Nazlı and the harem emerges. The exhibition of
her harem portraits and fantasy paintings configures Nazlı respectively as
an ethnographic curiosity and as the languid, exotic odalisque for a Western audience. The complexity of social change in harems that is registered
in Jerichau-Baumann's diary is absent from the harem fantasy paintings
she produced back in Europe. Whereas her portraits potentially challenged the Western sexualized harem stereotype and her diary incorpo-
rates a complex mix of social and sexual discourse, her fantasy paintings
reaffirm the trope of the sensual harem beauty. Her fantasy of the Orient
fundamentally challenges Western gender categories because the artist is
positioned as a desiring subject and yet she achieves this through works
that are surprisingly similar to the familiar trope of the languid odalisque.
This is an instance where women's Orientalism is, to quote Yeğenoğlu,
"implicated and caught within the masculinist and imperialist act of subject constitution."[26]

Yet it is too limiting to see the exchange between Jerichau-Baumann
and Princess Nazlı solely in terms of enabling this European painter to
claim her role in Orientalist discourse, for this is to ignore the agency of
the Ottoman patron. Instead, I would argue that Jerichau-Baumann's portraits are entangled objects, whose meanings shift and are displaced in the
differing cultural contexts they inhabit. Nicholas Thomas's characterization of cross-cultural exchange as a "movement and displacement of competing conceptions of things" that enables indigenous cultures to reinvent
and reinterpret objects is particularly pertinent here.[27] To date, the notion
of cultural exchange has seemed foreign to the analysis of harem paintings

because the Western fantasy of the seraglio has been seen as the archetype for Western appropriation of the Orient.[28] A consideration of the dual contexts for reception of Jerichau-Baumann's harem portraits necessitates a radical revision of this understanding of the harem genre, emphasizing cross-cultural exchange and the processes by which these harem paintings, like Mary Walker's portraits, were created in response to local Ottoman priorities. This becomes apparent when we consider the cultural milieu for Jerichau-Baumann's third portrait, which remained inside Mustafa Fazil Paşa's harem, and in particular when we address Nazlı's subsequent career.

So far, we have only considered the itinerary of the two portraits in Europe, but when the focus is shifted back to Istanbul, it becomes apparent that there were other consequences of Jerichau-Baumann's visit arising from the fifteen-year-old princess's fascination for the practice of easel painting. Evidence suggests that Nazlı's portrait sitting for Jerichau-Baumann was not for her an isolated encounter with easel painting. She grew up in an Islamic family milieu that was engaged with Western cultural practices, including painting, music, and sculpture. Her uncle, Prince Halim, commissioned and collected Western art. His collection, housed in his mansion on the shores of the Bosporus at Baltalimanı, included a portrait of his father, Muhammad Ali Paşa, by Horace Vernet, portraits by Jerichau-Baumann, and views of Istanbul by her son Harald that were purchased in 1875.[29] Nazlı spent much time in the company of her uncle's family and in all likelihood was very familiar with this art collection. Her husband, Halil Şerif Paşa, was also an important patron and collector. They married in 1872, after he returned to Istanbul from a diplomatic post in Vienna. He was a statesman and advocate for political reform and one of the most prominent Ottoman diplomats in Europe in the 1860s and 1870s (serving in Athens, St. Petersburg, Vienna, and Paris). Halil Paşa was renowned in Second Empire Paris for his flamboyant lifestyle and is remembered in the art historical literature for his collection of nearly one hundred modern and old masters, including Ingres's *Le Bain turc* and Courbet's *L'Origin du monde* and *Les Dormeuses*, which he acquired while living in Paris from 1865 to 1868.[30] Although most of his art collection was auctioned in January 1868 before he left Paris (and there are no records of what he continued to collect once he moved back to Istanbul from Vienna in 1872), there is every likelihood that he remained interested in art during his seven-year marriage to Princess Nazlı and that this in turn had an influence on her own artistic concerns.[31]

In 1880, the year after her husband's death, Nazlı's own art came to public prominence. She exhibited four still life paintings at the inaugural exhibition of the ABC Club (Artists of the Bosphorus and Constantinople). The salon held at the Greek Girls' School on the shores of the Bosporus in Tarabya was one of a very significant series of exhibitions for the development of easel painting in the Ottoman capital. These exhibitions, in which both European and Ottoman painters participated, laid the foundation for the development of modern Turkish art.[32] Nazlı's participation is a very early example of an Ottoman woman painter working within the Western easel-painting tradition, but she was certainly not the first female Ottoman artist. There were a number of Ottoman women skilled in the art of illumination, poetry, and other traditional arts such as music and dance.[33]

The reviews of the 1880 salon published in Denmark and Istanbul provide important insights into the differing cultural contexts for the reception of Ottoman and European Orientalist painting. In 1880, the Danish writer for *Dagbladet* completely disregarded the work of the thirty European and Ottoman painters who exhibited at the Istanbul salon, focusing instead on what was presumed to be most fascinating to his European audience: the fact that an Ottoman harem woman, Princess Nazlı Hanım, had exhibited there. In his review, the Danish critic reveals a distinct preference for biography over art. He stressed that Nazlı was the wife of Halil Bey, who, "as the envoy of the High Port in Paris, squandered an enormous fortune during the wildest of escapades." Reiterating a familiar cliché of the despotic Turk, this writer was preoccupied with a rumor that "at the side of this unworthy husband the unhappy Princess spent sad days: although she according to her education and upbringing was entirely European, she had to put up with being treated just like a Turkish wife by her husband, who was very far from being able to judge her according to her merit."[34]

A very different perspective on the Istanbul exhibition emerges once we consult a contemporary Ottoman source. The review in the Ottoman newspaper *Osmanlı* challenges an approach to Orientalist visual culture as being exclusively an expression of the politics of Western domination.

In contrast to the Danish reviewer's emphasis on Nazlı's biography as an exotic curiosity, the Ottoman reviewer pronounced the entire exhibition a source of Ottoman cultural pride. This cultural insider claimed the event as an Ottoman exhibition (despite the large number of European painters) because "the natural beauty of our country and ethics have been appreciated by the artists." The same writer also praised Mary Walker for rendering "a great service to our country" by training Ottoman women painters and wrote that the international recognition of Osman Hamdi Bey's art was a "source of pride for our country."[35] From an Ottoman perspective, this engagement with Western easel painting is a source of national pride and cultural exchange and is characterized as a productive collaboration between European and Ottoman painters. The difference between these two reviews indicates the disparities between Western and Ottoman perceptions of Ottoman culture. I would argue that while we cannot naïvely ignore the persistence of Western stereotypes of the exotic Orient, what is required is a radical revision of the paradigm of Orientalism in order to acknowledge productive cross-cultural collaborations and the priorities of Ottoman audiences.[36]

As far as I am aware, Nazlı did not pursue a public career as a painter—but neither did she disappear without a trace. She moved to Cairo after the death of Halil Paşa and was actively engaged in the cultural life of that city. She conducted a distinguished salon in the late nineteenth century and early twentieth where Arab nationalists, advocates for women's rights, British colonialists such as Lord Kitchener and Sir Evelyn Baring (Lord Cromer), and other members of the social elite were welcomed.[37] She is mentioned in several accounts from the period, including an article in the Arabic journal *al-Muqtataf* of 1897 praising her recently published book.[38] Throughout these sources, her shifting political allegiances are evident. She supported the nationalist leader Ahmad Urabi, but shifted her support to the British upon his defeat. Her allegiances appear to have been pragmatic and were most likely colored by khedival family politics; no doubt a primary motivation was her contempt for her cousin Tevfik.[39] Nazlı was reputedly a great friend of Kitchener's, but rather than being a compliant member of the Ottoman elite complicit with British imperial ambitions, there is evidence to suggest that she was vociferous and staunchly independent, often critical of Kitchener's ignorance of Egyptian culture.[40]

In this period, probably the 1880s, Princess Nazlı commissioned her most unusual portraits that satirize the Western stereotype of the harem. In an anonymous album in the *Sutherland Papers*, two portraits of Princess Nazlı sit next to one another on the album page (Plate 31). Against the same studio backdrop of pyramid and palm trees, the Egyptian princess has choreographed two distinct representations: on the left, an honorific portrait in contemporary European dress; on the right, a cross-dressed parody of the Western harem stereotype.

The photograph on the left conforms to familiar codes of honorific portraiture. This is cultural cross-dressing from the other side, but its significance is vastly different from that of the Western traveler going native. For Princess Nazlı, "going European" signals her social position as an Ottoman elite who, like Mary Walker's portrait patrons, embraced Western dress as a sign of her modernity.[41] The cut of her bodice and skirt are in the fashionable European bustle style. Her erect posture and the contours of her tight-waisted figure are formed by the corset, a notable contrast to the soft lines of traditional Ottoman dress that facilitated greater ease of movement. The decoration of her skirt is achieved through draping, pleating, and a fabric bow in line with the current fashions in Britain and France, rather than the profuse embroidery that was conventional in Ottoman dress. Her crossed legs lift the edge of her skirt, revealing the tips of her leather shoes, which she wears in place of the more traditional Ottoman slippers. Her hair style, however, represents a departure from European convention. A respectable European woman of Nazlı's age would tie up and pin back her hair, whereas Nazlı's long hair sweeps loosely around her neck, following the contours of her head scarf, wrapped tightly around her head, and falls gently across her chest. She is completely at ease in her hybrid European outfit. No doubt this confidence came from her lifelong engagement with European culture. Her upright bearing and direct look convey an ease and confidence indicating that she has taken command of this sitting. It is as if she is initiating a conversation with the viewer. Here is a self-assured woman addressing her viewer as an equal. Like a number of other Ottoman women of her social standing, Princess Nazlı was in the habit of presenting her photographic portrait as a gift to European women who visited her. Certainly the earlier carte de visite Nazlı presented to Jerichau-Baumann exemplifies the place of such photographs in harem visiting etiquette, and perhaps the *Sutherland Papers'* photograph was another such gift. This practice bespeaks a form of exchange in which, like the photographs themselves, Nazlı addresses her European visitors as social equals.

Nazlı's portrait is symptomatic of the way photographic technologies were harnessed by the Ottoman elites in the nineteenth century to present a new self-image. With the advent of the medium, portrait photography quickly became an instrument for the expression of bourgeois subjectivity in Britain and France. In the same period it was just as enthusiastically embraced as a means of self-fashioning by Ottoman elites.[42] Photography was harnessed by the Ottoman leaders as a medium for presenting a revised collective self-image to Europe. The most notable manifestations of this approach are Osman Hamdi Bey's costume book and the Adbülhamit II albums.[43] This state-sponsored redefinition of the collectivity emerged in tandem with changed concepts of individual identity. Individuals within the Ottoman elite, such as the members of Mustafa Fazil Paşa's family, embraced the new technology of photography, having their portraits taken in local photographic studios such as Sébah, Abdullah Frères, and Kargopoulo.[44] Extant honorific portraits produced by these studios are mostly of men; portraits of Ottoman women are rare. For women such as Nazlı, their honorific portraits had an inverse representation in the anonymous clichéd harem scenes that were produced in the same photographic studios and sold to the passing tourist trade. Non-Muslim women and women on the fringes of respectable Islamic society were co-opted to perform in the production of these harem photographs that catered to the Western tourist.[45] One such photograph, by Hippolyte Arnoux, generically titled *Odalisque, Egypt* (c. 1880, Fig. 7), forms a striking comparison with Nazlı's honorific portrait. The upright formality of Nazlı's portrait has its counterpoint in the erotic promise of Arnoux's recumbent odalisque. Nazlı's direct, impassive look differs markedly from the dreamy self-absorption of the odalisque, who is twisted into a suggestive pose with buttocks pushed forward, one slippered foot poking through the folds of her harem pants, and a delicately embroidered slipper casually shifting forward to reveal a slender ankle. Such stagings of erotic availability within the timeless, closed world of the harem had nothing in common with the experience of Ottoman domestic life for elite urban women. Thus the portrait of Prin-

FIGURE 7. Hippolyte Arnoux, *Odalisque, Egypte*, c. 1880. Albumen print, 20 × 26 cm. Collection of Jean-Pierre Evrard, Maurepas. Photograph by Jenni Carter.

cess Nazlı can be interpreted as participating in broader processes of Ottoman revisionary self-imaging, because her portrait entreats her viewer to acknowledge a more complex view of harem life.

Nazlı's honorific portrait expresses this desire to communicate with her viewer; however, the companion portrait is a photograph of a very different order. The same studio backdrop has been deployed, but the photographer has drawn back slightly to admit a second figure within the frame. This is a confronting photograph of Nazlı cross-dressed as an Ottoman gentleman, with her companion dressed as an Egyptian pottery seller, posed as though she is a part of Nazlı's imaginary harem. In contrast to Nazlı's openness to the viewer in the photograph on the left, on the right the two masquerading women appear to rally in defiance of the spectator. Nazlı has an imposing presence because of her commanding upright stance; her costume closes her body from the viewer and her look is impassive, withdrawing rather than actively engaging. The lower edge of her cloak encompasses the rock against which the pottery seller rests, emphasizing a unity of the two that is echoed by the implied narrative of harem master and his possession. Their gazes confront the viewer, further allying the two in their separation from us. This photograph implies an erotic subtext between the two women in which we, the viewer, are resolutely refused participation.

One way of interpreting this photograph is to consider its subversive relationship to existing Orientalist photographic codes as a parodic re-staging of tourist photographs. The context for the production of these two photographs remains a mystery; however, they invite us to speculate. Perhaps Nazlı visited the photographer's studio to commission the honorific portrait on the left and decided to play with the props that she found there. I imagine her in the studio cognizant of the degraded stereotypes of the harem that were on sale there, parodying such representations by playfully cross-dressing and posing with mock solemnity while the photographer registered her second image.

Cross-dressing is familiar as a practice popular among Western travelers, particularly with the fashion for *turqueries* from the late eighteenth century onward.[46] Here, however, the cross-dresser is an Ottoman woman, and the theatricality of the two figures burlesques the staginess of the Orientalist harem postcard. Her impassive look promises no insights into her psychological interiority; instead, our attention is focused on the theatrical staging of a performance. In this parodic photograph the illusion of Nazlı's transformation is incomplete; she has made no effort to disguise her long hair and the heavy cloth underneath her dark cloak has been hastily drawn across the front of her body (one assumes this was done to cover the dress which we see her wearing in the photograph on the left). The effect is to play up the theatricality of the performance and to remind us that underneath she remains the modern Ottoman woman, the sophisticated instigator of this parody. The staginess also underscores the theatricality of the photographs the parody satirizes. At first glance Arnoux's *Odalisque, Egypt* conforms seamlessly to the exotic stereotype, but closer inspection reveals the very theatricality of this conceit by indicating its makeshift production within the photographer's studio. The most obvious reminder of the studio is the artificiality of the landscape backdrop. Further reminders are the makeshift Ottoman divan that is clearly a buttoned leather chaise-longue converted by means of silk fabric draped over its base. The pearls on the odalisque's embroidered hat and flowing hair also appear to have been hastily draped there for the duration of the photograph. As a consequence, the exotic fiction of the harem seems barely sustained. By emphasizing the process of dressing up, Nazlı's photograph also underscores the notion of identity as a performance.[47] This irreverent performativity is a powerful testament to the agency of Princess Nazlı and profoundly challenges a notion of the silence or passivity of Ottoman women.

Nazlı's adoption of the costume of an Ottoman gentleman is a crossing of gender, not culture, as she assumes his powerful position, but metaphorically this can also be construed as a cultural crossing. By dressing to perform the clichéd harem, she inhabits a Western stereotype, both performing that stereotype and exceeding it. By gifting her photograph, Nazlı sent a satiric missive to England parodying the seemingly limitless Western fascination with the idea of the seraglio. In this way she emerges as a figure of resistance to a dominant scopic regime; she presents herself as a sophisticated, visually literate instigator of the clichéd codes of Orientalist visual culture who rewrites these codes as satire. The object of the joke is those Westerners who desire the fantasy seraglio. With whom did she share this joke? Certainly with her fellow collaborator and, in all likelihood, with other elite Ottoman women, who would have enjoyed her travesty. Was it shared with the Englishwoman to whom they were gifted, thereby forging an alliance between the two? Or was she poking fun at Western women's propensity to subscribe to the fantasy of the harem?

Following this latter proposition, there is another level at which I wish to read the erotic subtext of this photograph and that is specifically in relation to Jerichau-Baumann's fantasy paintings. There is a striking coincidence between Nazlı's pottery seller and Jerichau-Baumann's *An Egyptian Pottery Seller Near Gizeh* (1876–78, Plate 32). It is uncertain whether Nazlı saw this or the painter's other eroticized representations of Egyptian pottery sellers; however, both have a shared derivation in Orientalist stereotypes of the sexually available peasant woman: one reaffirms this cliché while the other mocks it. In both, the seller, a robust peasant woman, is seated near the vessels that so clearly signify her trade and lowly social status. What distinguishes the two is a difference in posture and demeanor. With her legs folded, arm outstretched, and torso alluringly visible beneath her translucent dress, Jerichau-Baumann's pottery seller exudes a robust, open physicality. This is a physicality made all the more enticing because of her shadowy face and penetrating stare and by her hand cautiously holding the edge of her head scarf, poised to draw it closed. With her sullen gaze, bent knees, and body covered by dark swathes of cloth, Nazlı's pottery seller, by contrast, is physically closed from the viewer's look. She seems to block the viewer. In Jerichau-Baumann's paintings there is a collapsing of any social distinctions between her pottery sellers and her odalisques as both become alluringly available to the viewer. In Nazlı's photograph the social distinction between elite Ottoman women and the poor pottery seller is reinscribed. These wealthy harem women who have commissioned this photograph can playfully enact various roles in the photographer's studio, distinct and distanced from the illiterate pottery seller whose role they play.[48] In contrast to the physical availability of the pottery seller and odalisque in Jerichau-Baumann's art, in Nazlı's photograph her body is covered and she is mischievously posed as Nazlı's possession rather than offering herself to the viewer.

Reading Nazlı's satiric performance in relation to the photograph that accompanies it we see a shift from earnest self-presentation in her honorific portrait on the left to parody in the harem travesty on the right. While the photograph on the left is an implicit revision of Orientalist stereotypes of the odalisque, the one on the right is a direct assault on such degrading tropes. Together these two photographs embody a vacillation: on the left, an opening out to dialogue; on the right, a closing off. Here the optimism and enthusiasm to communicate with her European female audience that characterized her earlier portrait photographs and paintings are tempered by experience. Perhaps this experience is the recognition of the persistent imperative of an exoticizing, Orientalizing gaze despite efforts to communicate otherwise. This photograph bespeaks an impatience with a Western attitude that returns dialogue to monologue and in which the Egyptian princess is reified as an odalisque of Western fantasy.

Next to one another on the album page, these two portraits of Princess Nazlı are like an uncanny stereoscopic plate, a popular device among armchair Orientalists that promised possession of the object. As Jonathan Crary argues, through the viewing process, these "mass-produced and monotonous cards are transubstantiated into a . . . seductive vision of the 'real.'"[49] Nazlı's stereoscopic pairing references this visual technology but does not offer reconciliation into the desired illusionistic effect. The spectators' certainty about the object of vision is disrupted and their position is called into question.

This pair of photographs brings together the strategies of both cultural and gendered cross-dressing to establish the authority of this Ottoman princess. The gap between the two photographs of Nazlı (as modern Ottoman woman and parodic harem master) sustains the humor of the image by making clear its author and target. The humor here is premised on a recognition that this is an elite, culturally sophisticated Ottoman woman occupying the position of the harem master in this travesty of Western fantasy. Indigenous agency is articulated through cross-dressing and thereby inhabiting a Western stereotype. The strategy for Princess Nazlı is not to didactically refute myth but to defuse its power by inhabiting and disrupting its effect and thereby usurping the position of mastery. The stereotype becomes masquerade. The power of the joke is premised on that gap between the stereotype and its knowing performance by the indigenous subject. What better demonstration of mastery of another culture than to parody that culture's stereotype of one's own. To joke in a foreign tongue displays a sophisticated grasp of that language; in Nazlı's case it is the degrading language of the harem stereotype that she returns as a joke. Once we are aware of this photograph, we cannot help but think of the range of her cartes de visite and portrait paintings as a playful, changing characterization of self, orchestrated by her.

This study of Nazlı's harem portraits introduces the entanglements of cross-cultural exchange to our understanding of the harem genre. The encounter between Jerichau-Baumann and Princess Nazlı in Istanbul in 1869–70 and 1874–75 was productive for the European artist and her audience but also for Nazlı. Yet this is not just a story of productive exchange; exchange here is about betrayal as much as collaboration. It is also about lacunas in communication and the overriding desire in Europe for a reaffirmation of the timeless, erotic Orient of Western fantasy. As Zeynep Çelik argues, the problem of "speaking back" might be as much about failure to listen and to hear.[50] Nonetheless, this narrative also touches on the currency of visual representations in late Ottoman culture and profoundly shifts our understanding of women's Orientalist art by introducing the harem as a context in which Ottoman women's identity and sociality was renegotiated via image making.

EPILOGUE

Having begun this book with the story of Elisabeth Jerichau-Baumann's entry into Istanbul, I believe it fitting to conclude with her homecoming. In both there is a disjunction between her prior imaginings of the event and the discomforting realities of the experience induced by the challenge of a transition between cultures.

When nearing Copenhagen, Jerichau-Baumann expressed her relief at the comfort and refuge anticipated by this homecoming to her family and her adopted hometown. The return she recounts, however, was devoid of such a welcome, inducing instead feelings of loneliness and dislocation. Because her family had not been alerted to her imminent arrival, no one was there to greet her; neither were they at home when she got there. She sought temporary consolation through the ritual of unpacking her suitcases, "those dumb travelling companions, whom I needed to make time pass,"[1] but even this could not shift her melancholy. Her paintings seemed to stare down at her from the walls, and the dust on the furniture provided a reminder of the length of time since the other occupants of the house had been there. Escaping for a meal at a nearby café lifted her spirits for a while as it enabled her to pretend she was still traveling.

This disconcerting experience of the time between arriving home and feeling at home made an encounter that she had the following morning seem all the more poignant. During a brisk stroll through one of Copenhagen's central squares, she came upon an "extraordinary sight . . . a genuine Turk in a fez, yellow pointed shoes, caftan and baggy trousers." The appearance of this man was so remarkable in the northern city that she believed for a moment she was walking through the streets of Istanbul. In a scene reminiscent of her own dockside experience upon entering the Ottoman capital, the foreigner was drawing a crowd of curious onlookers who thronged about regarding him "as a wild beast who had escaped from a menagerie."[2] She was disturbed to think what he made of all of this. Impatient with this unfriendly reception and unwilling to participate in this treatment of the man as an exotic spectacle, Jerichau-Baumann intervened. Using her few limited words of Ottoman and some Italian to communicate, she offered assistance and ascertained that he was awaiting his business partner's arrival to access the shop on the square that they jointly ran.

This story of an encounter between two strangers, foreign residents, in the center of Copenhagen is an apt metaphor for the complexities of cultural exchange between intimate outsiders with which this book has been concerned. Jerichau-Baumann was drawn to this man because his evident vulnerability as an outsider in Copenhagen resonated with her own sense of dislocation; hers was an empathy compelled by feelings of alienation in her adopted hometown. She felt a particular bond and extended the gesture of friendly solidarity because her recent travels to the Ottoman Empire gave her a sense that, unlike the other citizens of Copenhagen, she had some insight into his cultural context. His presence in Copenhagen also served to ameliorate her own sense of alienation by validating her recent experiences abroad.

Inside his shop, the artist was astonished and delighted to find a range of Ottoman domestic items: pipes, pipe bowls, rose oil, and Oriental beads. For her, these were not just exotic curios but familiar domestic objects similar to those she had seen inside Istanbul's elite harems, into which she had been recently welcomed. It was here, rather than in her home, that she found a reassuring confirmation of self. Her attention was drawn to a sign that advertised dried roses from the East that could be revivified by immersion in water; they were labeled "Jerichau Roses." This bizarre coincidence resonated comfortingly for her, and she thought to herself, "This is something for you and about you."[3] At last she was able to still her unease and reflect upon the mutually affirming relationship between travel and home.

Jerichau-Baumann's retrospective testament to the transformative possibilities of travel and the entanglement of objects with particular nostalgic memories of place is reminiscent of other travelers' experiences addressed in this book. There are some parallels, for example, with John Frederick Lewis's performance as an Ottoman paşa in the photographer's studio in England in the 1860s, which I addressed in the first part of this book. Lewis's nostalgic self-portrait demonstrates the role Ottoman costume could play in intimately evoking the artist's former life in Cairo. Julia Pardoe's account of her pleasure in conjuring memories of Istanbul by gazing at William Bartlett's sketches, which I analyzed in the second part of this book, is another example of the role that visual culture could play as a catalyst for memory. In each case we witness the emergence of the authority of the Orientalist traveler whose claim is based on an insider's knowledge that surpasses his or her countrymen's. And yet these encounters with Ottoman culture are not solely about its objectification. Travel not only consolidates authority, its transformative possibilities also encompass a challenge to reimagine the self.

This book has been concerned with tracking the processes of such self-representation and examining the ways those experiences also enabled transformations within Ottoman culture. Reimagining the self was not exclusively the preserve of the European traveler but was also experienced by those whom the traveler visited, prompting their own imaginings and desires. Such was the case in the encounter between Elisabeth Jerichau-Baumann and the Egyptian princess Nazlı Hanım. There is eloquent testimony to this in a short letter by Princess Nazlı that remains in the Jerichau-Baumann papers in the Royal Library in Copenhagen. This short note is the partial remnant of a correspondence between the Ottoman princess and Jerichau-Baumann's daughter. Written in November 1872 inside her father's harem in Istanbul, Nazlı writes briefly about her imminent marriage and wishes her correspondent happiness in her own forthcoming nuptials. The tone of the letter conveys the intimate bonds of friendship. The fluency of Nazlı's letter remains for us a testament to her sophisticated grasp of the foreign language, but more than this, it is her openness and youthful enthusiasm that is most remarkable. The note conveys her optimism for the future and her hope for the opportunity to travel: "I have never been out of my own country but still hope that happiness is in store for me one day. I do much desire to see Rome, Paris and London."[4]

This is only one remaining fragment of a larger correspondence, yet it is sufficient to indicate that Princess Nazlı's meeting with Elisabeth Jerichau-Baumann had sparked her imagination, fueling her desire to travel to Europe. It remains a testament to the fact that in the late nineteenth century, even within the secluded world of elite Ottoman harems, the potential for reimagining the self through exchanges with an outsider was not an exclusively Western preoccupation.

I have invoked the term "intimate outsiders" in this book to characterize those individuals whose unique social position and cultural interests provide scope for a more nuanced interpretation of Orientalist visual culture. This has proved a particularly useful way of envisaging the complex relationships between those Orientalists who had privileged or perceived access to Ottoman harems in the nineteenth century and those Ottomans who actively sought contact with Europeans, inviting them into their homes in order to satisfy their own interest in Western visual culture. At the same time, this term has particular resonance because of the semantic strains inherent in the pairing of intimacy and outsideness, which encapsulates the tensions and contradictions of the cross-cultural exchanges at play here. To focus solely on Western visual stereotypes of the harem and their reception in Europe, as has been the tendency in art historical studies of harem imagery, brings into view only the tip of the iceberg. Shifting the parameters of inquiry to include both Orientalist and Ottoman perspectives broadens its scope by introducing voices previously occluded from the field and by engaging with the Ottoman contexts for the production and reception of harem representations.

Throughout this book I have explored the legacy of these intimate outsiders and their importance in enabling a more subtle account of nineteenth-century harem imagery. A greater inclusiveness is achieved by focusing on the processes of journeying and the encounters inside harems as well as the myriad visual and textual inscriptions that are the result of such engagements. Tracking these experiences and mapping the shifting power relations entailed in these cross-cultural encounters and the transitions between cultures focus our attention on the heterogeneous outcomes for both the Ottoman and Orientalist interlocutors. At the core of this project is a challenge to any simple characterization of power relations in the analysis of nineteenth-century harem imagery. Examining the power of elite Ottoman women to commission and create representations of themselves presents a profound revision of any account of nineteenth-century harem imagery as exclusively an expression of the Western power to fantasize about the seraglio and consolidate a European identity. This project has not only involved a process of addressing such previously marginalized perspectives but has also engendered an alternative view of the West from those margins. One of the crucial outcomes of such an engagement is the emergence of a means of registering how European cultures appeared from the perspective of those inside the harems of Cairo and Istanbul.

Such an approach involves inserting the complexity of nineteenth-century Ottoman culture into the history of Orientalist art; doing so transforms our understanding of both. Ottoman harem women's art patronage emerges as a profound challenge to Western fantasies of the passive odalisque. Moreover, the controversial status of their harem portraits within Ottoman culture requires acknowledgment of how entangled these alternative harem paintings are within Ottoman debates about the value of engaging with Western cultural forms and with disputes about the impact of modernization on late Ottoman culture. Shifting the ground of inquiry in this way also offers a new vision of the West by bringing into view Western Orientalists, often expatriates, whose artistic practice has up until now been marginalized from the field. The harem representations that resulted from such cross-cultural encounters can thus be seen to have served both parties in various ways.

In contemporary analyses of nineteenth-century Orientalism, the Western trope of unveiling the Oriental woman and penetrating the harem has often provided a powerful visual metaphor for the Western Orientalist's assertion of power over the Orient. By inserting into this debate other kinds of harem encounters between Ottomans and Orientalists, this book has provided alternative metaphors of cultural exchange and resistance. Within this book there are numerous examples of such alternatives: the story retold by a British governess of a theatrical harem performance that exacted symbolic revenge on Western men who transgressed Ottoman harem sanctions; Fatma Sultan's destruction of Mary Walker's harem sketches; and Princess Nazlı's canny and parodic harem photographs. My intention is that these other kinds of encounters between Ottomans and Orientalists will begin to provide alternative metaphors that are accorded the appropriate interpretive weight in our understanding of relations between European and Ottoman culture in the nineteenth century. This is not to ignore the plethora of reductive harem stereotypes that circulated in Europe in this period, which undoubtedly had a powerful hold on the European imagination. Yet by bringing harem portraits into conjunction with Western harem fantasy images produced by those with some form of privileged access, and by tracking their processes of production and reception in Istanbul, Cairo, Copenhagen, and London, we begin to see how these, at times incompatible, notions of the harem were both mutually delimiting and defining.

Notes

INTRODUCTION

1. Jerichau-Baumann, *Brogede Rejsebilleder*, 8.
2. Ibid., 9.
3. Ibid., 8.
4. The literature on modernization during this period of Ottoman history is extensive. Key texts include S. J. Shaw and Shaw, *History of the Ottoman Empire*; Quataert, *The Ottoman Empire*, and "Part IV: The Age of Reform."
5. Pamuk, *Istanbul*, 218. My emphasis.
6. At another point in the same text, Pamuk reflects that when reading nineteenth-century European writings about Istanbul, there are moments when "I will lull myself into believing the accounts of Western outsiders are my own memories" (ibid.). Out of this multivalent engagement emerges a self-portrait, a portrait of Istanbul and the contemporary *Istanbullu* forged from "the ruins of Empire." This is a complex, ambivalent legacy based on a conflicted mix of Ottoman legacy and Turkish Westernization. Pamuk's book provides a far more complex meditation on the nineteenth-century legacy (forged through processes of Westernization and encompassing the dislocating transition from empire to republic) than I can do justice to here. The result of Westernizing processes within Turkish culture has been a certain dislocation from the past, a process Pamuk describes as allowing "me and millions of other Istanbullus the luxury of enjoying our own past as 'exotic,' of relishing the picturesque" (217).
7. Çelik, "Colonial/Postcolonial Intersections."
8. Çelik, *The Remaking of Istanbul*.
9. Faroqhi, "Elegance Alafranga"; Mardin, "Super Westernization"; Sönmez, *Turkish Women*.
10. The nineteenth-century governors were Ibrahim Paşa (1848), Abbas Paşa (1848–54), Sait Paşa (1854–63), Ismail Paşa (1863–79), and Tevfik Paşa (1879–92).
11. Muhammad Ali employed French and British experts to assist in the founding of factories and educational reforms, and the basis for his power was the strong modernized army that he created in the 1820s. For an account of Muhammad Ali's army, see Fahmy, *All the Pasha's Men*.
12. This is a much more complex history than I can do justice to here. For a fuller account of the period and contested claims about its political significance, see, for

example, al-Sayyid Marsot, *Egypt in the Reign of Muhammad Ali*; Mitchell, *Colonising Egypt*; Toledano, *State and Society*; Fahmy, *All the Pasha's Men*.

13. This restriction on the military changed in 1873; see S. J. Shaw and Shaw, *History of the Ottoman Empire*, 145.

14. For an account of the emergence of Ottoman-Egyptian identity in the middle years of the nineteenth century, see Toledano, *State and Society*.

15. S. J. Shaw and Shaw, *History of the Ottoman Empire*, 195.

16. Quataert, *The Ottoman Empire*, 66.

17. Ibid., 149. For analyses of the changes to Ottoman women's lives in the nineteenth century, see Duben and Behar, *Istanbul Households*; Davis, *The Ottoman Lady*; Şeni, "Fashion and Women's Clothing."

18. For a study of the powerful influence of palace women in the sixteenth and seventeenth centuries, see Peirce, *The Imperial Harem*.

19. These include Çelik, *The Remaking of Istanbul*, and *Displaying the Orient*; Germaner and İnankur, *Constantinople*; W. M. K. Shaw, *Possessor and Possessed*.

20. See Çelik, "Speaking Back to Orientalist Discourse," and "Speaking Back to Orientalist Discourse at the World's Columbian Exposition."

21. W. M. K. Shaw, *Possessor and Possessed*.

22. On women's harem literature, see Melman, *Women's Orients*; R. Lewis, *Gendering Orientalism*, and *Rethinking Orientalism*.

23. As Ruth Yeazell argues, "The more fantastic a harem the imagination builds . . . the stronger is the need to buttress the structure with fact" (*Harems of the Mind*, 8).

24. Ibid., 13.

25. Nochlin, "The Imaginary Orient."

26. R. Lewis, *Gendering Orientalism*, 129–144.

27. Melman, *Women's Orients*; Mills, *Discourses of Difference*; R. Lewis, *Gendering Orientalism*.

28. "Female networks sustained through formal visiting rituals provided women with information and sources of power useful to their male relatives" (Peirce, *The Imperial Harem*, 7).

29. Alloula, *The Colonial Harem*, 5.

30. DelPlato, *Multiple Wives*, 12–13.

31. Lewis, *Rethinking Orientalism*.

1 THE LANGUID LOTUS-EATER

1. The writer had secured a free passage on P & O steamships in exchange for some favorable publicity. Sarah Searight, introduction to Thackeray, *Notes of a Journey*, 1991, 13.

2. Thackeray, *Notes of a Journey*, 488. This book was first published in 1846; quotations throughout this chapter are from the 1869 edition.

3. Sarah Searight, introduction to Thackeray, *Notes of a Journey*, 1991, 156.

4. Thackeray, *Notes of a Journey*, 489–90, 491.

5. Key contributors to the analysis of cultural cross-dressing include Low, "White Skins/Black Masks"; Garber, "The Chic of Araby"; Macleod, "Cross-Cultural Cross-Dressing."

6. There are a number of recent analyses that have critically examined the role of Thackeray's text in constructing a mythology of the artist's biography. See Roberts, "Masquerade as Disguise and Satire," "Mythology as Biography," in "Travel, Transgression," 22–34, and "Cultural Crossings"; Weeks, "J. F. Lewis"; Weeks, "The 'Reality Effect'"; Llewellyn, "A 'Masquerade' Unmasked."

7. For an account of Lewis's early years, see M. Lewis, *John Frederick Lewis*, 11–20.

8. Thackeray, *Notes of a Journey*, 504.

9. Ibid., 504–505.

10. Ibid., 506–507.

11. Ibid., 504.

12. For an analysis of costume of this period, see Truman, "Empire and the Dandies."

13. The literature on the dandy is extensive. See in particular Wilson, "Oppositional Dress"; Black, "Baudelaire as Dandy."

14. "The ethno-linguistic 'division of labour' that characterized the Pasha's army was mirrored by a similar one in the civilian administration where the ruling elite remained 'Turkish' and where 'Arabs' were prevented from being promoted to higher posts" (Fahmy, *All the Pasha's Men*, 314).

15. The agha was the chief of the Janissary militia. Raymond, *Cairo*, 385.

16. Renda, "Portraits," 505.

17. Originating in Morocco, the fez had different names throughout the region. "Fez" was the name used in Istanbul, while "tarboosh" was the popular term in Egypt. Mohammed Ali mandated a Greek version of this headwear as part of the new military uniform and called for the establishment of facilities for their local manufacture. For an account of the contentious history of this headwear in the nineteenth century and early twentieth, see Samir Raafat, "The Tarboosh and the Turco-Egyptian Hat Incident of October 29, 1932," *Egyptian Mail*, October 26, 1996.

18. Thackeray, *Notes of a Journey*, 508.

19. For an analysis of the significance of Wilkie's portrait, see Weeks, "About Face."

20. For an account of this struggle, see Rustum, *The Struggle*.

21. Fahmy, *All the Pasha's Men*.

22. Günsel Renda analyzes Sultan Mahmut II's (1808–39) strategic use of his portraits, which hung in government offices and were gifted to foreign embassies. In doing so, Mahmut II used them to "institutionalise his reforms and persuade the general public to espouse them." Sultan Abdülmecit, who succeeded him in 1839, continued to have his portraits painted in the new military uniform and to gift them to visiting dignitaries. Renda, "Portraits," 505.

23. al-Sayyid Marsot, *Egypt in the Reign of Muhammad Ali*.

24. Muhammad Ali's expansionary aspirations in Syria were checked in 1840, when the British stepped in in defense of the Ottomans. "When the British navy paraded outside his bedroom window in Alexandria, Muhammad Ali admitted defeat, and he was forced to withdraw his army from Syria." As a concession he was granted the hereditary pashalik of Egypt, but was forced to abandon his industries related to weapons production and the embargoes and monopolies that protected his other infant industries. "Egypt was relegated to the status of a province, whose

sole commercial and economic function was to supply raw materials for European industry. From having become the centre of an empire, it was once again broken to the ranks of a mere province" (al-Sayyid Marsot, *A Short History*, 64). The events of 1841 have been interpreted slightly differently by Fahmy as heralding one of the great successes of his reign, whose overriding ambition was "seeking the establishment of a secure personal rule for himself and his household in Egypt. His efforts in this regard were crowned with success when in 1841 the Sultan, with the acquiescence of Britain, granted him a firman bestowing on him the hereditary rule of Egypt" (*All the Pasha's Men*, 311). Fahmy rejects al-Sayyid Marsot's proto-nationalist reading of Muhammad Ali's rule, seeing it as symptomatic of a dominant nationalist interpretation of this history.

25. Abu-Lughod, *Cairo*, 87.
26. Thackeray, *Notes of a Journey*, 488–489.
27. For an analysis of these reforms, see Abu-Lughod, *Cairo*, 94.
28. Thackeray, *Notes of a Journey*, 492–493. Muhammad Ali had commissioned the French architect Pascal Coste to design this mosque in 1820. His plans, in a neo-Mamluk style, were not realized. The final design, by an anonymous Armenian architect, was inspired by the Sultan Ahmet I mosque in Istanbul. See Raymond, *Cairo*, 304.
29. Thackeray, *Notes of a Journey*, 492, 482.
30. During Muhammad Ali's reign the Citadel compound housed not only the ruler's palace and mosque, but also an arsenal, a powder house, and the hall of currency. Raymond, *Cairo*, 304.
31. See Fahmy, *All the Pasha's Men*, 1–9.
32. A number of Europeans held advisory positions in the Ottoman Empire. Some of them wore the fez with their European military uniform.
33. For example, Randall Davies wrote:

    Other painters had been eastwards and returned with a respectable tan; but Lewis lived there and the sunshine was in his bones. In Spain he had for years been warming himself up, so that when he settled in Cairo he was fairly acclimatized, and during his long sojourn there so completely absorbed the atmosphere of the place that he was able to give it off on his return like a fire of coals. . . . Thackeray happened to visit Egypt, and in his account . . . has told us something about Lewis that we should never have known from other sources; and the interest of it is that the change he describes in Lewis's manner of living is in entire accordance with the change in his work. (Davies and Long, "John Frederick Lewis," 36–37)

    The same approach is also evident in an article by Hugh Stokes, quoting a critic of *The Hhareem*: "The novelty of the first drawings in this style was emphasised by the new spirit in which his subjects were treated—the spirit, not of a traveller in search of the picturesque, but one who by a long sojourn in a strange country had become intimate with the character of the inhabitants and familiar with their mode of life" ("John Frederick Lewis," 32).
34. For instance, this tendency is evident in Stevens, *The Orientalists*, 202–208; M. Lewis, *John Frederick Lewis*, 23; Green, *John Frederick Lewis*, 7.

35. *Portfolio*, 1892, 94.

36. For an account of these events, see M. Lewis, *John Frederick Lewis*, 22.

37. *Art Journal*, 1850, 179; *The Athenaeum*, May 4, 480.

38. *The Times*, May 1, 1850, 8.

39. This comment is made in conjunction with a critique of Lewis's treatment of the faces in this painting, but in general John Ruskin was extremely supportive of Lewis's painting. See *The Times*, May 30, 1851, 8. As Prettejohn argues, there is a shift in the critical reception of the Pre-Raphaelites after the publication of Ruskin's two letters to *The Times* and his pamphlet *Pre-Raphaelitism* published in 1851. His defense of the Pre-Raphaelites shifts the debate from an emphasis upon revivalism to realism through his assessment of the value of their art as exemplars of the principle of "truth to nature." See Prettejohn, *The Art of the Pre-Raphaelites*, 59. It is significant that although critics perceived a parallel between Lewis and the Pre-Raphaelites, in general his work was not caught up in these earlier critiques.

40. *The Athenaeum*, February 23, 1850, 210.

41. John Frederick Lewis, *Royal Scottish Academy Catalogue of the 27th Exhibition*, 1853, No. 494; Lane, *An Account*, 1836 ed.

42. *Illustrated London News*, May 4, 1850, 300; *The Athenaeum*, May 4, 1850, 480.

43. Praising this aspect of the composition, *The Athenaeum* critic wrote, "The figure of the slave is exceedingly fine; and the combination of the two, forming the principal dark mass of the picture, and surrounded by the sober tones of the background, make a magnificent group and give grandeur, firmness and repose to the whole composition" (May 4, 1850, 480).

44. *Illustrated London News*, May 4, 1850, 300.

2 "MR LEWIS'S ORIENTAL PARADISES"

The title of this chapter is from *The Athenaeum*, May 30, 1874, 740.

1. The change here from the *tarboosh* (fez) described in Thackeray's word-portrait of Lewis is significant. Perhaps it indicates Lewis's increased investment in notions of the traditional exotic East upon his return to England. For an analysis of the issue of self-portraiture in Lewis's harem paintings, see Llewellyn, "A 'Masquerade' Unmasked," 133–151; Williams, "John Frederick Lewis."

2. It is uncertain whether they are of equal status or whether this is a sultana and her servant. DelPlato, *From Slave Market to Paradise*, 239–240.

3. For instance, Llewellyn and Newton write about the unresolved tension in this picture, speculating that the legs in the mirror signal the presence of the husband in Turkish dress:

    The enigmatic smile of Marian and the implied silence of her statuesque companion leave the viewer to speculate about what is happening. . . . Could it be the theme of male jealousy again that reaches its full expression in *Intercepted Correspondence*? Lewis was much older than Marian; was he capable of coolly looking at his own feelings of jealousy? Or is he merely depicting coquettishness? Is he placing the (male) viewer in the fantasy? It could be all or none of these things. ("John Frederick Lewis," 46)

4. *Illustrated London News*, May 9, 1857, 444.

5. In his analysis of a range of influences on Lewis's art, including classicism and Persian miniature painting, John Sweetman notes that his interiors are reminiscent of Vermeer's domestic scenes. Lewis was also interested in Velasquez's *Las Meninas*; his fascination with mirrors may well have been inspired by this Spanish masterpiece, the lower part of which he copied in 1834 (the sketch is held in the Royal Scottish Academy collection). See Sweetman, *The Oriental Obsession*, 132. Both Ruth Yeazell and Joan DelPlato note the similarities between these intimate interiors and Dutch and Flemish painting. Yeazell, *Harems of the Mind*, 227–228; DelPlato, *From Slave Market to Paradise*, 234–238. Emily Weeks explores the entanglements of self-portraiture with Lewis's artistic sources through an intriguing analysis of *Hhareem Life, Constantinople* in relation to Jan Van Eyck's *Arnolfini Marriage Portrait*. See Weeks, "The 'Reality Effect,'" 198–202.

6. Alpers, *The Art of Describing*, 13, 44.

7. According to Alpers, in Dutch art there is a crucial interrelationship between the gaze and touch; the eye is the primary means of knowledge and yet it is linked with touch. Ibid., 17.

8. *The Athenaeum*, May 4, 1850, 480.

9. Using *The Language of Flowers* published in 1869, Caroline Bugler offers the following interpretation of the floral symbolism in the bouquet: "The pansy, or heart's ease, exhorts the receiver to think of the giver, the anemone signifies that the giver feels forsaken, the *Hibiscus syriacum* pays homage to the woman's delicate beauty and the roses probably symbolise love." Pushing the reading of floral symbolism in this painting further, she notes, "In the vase beside the master of the harem stand larkspur (haughtiness), a rose (love) and a scarlet dahlia (instability), suitable attributes for an outraged husband." Quoted in Stevens, *The Orientalists*, 207.

10. This critic assumes that the seated woman closest to the woman who has intercepted the bouquet is the culprit, and the young woman in green who stands on the other side and whose hand is being held by the informant is only the messenger. *The Athenaeum*, May 15, 1869, 674.

11. *The Times*, May 19, 1869, 5.

12. *Illustrated London News*, May 8, 1869, 471.

13. As with Lewis's earlier harem paintings there is a play between order and decorative floral profusion in this scene. The unity created by the strong green background was praised by the *Art Journal* critic (1865, 169). *The Athenaeum* critic also praised the balance between detail and breadth of effect: "If we stand near this work its details are singularly rich and beautiful in treatment; when we are a little removed it appears as broad as it is brilliant" (May 6, 1865, 626–627).

14. This critic reproaches the painter because of the vacancy in the face of the harem woman but is not too concerned about this shortcoming because the vacuousness was not considered inappropriate for this "pretty plaything" of the harem:

> [This] picture is perhaps the greatest triumph yet achieved by J. F. Lewis, R.A. elect. A favourite of the harem comes to gather flowers, which bloom in gay profusion in the garden of her lord. The girl, a pretty plaything, is herself a flower, but deficient, no doubt, in intellect, her face vague and vacant, defects for which the artist is perhaps more to blame than the lady herself. As for the flowers, nothing more lovely ever grew or was ever painted; each petaled

cup is brimful of light and sunshine, and each leaf enjoys the air it breathes. The abounding detail, which otherwise might have been scattered, is brought together by a cool green background. (*Art Journal*, 1865, 169)

15. *The Athenaeum*, May 11, 1872, 597.

16. *The Times*, May 21, 1872, 7. The critic for the *Illustrated London News* also condemned the painter, asserting that such aesthetic effects in Lewis's art were nothing more than clever trickery:

> lilies and other flowers serving to enrich the composition to the extreme of possible decoration, even in Arabesque. Many of the passages imitative of ornamental details, in both pictures, are, taken alone, not only captivatingly resplendent in colour, but likewise almost illusive in truth of effect. Yet sound criticism cannot accept pictures constructed on the principles which this painter has adopted as works of fine art in the strictest and highest sense. There is here little artistic interpretation in the best acceptation of the word, little power of seizing the more central or generalised artistic facts of relative aspect and impression, little more than hard, toilsome, piecemeal copyism, weakest where it should be strongest, as in the faces, and addressing itself to no higher capability of our nature than that of the wonder we experience as children at the illusions and colour play of the mirror, the camera and the kaleidoscope. (May 25, 1872, 502)

17. For an analysis of Lewis's relationship to the aestheticism of Albert Moore, see Bendiner, "Albert Moore and John Frederick Lewis," 76–79. See also DelPlato, *From Slave Market to Paradise*, 348–350. Aestheticism was an extremely disparate movement that spanned a long period and included a diverse range of artists; its formative years were the 1860s and 1870s. On aestheticism, see Prettejohn, *After the Pre-Raphaelites*.

18. There was a notable time lag between the development of aestheticism in British art and the acceptance of it as a set of evaluative criteria in mainstream art criticism. For an analysis of the attitudes of the conservative critics, see Flint, "The English Critical Reaction," 8. While Lewis's later harem paintings were receiving an ambivalent critical response in the 1870s, his harem paintings remained in demand on the private art market.

19. John Ruskin's attitude to Lewis changed significantly. By the 1870s he had distanced himself from his initial enthusiastic embrace, becoming discontented with the direction of Lewis's art. In 1876 he was still praising Lewis's narrative painting *A Frank Encampment* of 1856, and yet a year earlier he had asserted that in his most recent painting, "Lewis loses his animal power among the arabesques of Cairo" ("Academy Notes, 1875," in *The Works of John Ruskin*, 291). Ruskin also chose to delete his references to Lewis in his 1873 edition of *Modern Painters*. See DelPlato, *From Slave Market to Paradise*, 338. Ruskin's opposition to aestheticism is well-known, particularly through the notorious Ruskin-Whistler trial of 1878.

20. The lilies are of Japanese origin, the bulbs imported into Europe in the nineteenth century. The abutilan and fuchsia on the extreme left and right are native to South America and wouldn't have been grown in Egypt at that time. They were grown in England as hothouse plants. The trees in the background also look English rather than Eastern. Catalogue information from Birmingham City Gallery.

21. *The Times*, April 29, 1865, 12.

22. *The Athenaeum*, May 30, 1874, 740.

23. Repetition is most apparent in the duplication of objects and costumes; for example, the green jacket with ermine cuffs appears in *Hhareem Life, Constantinople, In the Bey's Garden, The Reception*, and *The Bouquet*. Other elements such as vases reappear in his works.

24. *The Athenaeum*, May 30, 1874, 740.

25. *The Academy*, May 16, 1874, 555.

26. The stereoscope, invented by Charles Wheatstone in 1832, achieved widespread popularity after the Parisian firm Duboscq exhibited it at the Crystal Palace exhibition of 1851. It was popularized in Victorian drawing rooms after Queen Victoria became interested in it. Turner, *Nineteenth-Century Scientific Instruments*, 300. In 1858 a lending library for stereoscopic slides was established in London. Gernsheim and Gernsheim, *The History of Photography*, 258.

27. In Britain, a range of subjects could be viewed on stereoscopic slides, including foreign countries and places of interest. Gernsheim and Gernsheim, *The History of Photography*, 257. For an analysis of this technology as an apparatus of colonial authority, see Dennis, "Ethno-Pornography," 22–28.

28. Crary, *Techniques of the Observer*, 123–124. For an analysis of the relationship between the stereoscope and Pre-Raphaelite painting (especially Millais's *The Woodman's Daughter*), see Smith, "The Elusive Depth of Field."

29. Walter Benjamin has characterized this as a condition of visuality within emergent modernity. Cited in Crary, *Techniques of the Observer*, 127.

30. Roberts, "Stereoscopic Vision and *The Reception*," in "Travel, Transgression," 66–69.

31. Sweetman argues that some of Lewis's paintings (especially *A Frank Encampment*) evoke "Persian rather than European attitudes to space-representation: space is seen in terms of adjoining sectors rather than as a continuum defined by perspective" (*The Oriental Obsession*, 136–139).

32. Weeks, "The 'Reality Effect,'" 224–225.

3 PLEASURES IN DETAIL

1. Collected in Montagu, *The Selected Letters*.

2. There is a considerable body of literature about women's travel writing. Sara Mills, *Discourses of Difference*, offers a feminist Foucauldian analysis of women's travelogues. Billie Melman, *Women's Orients*, attends to the impact of class and gender on women's travel writing. See also Marcus, *A World of Difference*; R. Lewis, *Gendering Orientalism*, and *Rethinking Orientalism*.

3. For example, Mary Walker emphasized her ability to cross the veiled threshold of the harem and established the veracity of her testimony by discrediting the reports of those who hadn't been inside. She observed that at the time she was in a harem painting the portrait of the favorite of Sultan Abdul Medjid (her spelling), a Western newspaper was printing sensational reports about this woman's recent escape from the harem with her Italian lover and their travels in Europe. Walker, *Eastern Life and Scenery*, 1: 41.

4. Melman, *Women's Orients*, 18.

5. This was particularly the case in their observations about child rearing in harems, as evident in Mary Walker's comment, "The mode of bringing up little children . . . is sadly deficient in the careful moral training which, with religious teaching, we in England consider as the indispensable basis of sound education" (*Eastern Life and Scenery*, 2: 45).

6. Baillie, *A Sail to Smyrna*, 175.

7. For an extended analysis of the influence of *The Arabian Nights Tales* on British travel literature, see Moussa-Mahmoud, "English Travellers."

8. Herbert, *Cradle Lands*, 16.

9. Ali, *Scheherazade in England*, 14.

10. Walter Bagehot wrote:

> [There] was a time with us . . . when the *Arabian Nights* were not so much a story as a dream, when, with the same dim mingling of identities which we sometimes have in sleep, it is not Aladdin but ourself, and yet not ourself but Aladdin, who gazes on the jewel-bearing fruit-trees, marries the Vizier's daughter, and controls the resources of the lamp. . . . We suffer and triumph with Sindbad, taste vicissitude with Cameralzaman, enjoy the shrinking fondness of Zutulbe, travel upon the enchanted carpet, or mount the flying horse. ("The People of the Arabian Nights," 46–47)

11. Lane wrote:

> There is one work, however, which presents most admirable pictures of the manners and customs of the Arabs, and particularly of those of the Egyptians; it is "The Thousand and One Nights; or Arabian Nights' Entertainments": if the English reader had possessed a close translation of it with sufficient illustrative notes, I might almost have spared myself the labour of the present undertaking." ("Author's Preface, Cairo 1835," in *An Account*, 2003 ed., xiv, n. 2)

12. Ali, *Scheherazade in England*, 43.

13. Hornby, *In and around Stamboul*, 1: 316, 320, 305–306.

14. For an analysis of the harem as a focus for European women's sapphic fantasies at the turn of the century, see Apter, "Acting Out Orientalism," 15–34.

15. Hornby, *In and around Stamboul*, 1: 306, 307.

16. Harvey, *Our Cruise in the Claymore*, 82–83.

17. Grey, *Journal*, 134.

18. Harvey, *Turkish Harems*, 79–80.

19. Hornby, *In and around Stamboul*, 1: 302–303.

20. Ibid., 1: 314.

21. On the "reality effect," see Barthes, "The Reality Effect."

22. "The jacket and loose quilted trousers may be painted on canvas to look graceful, but they fail in reality to be so, at least so we thought, and it was not from this single visit that our conclusions were drawn." Blackwood, *A Narrative*, 85.

23. Montagu, *Selected Letters*, 91.

24. Pardoe, *The Beauties of the Bosphorus*, 3, 4.

25. Ibid., 125.

26. Grey, *Journal*, 124.

27. Harvey, *Turkish Harems*, 65–66.

28. Rogers, *Domestic Life in Palestine*, 224.

29. Skene, *Wayfaring Sketches*, 2: 275.

30. Merleau-Ponty, "The Intertwining," 143.

31. The effect in this painting is similar to what Martin Jay identifies as "a performative critique of the reality-effect itself. In painting I suppose this is produced by the painter or the beholder entering the picture in some metaphorical way; this makes it impossible to see painting as a scene out there viewed with either the realist or the naturalist eye" ("Scopic Regimes," 26). Michael Fried is the art historian who has most thoughtfully developed these questions of the painter and the beholder's identification, entry, and merger. See Fried, *Courbet's Realism*. For an analysis of the feminist implications of Fried's argument, see Roberts, "Difference and Deferral."

32. Murray, *A Handbook*, 88. The connection between traditional costume and the *Arabian Nights* is also expressed by Washington Irving when he writes of his disappointment at seeing a Turkish minister in Barcelona in European dress: "I confess I should rather have seen him in the magnificent costume of the East; and I regret that that costume, endeared to me by the Arabian Nights' Entertainments, that joy of my boyhood, is fast giving way to the levelling and monotonous prevalence of French and English fashions." Quoted in Ali, *Scheherazade in England*, 46.

33. Blunt, *The People of Turkey*, 2: 63. See also 2: 67, 70.

4 BEING SEEN

1. Tickner, "Feminism, Art History," 105.

2. Griffith, *A Journey*.

3. Ibid., 297.

4. Poole, *The Englishwoman in Egypt*, 1846 ed., 89.

5. Martin Jay characterized the labyrinth as "that potent figure . . . used to challenge the putative clarity of a God's-eye view of the world" (*Downcast Eyes*, 364).

6. Emmeline Lott was employed as a governess to Ibrahim, son of Ismail Paşa from his second wife. For further biographical information on Lott, see Robinson, *Wayward Women*, 141–142; Melman, *Women's Orients*, 150. Lott, *The Mohaddetyn*, 1: 31–32, 50.

7. Anonymous, *The Lustful Turk*.

8. *Harem*, directed by Arthur Joffe, 1986.

9. The relationship between fear and the experience of colonized space has been analyzed by several postcolonial writers. Homi Bhabha argues that fear and paranoia are integral to the ambivalence at the origins of colonial authority: "The colonialist demand for narrative carries, within it, its threatening reversal. . . . The hybrid tongues of the colonial space make even the repetition of the *name* of God uncanny" ("Sly Civility," 100–101).

10. Lacan, *The Four Fundamental Concepts*, 96.

11. Ibid., 106. As Kaja Silverman argues, this is a "monumental challenge to all such notions of mastery . . . [because] the geometrical point is only a 'partial dimension in the field of the gaze'" ("Fassbinder and Lacan," 146).

12. Silverman, "Fassbinder and Lacan," 150.

13. Lacan, *The Four Fundamental Concepts*, 105–112.

14. Mulvey, "Visual Pleasure." For an analysis of the early feminist film theory align-

ment of gaze and eye with masculine privilege and the later revisions of this assumption, see Saper, "A Nervous Theory."

15. Writing about this effect in the visual arts, Lacan states, "This is the pacifying, Apollonian effect of painting. Something is given not so much to the gaze as to the eye, something that involves the abandonment, the *laying down*, of the gaze" (*The Four Fundamental Concepts*, 101).

16. Starr, "Ladies of the Harem," 318.

17. Cubley, *The Hills and Plains*, 34.

18. Elwood, *Narrative*, 1: 155.

19. Wendy Leeks had noted an exception to this in Ingres's bather paintings, particularly the first in the series, the 1807 *Bather*. Leeks argues that this figure appears startled by an onlooker (the viewer) from which she attempts to cover herself. Leeks, "Ingres Other-Wise," 31.

20. Romer, *A Pilgrimage*, 1: 222–223. Saint Bartholomew was one of the twelve apostles; tradition asserts that he was flayed alive in Armenia. Attwater, *The Penguin Dictionary of Saints*, 56.

21. "He maps himself in it. How? In so far as he isolates the function of the screen and plays with it. Man, in effect, knows how to play with the mask as that beyond which there is the gaze. The screen is here the locus of mediation." Lacan, *The Four Fundamental Concepts*, 107.

22. Montagu, *Selected Letters*, 91. For an analysis of the portraits of Lady Montagu, see Pointon, "Killing Pictures."

23. Romer, *The Bird of Passage*, 2: 261.

24. Blackwood, *A Narrative*, 86. The comments Blackwood recorded contrast with a conversation about Western fashion among women at an Armenian wedding that Fanny Blunt attended: "'Doudou, do you notice how stiff and stately Mariemme Hanoum sits in her new polka? Her husband, Baron Carabet, who has just returned from Constantinople, has brought her a machine made of whalebone and steel, in which the Franks cage their wives in order to fill up what is missing, and tone down what is superfluous'" (*The People of Turkey*, 2: 69).

25. Female narcissism is attractive to men, "not only for aesthetic reasons. . . . For it seems very evident that another person's narcissism has a great attraction for those who have renounced part of their own narcissism and are in search of object-love." Freud, *On Metapsychology*, 82–83.

26. Lacan's model "calls radically into question the possibility of separating vision from the image—of placing the spectator *outside* the spectacle, in a position of detached mastery." Silverman, "Fassbinder and Lacan," 146.

5 SARTORIAL ADVENTURES

1. For those women who did travel in disguise (and these were usually women who spent some years abroad, such as Hester Stanhope) they found that it was more effective, indeed more practical, to dress as Oriental men than as Oriental women. Initially Hester Stanhope adopted Turkish male dress out of necessity because of a shipwreck in 1812 in which she lost all of her possessions. Explaining why she continued to dress in this fashion, James Silk Buckingham wrote in his diary of 1823:

Had she retained the dress of an English lady, she could never have ventured into the open air, even for the purpose of exercise, without attracting a crowd of peasantry, and others, to witness such a curiosity. . . . This would be a perpetual impediment to all her movements abroad. Had she adopted the dress of a Turkish lady, she could never have ventured out except in the ample garments worn by these. . . . The dress of an English gentleman . . . would be liable to still stronger objections . . . so that the Turkish male dress appeared the only one that could be adopted with delicacy and advantage combined . . . [for] it conceals the whole figure and person of the wearer. . . . Nothing can be more consistent with the most feminine delicacy so that the choice was wise and prudent and in every other respect quite unexceptionable. (*Travels in Mesopotamia*, 1827, quoted in Aitken, *A Girdle round the Earth*, 166)

2. For example, see Alloula, *The Colonial Harem*, 13.

3. For an analysis of the images of excursion sites around Istanbul, see Germaner and İnankur, "Excursion Sites," in *Constantinople*, 263–275.

4. Montagu, *Selected Letters*, 96–97.

5. Elwood, *Narrative*, 1: 340.

6. Hornby, *In and around Stamboul*, 2: 39–40.

7. Elwood, *Narrative*, 1: 339, 338.

8. The Islamic veil functioned as a compelling provocation to masculine desire. Emily Apter refers to this as the "erotics of claustration." Apter, "Female Trouble," 212. In Western feminism, by contrast, there has been a tendency to read the Islamic practice of veiling as a symbol of women's oppression within Islamic cultures. This issue has been the subject of much debate. A number of postcolonial feminist writers have argued for a more nuanced reading of the veil as a mutable signifier that requires site-specific interpretation. As Frantz Fanon and Barbara Harlow, among others, have argued, there has been a "historic dynamism of the veil." See Fanon, *Studies in a Dying Colonialism*, 63. The literature on this subject is vast. For a summary of some of these debates and essays on the veil in visual culture, see Bailey and Tawadros, *Veil*; and Yeğenoğlu, *Colonial Fantasies*.

9. "She was probably employed for one year only and may have been forced to leave her post." Melman, *Women's Orients*, 150. For further biographical information about Emmeline Lott, see Robinson, *Wayward Women*, 141–142. Lott published the following memoirs of her time in Egypt: *The English Governess in Egypt*; *The Mohaddetyn in the Palace of the Ghezire*; and *The Grand Pasha's Cruise on the Nile in the Viceroy of Egypt's Yacht*.

10. Lott, *The English Governess*, 1: xxiii. Lott notes, despite the conspicuous wealth of her employer, she endures conditions worse than that of a governess in Europe (1: 255).

11. Yusef was in Istanbul having accompanied Princess Fatimah Hanım, who was spending Ramadan at the Ottoman court. Lott, *The Mohaddetyn*, 1: 103.

12. Slade, *Records of Travels*.

13. Burton, *Personal Narrative*.

14. Lott, *The Mohaddetyn*, 1: 113, 124, 106.

15. Ibid., 1: 117–118, 121.

16. Said, *Orientalism*, 196. See also Low, "White Skins/Black Masks," 90.

17. Lott, *The Mohaddetyn*, 1: 140–141.

18. Ibid., 1: 142, 145–146.

19. Indeed, the complex interactions between the two storytellers appears in Lott's account; she interjects with asides elaborating on points made to educate her readers, who are less familiar with particular customary practices in the harem.

20. It is noted that "at one time [the library was] the favourite resort of the *Sheik-el-Islam* (the Moslem Patriarch)." Lott, *The Mohaddetyn*, 1: 136–137.

21. Ibid., 1. 138.

22. See also Caroline Jordan's important catalogue entry on this painting in Benjamin, *Orientalism*, 103.

6 THE POLITICS OF PORTRAITURE

1. Walker, *Eastern Life and Scenery*, 1: 8–39.

2. Sakaoğlu and Akbayar, *Sultan Abdülmecid*, 88–90, 215–219; Leyla (Saz) Hanımefendi, "The Tragic Celebration of Fatma Sultane's Confinement," in *The Imperial Harem*, 147–157.

3. See Salaheddin Bey, *La Turquie*, 143; Germaner, "Osmanlı İmparatorluğu'nun Uluslararası Sergilere Katılımı ve Kültürel Sonuçları," 36; Pamukciyan, "1867 Yılı Paris Sergisine Katılan Osmanlı Sanatkârları," 37. Mary Walker had considerable standing within the artistic community of Istanbul. She exhibited alongside Ottoman and European artists in 1880 and 1881 at two exhibitions in Istanbul that were key events for the development of Western-style easel painting in the capital. The exhibitions were held at the Greek Girls' School in Tarabya in 1880 and at the Municipal Hall of the Petit Champs in Tepebaşı in 1881 and were extensively reviewed in the expatriate and Ottoman press. In 1880, Walker exhibited *A Negro Boy Carrying Fruit* along with a number of other watercolor and pencil sketches. *Constantinople Messenger*, September 11, 1880. In 1881 Walker exhibited *Jeune Bulgare*, *Jerry*, *Étude au pastel*, *Child in a Cradle*, and *Tour de Galata*. *Constantinople Messenger*, April 26, 1881, 2. Walker also developed a considerable reputation as a teacher, privately tutoring women artists and teaching drawing at the Turkish Girls' School at Yerebatan. For an account of her experiences teaching drawing to young Ottoman women, see Walker, *Eastern Life and Scenery*, 1: 221–248.

4. Walker's sitters include the wife of Riza Paşa, Fatma Sultan, Serfiraz Hanım (favorite of Sultan Abdülmecit), and Eminé Hanım (wife of Ziya Paşa) and her two children, Eminé Faika Lutfié Hanım and Mushaver Bey. Walker chose to conceal the identity of her sitters through the convention of listing their initials only, except in the case of Sultan Abdülmecit's daughter, for whom she uses the pseudonym "Zeïneb." The sultan did not have a daughter by this name; however, it is possible to deduce her identity, Fatma Sultan, and the identity of the others through the circumstantial evidence Walker provides. My thanks to Aykut Gürçağlar and Zeynep İnankur for confirming these names.

5. To my knowledge there are two extant portraits of Fatma Sultan, one a photograph and the other a print. See Germaner and İnankur, *Constantinople*, 178; Sakaoğlu and Akbayar, *Sultan Abdülmecid*, 217. The earlier portrait engraving by Ruben held in

the Topkapı Palace Museum shows a much younger Fatma Sultan demurely dressed in traditional Ottoman clothing with sumptuous fabrics and delicate embroideries that denote her wealth and privilege, but with few of the signs of social rank that were indicated in Walker's portrait. These two portraits are not only distinguishable by their relative formality, but also by the circumstances of their commission. The earlier portrait was completed while she was living within her father's household and was most likely supervised by more senior members of the palace, whereas the later portrait was clearly determined by Fatma Sultan herself. It is significant, therefore, that when she was of an age to supervise her own commission, she chose to express her elevated position and eminent social standing through her portrait.

6. Walker, *Eastern Life and Scenery*, 1: 16.
7. Sakaoğlu, "Record of a Royal Wedding."
8. Renda, "Portraits," 454, 514.
9. For an analysis of the varied attitudes toward figural representation within Islam, see Isma'il R. al-Faruqi, "Figurative Representation and Drama: Their Prohibition and Transfiguration in Islamic Art," in Issa and Tahaoğlu, *Islamic Art*, 261–269.
10. Gentile Bellini's *Portrait of Mehmed II*, 1480, is held by the National Gallery in London.
11. Raby, *Qajar Portraits*; *The Sultan's Portrait*; Günsel Renda, "Portraiture in Islamic Painting," in Issa and Tahaoğlu, *Islamic Art*, 225–235; Giray, "Introduction," 185; Weeks, "About Face," 46–62.
12. W. M. K. Shaw, *Possessors and Possessed*, 16–17.
13. Renda, "Portraits," 450–455.
14. Walker, *Eastern Life and Scenery*, 1: 2.
15. Ibid., 1: 17.
16. Chennells, *Recollections*, 2: 114. For an analysis of the Ottoman engagement with portrait photography in the late nineteenth century and early twentieth, see Mickelwright, "Personal, Public and Political (Re)Constructions."
17. Walker, *Eastern Life and Scenery*, 1: 4.
18. The same issue arose in her portrait of Fatma Sultan in which it was noted that "shade was highly objectionable." Ibid., 1:16.
19. Ibid., 1: 16, 17.
20. Ibid., 1: 120–121.
21. Ibid., 1: 311.
22. Ibid., 1: 310.
23. Scarce, *Women's Costume*, 81. For an analysis of Ottoman women's fashion in this period, see also Mickelwright, "Public and Private."
24. The torba çarşaf was introduced from Syria in 1872. "It was regarded as a reaction of conservative sections of society, since it enveloped the woman's body entirely." *Woman in Anatolia*, 256.
25. Şeni, "Fashion and Women's Clothing," 30.
26. As Linda Nochlin argues, the absence of history and of social change in the East is a consistent trope of Orientalist painting. Nochlin, "The Imaginary Orient."
27. Hamdy Bey and de Launay, *Les Costumes Populaires*, 24. (My thanks to Hannah Wil-

liams for this French translation.) For an analysis of this album, see Ersoy, "A Sartorial Tribute."

28. On the revisionary nature of Osman Hamdi Bey's realist painting, see Çelik, "Speaking Back to Orientalist Discourse."

29. Walker, *Eastern Life and Scenery*, 1: 3–4.

30. The literature on the Tanzimat reforms is extensive. See, for example, S. J. Shaw and Shaw, *History of the Ottoman Empire*; Mardin, "Super Westernization."

31. Renda, "Portraits," 505.

32. Şeni, "Fashion and Women's Clothing." For an analysis of the shifting attitudes to Western consumer culture as reflected in the Ottoman women's press in the Abdülhamit era, see Frierson, "Cheap and Easy."

33. Fatma's husband drowned four years into their marriage. Fatma Sultan married Nuri Paşa in 1859, a marriage which lasted 22 years until his death in 1882. Sakaoğlu and Akbayar, *Sultan Abdülmecid*, 218–219.

34. Like other women of her generation, Fatma Sultan would have been trained in the traditional Ottoman arts of embroidery and music, and yet she was very familiar with Western art forms because of her father's interest.

35. Walker, *Eastern Life and Scenery*, 1: 99.

36. Alloula, *The Colonial Harem*, especially 3–5.

37. Walker, *Eastern Life and Scenery*, 1: 10, 22.

38. Ibid., 1: 312.

39. Hornby, *Constantinople*.

7 ORIENTAL DREAMS

1. Princess Alexandra had visited the Ottoman Empire with the Prince of Wales on their tour in early 1869. In Egypt they met with Khedive Ismail and visited the Suez Canal with Ferdinand de Lesseps. In Istanbul they met with Sultan Abdülaziz and senior dignitaries of state. Princess Alexandra visited the Valide Sultan (the sultan's mother) and his wife at the Dolmabahçe Palace harem and was entertained by Mustafa Fazil Paşa's daughters at his *yalı* (waterside mansion) on the Asian shore of Istanbul. In Cairo Princess Alexandra visited Khedive Ismail's mother, dined with his wives in the harem, and met the wife of Mourad Paşa in his harem. Grey, *Journal*.

2. Mustafa Fazil Paşa lived in luxurious exile in Istanbul after his failed attempt, in collaboration with his uncle, Prince Halim Paşa, to depose Khedive Ismail after the Egyptian ruler displaced their right to succession. In 1866 Ismail persuaded Sultan Abdülaziz to change the law of succession enshrining primogeniture, thus ensuring that his son Tevfik Paşa was the heir presumptive rather than Prince Halim. See S. J. Shaw and Shaw, *History of the Ottoman Empire*; Çetin, "Hidiv Ailesi."

3. Mustafa Fazil Paşa, *Lettre*; see Davison, "Halil Şerif Paşa: The Influence of Paris," 59. In 1857 Mustafa Fazil Paşa was appointed a member of the Meclis-i-Tanzimat (Council for the Reforming of Old and Promulgation of New Laws). After his involvement in the failed attempt to depose the khedive, and while exiled in Paris, Mustafa Fazil Paşa funded Yeni Osmanlılar, the "Young Ottomans," a politically radical group of young Turkish writers. In 1867 he was reconciled with the sultan

and Grand Vizier Ali Paşa and returned to Istanbul resuming various parliamentary appointments. When Jerichau-Baumann first visited Istanbul in 1869 Mustafa Fazil was a parliamentary minister. Mehmed Süreyya, *Sicill-i Osmanî* (İstanbul: Kültür Bakanlığı ile Türkiye Ekonomik ve Toplumsal Tarih Vakfı, 1996), 2: 511; Özel, "Tanzimatın Getirdiği 'Aydın,'" 65; Tugay, *Three Centuries*, 109–111; Kuntay, *Namık Kemal*, 1: 311–339. William Howard Russell characterizes Mustafa Fazil Paşa as a "very clever, bold and subtle man" (*A Diary in the East*, 501).

4. *Dünden Bugüne İstanbul Ansiklopedisi* (İstanbul: Kültür Bakanlığı ve Tarih Vakfı, 1995), 2: 464, 3: 172.

5. Tugay, *Three Centuries*, 110–111.

6. Letter from Constantinople to her husband Adolf and children, November 19, 1869. Elisabeth Jerichau-Baumann papers, Royal Library, Copenhagen.

7. Writing home about her portrait commissions for the vice king's (Khedive Ismail's) children, Jerichau-Baumann stated, "I have made so incredibly much money." Elisabeth Jerichau-Baumann, Letter from Cairo to her children, March 3, 1870, Elisabeth Jerichau-Baumann papers, Royal Library, Copenhagen.

8. Jerichau-Baumann, *Brogede Rejsebilleder*, 22.

9. In other circumstances Jerichau-Baumann had written of the hybrid fashions that were popular among Ottoman women in Constantinople as an unlucky reunion and a misalliance: Turkish ladies look

> just like a motley array of blooming tulips. With their indispensable parasols up and with bundles under their arms . . . waddling like geese in their yellow slippers across the deck. Occasionally one sees a fat ankle protruding nakedly over the fine, modern, Parisian high-heeled boot, for curiously enough it is with the woman that the conservative adherence to the old traditions is barbarically mixed with the all-conquering progress of the new fashion. It is only a shame that both the Old Turkish elements and the fashion, accustomed to being victorious, suffer from the unfortunate combination which, more than anything else, has the aspect of a *mésalliance*. (Ibid., 123)

10. Ibid., 22.

11. Davis, *The Ottoman Lady*. For an analysis of debates about Westernization in Ottoman novels of the period, see Mardin, "Super Westernization." One of the few Ottoman accounts of harem life is Leyla (Saz) Hanımefendi, *The Imperial Harem of the Sultans*.

12. Jerichau-Baumann, *Brogede Rejsebilleder*, 25. Lamenting Nazlı's future within the harem, Jerichau-Baumann writes:

> Oh Nazili, to have to languish among barbarians! You budding rose surrounded by thorns, you who dream about the unknown, about this world, of which you have only an inkling, you resemble a true pearl concealed between the hard, tightly closed blades of the shimmering mother shell. What will be your destiny? Will you be passed from hand to hand like a chattel, to be concealed and forgotten, or shimmer like the rest of your sisters. (24)

13. It was the wife of the minister of finance, Cabouli Paşa ("a champion of women's emancipation in the harems") who was the focus of Jerichau-Baumann's disapprobation:

Madame Cabouli Pasha was the misbegotten offspring of women's emancipation in the fairy-tale existence of the wholly or half-veiled Turkish *hanums*. Her doctrines had the fragrance and taste of the sweet poison from which the unfortunate flies nip until at last they become giddy and drown therein. Madame Cabouli Pasha was "*La fable de la ville*," as the saying goes. There were those who applauded her new principles, particularly the young, the *hanums*, who had had a half-European upbringing. Madame Cabouli Pasha was a medium, an agreeable, elegant and aristocratic medium between the *harems* and the outside world, but she was exceedingly unpopular and only spoken about with disfavour. (Ibid., 98)

14. For an analysis of the trope of Eastern despotism in liberal feminist discourse, see Zonana, "The Sultan and the Slave." For an analysis of feminist artists and Orientalism, see Cherry, *Beyond the Frame*.

15. Jerichau-Baumann clarified the purpose of her visit when she wrote, "There were considerable difficulties involved if private individuals requested admittance to the harems, and particularly so if one wished to paint the women. That, however, was my wish, and I was determined to achieve this objective of my journey" (*Brogede Rejsebilleder*, 20).

16. Ibid., 23.

17. Bukana Hanım's stature in the harem is indicated by the fact that she had 175 slaves at her command. Ibid., 22. Leslie Peirce notes that "the segregation of the sexes [in Islamic society] permitted the articulation of a hierarchy of status and authority among women, parallel to that which existed among men" (*The Imperial Harem*, ix).

18. Jerichau-Baumann, *Brogede Rejsebilleder*, 24.

19. Ibid., 25.

20. Ibid., 24.

21. "This lady is impelled upwards into the epic vein by her tastes and feelings, and, at the same time, is more pronouncedly ethnological than perhaps any artist of the day." *Art Journal*, 1871, 165.

22. The critic also applauded the veracity of her Fellaheen paintings: "There are also one or two female studies of Fellaheen, in which truth and genuine nationality prevail over poets' dreams of matchless houris and peerless Egyptian maids." *Art Journal*, 1871, 165. In Jerichau-Baumann's papers there is another review transcribed by the artist that corroborates this ethnographic reading:

    Mme Jerichau's gallery at 142 New Bond Street where the artist brings before the public several of her eastern studies very remarkable as to the different Egyptian types displayed. . . . Mme Jerichau has also been able, thanks to HRH the Princess of Wales, and HM the King of Greece introductions, to enter the private Harems of highest rank. She has been favoured with portrait orders of H. Highness the Khedive's sons and daughters and her two eastern pictures of *immense* value as being the very first ever seen and ever painted, are portraits of Ladies of highest rank inhabitants of the Harem. Mme Jerichau was allowed to lift the edge of its veil. (Untitled and undated letter, Elisabeth Jerichau-Baumann papers, Royal Library, Copenhagen)

23. For analysis of this painting, see Larsen, "Fra Nationalromantisk Bondeliv til Orientens Haremsmystik"; Von Folsach, *By the Light of the Crescent Moon*, 86. Although her hair color is darker than Jerichau-Baumann describes, this painting has parallels with Jerichau-Baumann's account of Nazlı in her diary:

> In her bedroom hung with blue satin, where a blue hanging lamp spread a gentle light she was half hidden by the blue hangings garnished with costly guipure, on a lovely carved ebony bed, which stood on a dais. For me she was unforgettable. In these forget-me-not coloured, aromatic surroundings Nazili lay on the soft pillow, her fragrant hair encircling her face like a halo. From the linen edged with real lace, one pink toe peeped out, and on the platform stood her white, silver and pearl embroidered slippers; while at the door, the black slave woman Lalla watched her like a dog—vigilant and faithful. (*Brogede Rejsebilleder*, 26)

24. Jerichau-Baumann exhibited at the Paris Salon, the Royal Academy in London, in Düsseldorf, the Royal Academy of Fine Arts, Stockholm, and at the Charlottenborg Salon in Copenhagen. She sold work to the empress of Russia, Empress Eugénie of France, Napoleon III, King George of Greece, the German kaiser, and Princess Anna of Hesse. Christensen, "Elisabeth Jerichau-Baumann."

25. For an analysis of Jerichau-Baumann's position in relation to these divisions in the Danish art world in the nineteenth century, see Von Folsach, *By the Light of the Crescent Moon*, 83–89; Christensen, "Elisabeth Jerichau-Baumann." Despite these divisions in the Danish art world, Jerichau-Baumann did secure a reputation through her portraits of key figures, including politicians, actresses, and members of the literary world such as her friend, Hans Christian Andersen. She also enhanced her reputation by securing patronage from the Danish royal court. It was these contacts that facilitated many of her commissions from other European royal households into which many of the Danish royal family were married.

26. Yeğenoğlu, *Colonial Fantasies*, 82.

27. Thomas, *Entangled Objects*, 123.

28. Richon, "Representation"; Kabbani, *Europe's Myths of Orient*.

29. Jerichau-Baumann observed the art works owned by Prince Halim when she visited Baltalimanı to paint portraits and work as an art tutor for the prince and his wife, Princess Viduar. Jerichau-Baumann, *Brogede Rejsebilleder*, 101, 126–188.

30. In France he was referred to as Khalil Bey. (He was promoted in rank from bey to paşa in 1871.) For an account of his involvement in the Parisian art world and notoriety in Second Empire Paris, see Haskell, "A Turk and His Pictures." Davison provides the most comprehensive account of Halil Şerif Paşa's political career in two articles: "Halil Şerif Paşa, Ottoman Diplomat and Statesman" and "Halil Şerif Paşa: The Influence of Paris and the West on an Ottoman Diplomat." See also İnankur, "Halil Şerif Paşa"; Haddad, *Halil Şerif Paşa*.

31. When de Villemessant visited Halil Paşa in his Vienna residence between 1870 and 1872, he observed that the Ottoman diplomat had a fine collection of French painting and sculpture as well as family portraits. It is likely that these paintings returned with him when he journeyed from Vienna to Istanbul in 1872, the year he married Princess Nazlı. See de Villemessant, *Mémoires*, 106.

32. Öner, "Tanzimat Sonrası Osmanlı Saray Çevresinde Resim Etkinliği," and "The Role of the Ottoman Palace."

33. Filiz Çağman, "Women and the Arts," in *Woman in Anatolia*, 242–255. In the 1880 Salon, Osman Hamdi Bey exhibited *İki Müzisyen Kız*, a painting representing skilled young Ottoman women playing traditional Turkish instruments. This painting is reproduced in Cezar, *Sanatta Batı'ya Açılış ve Osman Hamdi*, 2: 668.

34. *Dagbladet*, November 11, 1880.

35. "A Fine Arts Exhibition in Tarabya," *Osmanlı*, 11 Şevval 1297, 1880: 14.

36. Zeynep Çelik has advocated this shift in focus for the study of Orientalism. Çelik, "Colonialism, Orientalism," and "Speaking Back to Orientalist Discourse." See also Benjamin, "Post-colonial Taste: Non-Western Markets for Orientalist Art," in *Orientalism*, 32–40.

37. Afaf Lutfi al-Sayyid notes that Princess Nazlı's salon was one of the three famous salons in late-nineteenth-century Cairo in which there were signs of political activity. al-Sayyid, *Egypt and Cromer*, 95.

38. *al-Muqtataf*, 1897, 21. Princess Nazlı is also mentioned in Rumbold, *Recollections*, 2: 331–332.

39. al-Sayyid, *Egypt and Cromer*, 95. Again her animosity seems to have been prompted by the fact that Tevfik's father, Khedive Ismail, had usurped her father's and uncle's right of succession to the khedivate.

40. Lord Kitchener's secretary, Ronald Storrs, recorded the following feisty exchange between Princess Nazlı and Kitchener:

> Against the combined volume and velocity of her conversation in English, French, Arabic and Turkish, the protests of the Field-Marshal rang surprisingly mild. "You think, I suppose, that the Egyptians are afraid of you, Lord Kitchener, sitting in Kasr al-Dubara? They laugh. And how should they not laugh when you allow to be made Minister a dirty, filthy kind of a man like . . ." "Really, Princess Nazlı! I don't think . . ." "You don't, and if you had . . . ," and the next victim would come up for dissection. (Storrs, *Memoirs*, 124–125)

Emine Tugay reports a similar heated exchange that was recounted to her by Ronald Storrs:

> Lord Kitchener and Storrs were having tea with Princess Nazlı when the conversation turned on a recent event in Egyptian politics. The Princess, whose views differed from those of her guest, in vain tried to bring him round to her own opinion. Finally Lord Kitchener tactfully said: "I do not understand what you mean." Whereupon Nazlı tartly replied: "You never understand anything." According to Sir Ronald, the rebuke was meekly received. (Tugay, *Three Centuries*, 112)

41. Scarce, *Women's Costume*, 81.

42. Even in the earliest years of photography's advent, the Egyptian rulers were fascinated by the medium. Muhammad Ali is rumored to have experimented with photography inside his harem. Perez, *Focus East*, 196.

43. Hamdy Bey and de Launay, *Les Costumes Populaires*. For an analysis of the Abdülhamit II albums, see Çelik, "Speaking Back to Orientalist Discourse at the World's Columbian Exposition," 77–95.

44. Özendes, *From Sébah*; Öztuncay, *Vassilaki Kargopoulo*.
45. For an analysis of Nazlı's other photographic portraits, see Roberts, "Karşıtlıklar." As Sekula, "The Body and the Archive," has astutely noted, the photographic portrait as an expression of bourgeois subjectivity in British culture in this period had its inverse in the instrumentalist use of photography for disciplinary purposes: as a record of the criminal, the insane, and the colonized subject. I am intrigued by this cross-cultural counterpart with Ottoman portraits and harem postcards. On harem postcards, see Alloula, *The Colonial Harem*.
46. On the practice of cultural cross-dressing, see Low, "White Skins/Black Masks."
47. I am struck by the parallels between the theatricality of Nazlı's photographs and the Countess de Castiglione's photographic self-portraits. See Abigail Solomon-Godeau's essay, which addresses the complex issues of masquerade and self-representation in the countess's oeuvre: "The Legs of the Countess," 77.
48. On the photographic studios in Istanbul and Cairo, see Perez, *Focus East*; Özendes, *From Sébah*; Öztuncay, *Vassilaki Kargopoulo*.
49. Crary, *Techniques of the Observer*, 132.
50. Çelik, "Speaking Back to Orientalist Discourse at the World's Columbian Exposition," 96.

EPILOGUE

1. Jerichau-Baumann, *Brogede Rejsebilleder*, 152.
2. Ibid.
3. Ibid.
4. Letter from Princess Nazlı Hanım to "My dear Mademoiselle," Stamboul, November 26, 1872, Jerichau-Baumann papers, Royal Library, Copenhagen.

Selected Bibliography

Abu-Lughod, Janet L. *Cairo: 1001 Years of the City Victorious*. Princeton: Princeton University Press, 1971.

Aitken, Maria. *A Girdle round the Earth*. London: Constable, 1987.

Ali, Muhsin Jassim. *Scheherazade in England: A Study of Nineteenth-Century English Criticism of the Arabian Nights*. Washington: Three Continents Press, 1981.

Alloula, Malek. *The Colonial Harem*. Minneapolis: University of Minnesota Press, 1986.

Alpers, Svetlana. *The Art of Describing: Dutch Art in the Seventeenth Century*. New York: Penguin Books, 1983.

Anonymous. *The Lustful Turk*. 1828; New York: Carroll and Graf, 1983.

Apter, Emily. "Acting Out Orientalism: Sapphic Theatricality in Turn-of-the-Century Paris." In *Performance and Cultural Politics*, ed. Elin Diamond. London: Routledge, 1996, 15–34.

———. "Female Trouble in the Colonial Harem." *Differences* 4, no. 1 (spring 1992): 205–224.

Attwater, Donald. *The Penguin Dictionary of Saints*. Harmondsworth: Penguin Books, 1983.

Bagehot, Walter. "The People of the Arabian Nights." *National Review* 9 (July 1859): 46–71.

Bailey, David A., and Gilane Tawadros, eds. *Veil: Veiling, Representation and Contemporary Art*. Cambridge, Mass.: MIT Press, 2003.

Baillie, E. *A Sail to Smyrna, or an English woman's journal, including impressions of Constantinople, A visit to a Turkish Harem and a Railway journey to Ephesus, Illustrated from Original Sketches*. London: Longmans, Green, 1873.

Barthes, Roland. "The Reality Effect." In *The Rustle of Language*. Trans. Richard Howard. Berkeley: University of California Press, 1989, 141–148.

Bendiner, Kenneth. "Albert Moore and John Frederick Lewis." *Arts* 5 (February 1980): 76–79.

Benjamin, Roger, ed. *Orientalism: Delacroix to Klee*. Sydney: Art Gallery of New South Wales and Thames and Hudson, 1997.

Bhabha, Homi. "Sly Civility." In *The Location of Culture*. London: Routledge, 1994, 93–101.

Black, Lynette C. "Baudelaire as Dandy: Artifice and the Search for Beauty." *Nineteenth-Century French Studies* 17, nos. 1–2 (fall–winter 1988–89): 186–195.

Blackwood, Alicia. *A Narrative of Personal Experiences and Impressions during my sojourn in the East throughout the Crimean War*. London: Hatchard, 1881.

Blunt, Fanny Janet. *The People of Turkey: Twenty years Residence among Bulgarians, Greeks, Albanians, Turks and Armenians, by a Consul's Daughter and Wife*. Ed. Stanley Lane Poole. 2 vols. London: John Murray, 1878.

Burton, Richard. *Personal Narrative of a Pilgrimage to Al-Madinah and Meccah, 1855–56*. 2 vols. New York: Dover, 1964.

Çelik, Zeynep. "Colonialism, Orientalism and the Canon." *Art Bulletin* 78, no. 2 (June 1996): 202–205.

———. "Colonial/Postcolonial Intersections: *Lieux de mémoire* in Algiers." *Historical Reflections/Reflexions Historiques* 28, no. 2 (summer 2002): 143–162.

———. *Displaying the Orient: Architecture of Islam at Nineteenth-Century World's Fairs*. Berkeley: University of California Press, 1992.

———. *The Remaking of Istanbul: Portrait of an Ottoman City in the Nineteenth Century*. Seattle: University of Washington Press, 1986; reprinted Berkeley: University of California Press, 1993.

———. "Speaking Back to Orientalist Discourse." In *Orientalism's Interlocutors: Painting, Architecture, Photography*, ed. Jill Beaulieu and Mary Roberts. Durham: Duke University Press, 2002, 19–41.

———. "Speaking Back to Orientalist Discourse at the World's Columbian Exposition." In *Noble Dreams, Wicked Pleasures: Orientalism in America, 1870–1930*, ed. Holly Edwards. Princeton: Princeton University Press, and Sterling and Francine Clark Art Institute, 2000, 77–97.

Çetin, Atilla. "Hidiv Ailesi." *Dünden Bugüne İstanbul Ansiklopedisi* 4 (1994): 59–61.

Cezar, Mustafa. *Sanatta Battı'ya Açılış ve Osman Hamdi*. 2 vols. 1971; Istanbul: Erol Kerim Aksoy Kültür Eğitim, Spor ve Sağlık Vakfı Yayınları, 1995.

Chennells, Ellen. *Recollections of an Egyptian Princess by Her English Governess. Being a Record of Five Years Residence at the Court of Ismael Pasha, Khédive*. 2 vols. Edinburgh: William Blackwood and Sons, 1893.

Cherry, Deborah. *Beyond the Frame: Feminism and Visual Culture, Britain 1850–1900*. London: Routledge, 2000.

Christensen, Charlotte. "Elisabeth Jerichau-Baumann." In *Dictionary of Women Artists*, ed. Delia Gaze. London: Fitzroy Dearborn, 1997, 2: 737–739.

Crary, Jonathan. *Techniques of the Observer: On Vision and Modernity in the Nineteenth Century*. Cambridge, Mass.: MIT Press, 1990.

Cubley, Lucy Matilda. *The Hills and Plains of Palestine. With Illustrations and descriptions by Miss L. Cubley*. London: Day and Son, 1860.

Davies, Randall, and Basil S. Long. "John Frederick Lewis, R.A. (1805–1876)." *The Old Watercolour Society's Club* 3 (1925–26): 31–50.

Davis, Fanny. *The Ottoman Lady: A Social History from 1718 to 1918*. Westport, Conn.: Greenwood Press, 1986.

Davison, Roderic H. "Halil Şerif Paşa: The Influence of Paris and the West on an Ottoman Diplomat." *Osmanlı Araştırmaları* (*Journal of Ottoman Studies*, Istanbul) 6 (1986): 47–65.

———. "Halil Şerif Paşa, Ottoman Diplomat and Statesman." *Osmanlı Araştırmaları* (*Journal of Ottoman Studies*, Istanbul) 2 (1981): 203–221.

DelPlato, Joan. *From Slave Market to Paradise: The Harem Pictures of John Frederick Lewis and Their Traditions.* Ann Arbor: UMI, 1987.

———. *Multiple Wives, Multiple Pleasures: Representing the Harem, 1800–1875.* Cranbury, Ontario: Associated University Presses, 2002.

Dennis, Kelly. "Ethno-Pornography: Veiling the Dark Continent." *History of Photography* 18, no. 1 (spring 1994): 22–28.

de Villemessant, H. *Mémoires d'un journaliste. 6éme série: Mes voyages et mes prisons.* Paris: E. Dentu, Libraire-Éditeur, 1876.

Duben, Alan, and Cem Behar. *Istanbul Households: Marriage, Family and Fertility, 1880–1940.* Cambridge: Cambridge University Press, 1991.

Elwood, Anne. *Narrative of a Journey Overland from England, by the Continent of Europe, Egypt, and the Red Sea, to India; including a residence there, and Voyage Home, in the Years 1825, 26, 27 and 28.* 2 vols. London: Henry Colburn and Richard Bentley, 1830.

Ersoy, Ahmet. "A Sartorial Tribute to Late *Tanzimat* Ottomanism: The *Elbise-i Osmaniyye* Album." In *Ottoman Costumes: From Textile to Identity*, ed. Suraiya Faroqhi and Christoph K. Neumann. Istanbul: Eren, 2004, 253–270.

Fahmy, Khaled. *All the Pasha's Men: Mehmed Ali, His Army and the Making of Modern Egypt.* Cambridge: Cambridge University Press, 1997.

Fanon, Frantz. *Studies in a Dying Colonialism.* London: Earthscan, 1989.

Faroqhi, Suraiya. "Elegance Alafranga, Social Criticism and Tomatoes: Transformations in the Culture of the Ottoman Upper Class, 1840–1914." In *Subjects of the Sultan: Culture and Daily Life in the Ottoman Empire.* London: I. B. Tauris, 2000, 247–271.

Flint, Kate. "The English Critical Reaction to Contemporary Painting, 1878–1910." Ph.D. thesis, Brasenose College, 1983.

Freud, Sigmund. *On Metapsychology: The Theory of Psychoanalysis.* Middlesex, England: Penguin Books, 1984.

Fried, Michael. *Courbet's Realism.* Chicago: University of Chicago Press, 1990.

Frierson, Elizabeth B. "Cheap and Easy: The Creation of Consumer Culture in Late Ottoman Society." In *Consumption Studies and the History of the Ottoman Empire, 1550–1922: An Introduction*, ed. Donald Quataert. Albany: State University of New York Press, 2000, 243–260.

Garber, Marjorie. "The Chic of Araby: Transvestism and the Erotics of Cultural Appropriation." In *Vested Interests: Cross-Dressing and Cultural Anxiety.* New York: Routledge, 1997, 304–352.

Germaner, Semra. "Osmanlı İmparatorluğu'nun Uluslararası Sergilere Katılımı ve Kültürel Sonuçları." *Tarih ve Toplum* 95 (1991): 33–40.

Germaner, Semra, and Zeynep İnankur. *Constantinople and the Orientalists.* Istanbul: İşbank, 2002.

Gernsheim, Helmet, and Alison Gernsheim. *The History of Photography: From the Camera Obscura to the Beginning of the Modern Era.* London: Thames and Hudson, 1969.

Giray, Kiymet. "Introduction to the History of Turkish Painting." In *The Sabanci Collection.* Istanbul: Akbank, Culture and Art Department, 1995, 182–210.

Green, Richard. *John Frederick Lewis R.A. 1805–1876.* Newcastle-upon-Tyne: Laing Art Gallery, 1971.

Grey, Theresa. *Journal of a Visit to Egypt, Constantinople, The Crimea, Greece &c. in the suite of the Prince and Princess of Wales.* London: Smith, Elder, 1869.

Griffith, Lucinda Darby. *A Journey across the Desert, from Ceylon to Marseilles: Comprising Sketches of Aden, the Red Sea, Lower Egypt, Malta, Sicily and Italy.* With illustrations by Major George Darby Griffith. 2 vols. London: Henry Colburn, 1845.

Haddad, Michèle. *Halil Şerif Paşa, Bir İnsan, Bir Koleksiyon.* Istanbul: P. Kitaplığı, 2001.

Hamdy Bey, Osman, and Marie de Launay. *Les Costumes Populaires de la Turquie en 1873 Ouvrage Publié sous le Patronage de la Commission Impériale Ottomane pour l'Exposition Universelle de Vienne. Phototypie par P. Sébah.* Constantinople: Imprimerie du "Levant Times and Shipping Gazette," 1873.

Harvey, Annie Jane. *Our Cruise in the Claymore, with a Visit to Damascus and the Lebanon.* London: Chapman and Hall, 1861.

———. *Turkish Harems and Circassian Homes.* London: Hurst and Blackett, 1871.

Haskell, Francis. "A Turk and His Pictures in Nineteenth-Century Paris." In *Past and Present in Art and Taste: Selected Essays.* New Haven: Yale University Press, 1987, 175–185.

Herbert, Mary Elizabeth. *Cradle Lands.* London: Richard Bentley, 1867.

Hornby, Emilia Bithynia. *Constantinople during the Crimean War.* London: Richard Bentley, 1863.

———. *In and around Stamboul.* 2 vols. London: Richard Bentley, 1858.

İnankur, Zeynep. "Halil Şerif Paşa." *P* 2 (summer 1996): 72–80.

Issa, Ahmed Mohammed, and Jahsin Ömer Tahaoğlu, eds. *Islamic Art: Common Principles, Forms and Themes.* Proceedings of the International Symposium, Istanbul, April 1983. Research Centre for Islamic History, Art and Culture. Damascus: Dar-Al-Fikr, 1989.

Jay, Martin. *Downcast Eyes: The Denigration of Vision in Twentieth-Century French Thought.* Berkeley: University of California Press, 1993.

———. "Scopic Regimes of Modernity." In *Vision and Visuality*, ed. Hal Foster. Seattle: Bay Press, 1988, 3–27.

Jerichau-Baumann, Elisabeth. *Brogede Rejsebilleder* (Motley Images of Travel). Copenhagen: Forlagsbureauet, 1881.

Kabbani, Rana. *Europe's Myths of Orient.* 1986; London: Pandora, 1988.

Kuntay, Midhat Cemal. *Namık Kemal, Devrinin İnsanları ve Olayları Arasında.* Istanbul: Maarif Mataası, 1944.

Lacan, Jacques. *The Four Fundamental Concepts of Psycho-Analysis.* London: Penguin Books, 1991.

Lane, Edward. *An Account of the Manners and Customs of the Modern Egyptians.* 2 vols., London: Charles Knight, 1836.

———. *An Account of the Manners and Customs of the Modern Egyptians. The Definitive 1860 Edition.* Cairo: American University in Cairo Press, 2003.

Larsen, Peter Nørgaard. "Fra Nationalromantisk Bondeliv til Orientens Haremsmystik: Elisabeth Jerichau Baumann i Dansk og Europæisk 1800-tals Kunst." In *Elisabeth Jerichau Baumann.* Denmark: På Øregaard Museum and på Fyns Kunstmuseum, 1997.

Leeks, Wendy. "Ingres Other-Wise." *Oxford Art Journal* 9, no. 1 (1986): 29–37.

Lewis, Major-General Michael. *John Frederick Lewis R.A. 1805–1876.* Leigh-on-Sea, England: F. Lewis Publishers, 1978.

Lewis, Reina. *Gendering Orientalism: Race, Femininity and Representation.* London: Routledge, 1996.

———. *Rethinking Orientalism: Women, Travel and the Ottoman Harem.* London: I. B. Tauris, 2004.

Leyla (Saz) Hanımefendi. *The Imperial Harem of the Sultans: Daily Life at the Çırağan Palace during the 19th Century. Memoirs of Leyla (Saz) Hanımefendi.* Istanbul: PEVA, 1995.

Llewellyn, Briony. "A 'Masquerade' Unmasked: An Aspect of John Frederick Lewis's Encounter with Egypt." *Egyptian Encounters: Cairo Papers in Social Sciences* 23, no. 3 (2000): 133–151.

Llewellyn, Briony, and Charles Newton. "John Frederick Lewis: 'In Knowledge of the Orientals Quite One of Themselves.'" In *Interpreting the Orient: Travellers in Egypt and the Near East*, ed. Paul and Janet Starkey. Reading, U.K.: Ithaca Press, 2001, 35–50.

Lott, Emmeline. *The English Governess in Egypt: Harem Life in Egypt and Constantinople.* 2 vols. London: R. Bentley, 1866.

———. *The Grand Pasha's Cruise on the Nile in the Viceroy of Egypt's Yacht.* 2 vols. London: T. Cautley Newby, 1869.

———. *The Mohaddetyn in the Palace of Ghezire: Nights in the Harem.* 2 vols. London: Chapman and Hall, 1867.

Low, Gail Ching-Liang. "White Skins/Black Masks: The Pleasure and Politics of Imperialism." *New Formations*, no. 9 (winter 1989): 83–103.

Macleod, Dianne Sachko. "Cross-Cultural Cross-Dressing: Class, Gender and Modernist Sexual Identity." In *Orientalism Transposed: The Impact of the Colonies on British Culture*, ed. J. F. Codell and D. S. Macleod. Aldershot, England: Ashgate, 1998, 63–85.

Marcus, Julie. *A World of Difference: Islam and Gender Hierarchy in Turkey.* Sydney: Allen and Unwin, 1992.

Mardin, Şerif. "Super Westernization in Urban Life in the Ottoman Empire in the Last Quarter of the Nineteenth Century." In *Turkey: Geographic and Social Perspectives*, ed. Peter Benedict, Erol Tümertekin, and Fatma Mansur. Leiden: E. J. Brill, 1974, 403–446.

Melman, Billie. *Women's Orients: English Women and the Middle East, 1718–1918. Sexuality, Religion and Work.* London: Macmillan, 1992.

Merleau-Ponty, Maurice. "The Intertwining—The Chiasm." In *The Visible and the Invisible: Followed by Working Notes.* Evanston: Northwestern University Press, 1968, 130–155.

Micklewright, Nancy. "Personal, Public and Political (Re)Constructions: Photographs and Consumption." In *Consumption Studies and the History of the Ottoman Empire, 1550–1922: An Introduction*, ed. Donald Quataert. Albany: State University of New York Press, 2000, 261–287.

———. "Public and Private for Ottoman Women of the Nineteenth Century." In *Women, Patronage and Self-Representation in Islamic Societies*, ed. D. Fairchild Ruggles. Albany: State University of New York Press, 2000, 155–176.

Mills, Sara. *Discourses of Difference: An Analysis of Women's Travel Writing and Colonialism.* London: Routledge, 1991.

Mitchell, Timothy. *Colonising Egypt.* Berkeley: University of California Press, 1988.

Montagu, Mary Wortley. *The Selected Letters of Lady Mary Wortley Montagu*. Ed. Robert Halsband. Middlesex, England: Penguin Books, 1986.

Moussa-Mahmoud, Fatma. "English Travellers and the *Arabian Nights*." In *The* Arabian Nights *in English Literature: Studies in the Reception of* The Thousand and One Nights *into British Culture*, ed. P. Caracciolo. New York: St. Martin's Press, 1988, 95–110.

Mulvey, Laura. "Visual Pleasure and Narrative Cinema." In *Visual and Other Pleasures*. London: Macmillan, 1989, 14–26.

Murray, John. *A Handbook for Travellers in Turkey: Describing Constantinople, European Turkey, Asia Minor, Armenia and Mesopotamia. With New Travelling Maps and Plans*. 3rd ed. London: John Murray, 1854.

Mustafa Fazil Paşa. *Lettre adressée à Sa Majesté le Sultan par S. A. le Prince Mustapha-Fazil-Pacha*. Paris, 1867.

Nochlin, Linda. "The Imaginary Orient." *Art in America* 71, no. 5 (May 1983): 118–131, 187–191.

Öner, Sema. "The Role of the Ottoman Palace in the Development of Turkish Painting Following the Reforms of 1839." *National Palaces* (Istanbul), no. 4 (1992): 58–77.

———. "Tanzimat Sonrası Osmanlı Saray Çevresinde Resim Etkinligi." Ph.D. thesis, Mimar Sinan University, Istanbul, 1991.

Özel, İsmet. "Tanzimatın Getirdiği 'Aydın.'" *Tanzimat'tan Cumhuriyet'e Türkiye Ansiklopedisi* (İletişim Yayınları, Istanbul) 1 (1985): 61–66.

Özendes, Engin. *From Sébah and Joaillier to Foto Sabah: Orientalism in Photography*. Istanbul: Yapı Kredi Yayınları, 1999.

Öztuncay, Bahattin. *Vassilaki Kargopoulo: Photographer to His Majesty the Sultan*. Istanbul: Birleşik Oksijen Sanayi A.Ş., 2000.

Pamuk, Orhan. *Istanbul: Memories of a City*. Trans. Maureen Freely. London: Faber and Faber, 2005.

Pamukciyan, Kevork. "1867 Yılı Paris Sergisine Katılan Osmanlı Sanatkârları." *Tarih ve Toplum* 105 (1992): 35–37.

Pardoe, Julia. *The Beauties of the Bosphorus. Illustrated in a series of views of Constantinople and its environs, from Original Drawings by W. H. Bartlett*. London: George Virtue, 1838.

Peirce, Leslie P. *The Imperial Harem: Women and Sovereignty in the Ottoman Empire*. Oxford: Oxford University Press, 1993.

Perez, Nissan N. *Focus East: Early Photography in the Near East (1839–1885)*. New York: Harry N. Abrams, 1988.

Pointon, Marcia. "Killing Pictures." In *Painting and the Politics of Culture: New Essays on British Art, 1700–1850*, ed. John Barrell. Oxford: Oxford University Press, 1992, 39–72.

Poole, Sophia. *The Englishwoman in Egypt: Letters from Cairo written during a Residence there in 1842, 3 and 4, with E. W. Lane Esq*. 2 vols., London: Chas. Knight, 1844.

———. *The Englishwoman in Egypt: Letters from Cairo Written during a residence there in 1845–46*. 2nd series. London: Chas. Knight, 1846.

Prettejohn, Elizabeth, ed., *After the Pre-Raphaelites: Art and Aestheticism in Victorian England*. Manchester: Manchester University Press, 1999.

———. *The Art of the Pre-Raphaelites*. London: Tate Publishing, 2000.

Quataert, Donald. *The Ottoman Empire, 1700–1922*. Cambridge: Cambridge University Press, 2000.

———. "Part IV: The Age of Reform 1812–1914." In *An Economic and Social History of the Ottoman Empire, 1300–1914*, ed. Halil İnalcık and Donald Quataert. Cambridge: Cambridge University Press, 1994, 759–933.

Raby, Julian. *Qajar Portraits*. London: Azimuth Editions, 1999.

Raymond, André. *Cairo*. Cambridge, Mass.: Harvard University Press, 2000.

Renda, Günsel. "Portraits: The Last Century." In *The Sultan's Portrait: Picturing the House of Osman*. Topkapı Palace Museum, Istanbul: İşbank, 2000, 442–542.

Richon, Olivier. "Representation, the Despot and the Harem: Some Questions around an Academic Orientalist Painting by Lecomte-du-Nouy (1885)." In *Europe and Its Others: Proceedings of the Essex Sociology of Literature Conference*, ed. Francis Barker et al. Colchester: University of Essex, 1985, 1: 1–13.

Roberts, Mary. "Karşıtlıklar: Said, Sanat Tarihi ve 19. Yüzyıl İstanbul'unda Osmanlı Kimliğini Yeniden Keşfetmek." In *Uluslararası Oryantalizm Sempozyumu (Papers of the International Orientalism Symposium)*, Istanbul: İstanbul Büyükşehir Belediyesi, 2007, 269–285.

———. "Cultural Crossings: Sartorial Adventures, Satiric Narratives and the Question of Indigenous Agency in Nineteenth-Century Europe and the Near East." In *Edges of Empire: Orientalism and Visual Culture*, ed. Jocelyn Hackforth-Jones and Mary Roberts. Oxford: Blackwell, 2005, 70–94.

———. "Difference and Deferral: The Sexual Economy of Courbet's 'Femininity.'" In *Refracting Vision: Essays on the Writings of Michael Fried*, ed. Jill Beaulieu, Mary Roberts, and Toni Ross. Sydney: Power Publications, 2000, 211–245.

———. "Masquerade as Disguise and Satire in Two Travellers' Tales of the Orientalist's Harem." *Olive Pink Society Bulletin: Anthropology, Race, Gender* 5, no. 1 (1993): 23–29.

———. "Travel, Transgression and the Colonial Harem: The Paintings of J. F. Lewis and the Diaries of British Women Travellers." Ph.D. thesis, University of Melbourne, 1995.

Robinson, Jane. *Wayward Women: A Guide to Women Travellers*. Oxford: Oxford University Press, 1990.

Rogers, Mary Eliza. *Domestic Life in Palestine*. 1861; London: Bell and Daldy, 1862.

Romer, Isabella. *The Bird of Passage; or Flying Glimpses of Many Lands*. 3 vols. London: Richard Bentley, 1849.

———. *A Pilgrimage to the Temples and Tombs of Egypt, Nubia and Palestine, in 1845–1846*. 2 vols. London: Richard Bentley, 1846.

Rumbold, Horace. *Recollections of a Diplomatist*. 2 vols. London: Edward Arnold, 1902.

Ruskin, John. *The Works of John Ruskin*. Ed. E. T. Cook and Alexander Wedderburn. La Crosse, Wisc.: Brookhaven Press, 1981.

Russell, William Howard. *A Diary in the East during the tour of the Prince and Princess of Wales*. London: George Routledge and Sons, 1869.

Rustum, Asad J. *The Struggle of Mehemet Ali Pasha with Sultan Mahmud II and some of its geographical aspects*. Notes prepared for the International Geographical Congress of Cairo, April 1925.

Said, Edward. *Orientalism*. Middlesex, England: Penguin Books, 1978.

Sakaoğlu, Necdet. "Record of a Royal Wedding During the Tanzimat Period." *National Palaces*, no. 4 (1992): 168–173.

Sakaoğlu, Necdet, and Nuri Akbayar. *Sultan Abdülmecid: A Milestone on Turkey's Path of Westernization.* Istanbul: DenizBank Publications, 2002.

Salaheddin Bey. *La Turquie à L'Exposition Universelle de 1867.* Paris: Libraire Hachette, 1867.

Saper, Craig. "A Nervous Theory: The Troubling Gaze of Psychoanalysis in Media Studies." *Diacritics* 21, no. 4 (winter 1991): 33–52.

Sayyid, Afaf Lutfi, al-. *Egypt and Cromer: A Study in Anglo-Egyptian Relations.* London: John Murray, 1968.

Sayyid Marsot, Afaf Lutfi, al-. *Egypt in the Reign of Muhammad Ali.* Cambridge: Cambridge University Press, 1984.

———. *A Short History of Modern Egypt.* Cambridge: Cambridge University Press, 1985.

Scarce, Jennifer. *Women's Costume of the Near and Middle East.* London: Unwin Hyman, 1987.

Sekula, Alan. "The Body and the Archive." *October*, no. 39 (winter 1986): 3–64.

Şeni, Nora. "Fashion and Women's Clothing in the Satirical Press of Istanbul at the End of the Nineteenth Century." In *Women in Modern Turkish Society: A Reader*, ed. Şirin Tekeli. London: Zed Books, 1995, 25–45.

Shaw, Stanford J., and Ezel Kural Shaw. *History of the Ottoman Empire and Modern Turkey.* Vol. 2, *Reform, Revolution, and Republic: The Rise of Modern Turkey, 1808–1975.* 1977; Cambridge: Cambridge University Press, 1995.

Shaw, Wendy M. K. *Possessor and Possessed: Museums, Archaeology, and the Visualization of History in the Late Ottoman Empire.* Berkeley: University of California Press, 2003.

Silverman, Kaja. "Fassbinder and Lacan: A Reconsideration of Gaze, Look and Image." In *Male Subjectivity at the Margins.* New York: Routledge, 1992, 125–156.

Skene, Felicia Mary Frances [Erskine Moir]. *Wayfaring Sketches among the Greeks and Turks, and on the shores of the Danube. By a Seven Years' Resident in Greece.* 2 vols. London: Chapman and Hall, 1847.

Slade, Captain Adolphus, R.N., F.R.A.S. *Records of Travels in Turkey, Greece etc. and of a Cruise in the Black Sea with the Captain Pacha.* London: Saunders and Otley, 1854.

Smith, Lindsay. "The Elusive Depth of Field: Stereoscopy and the Pre-Raphaelites." In *Pre-Raphaelites Re-viewed*, ed. Marcia Pointon. Manchester: Manchester University Press, 1989, 83–99.

Solomon-Godeau, Abigail. "The Legs of the Countess." *October* 39 (winter 1986): 65–105.

Sönmez, Emel. *Turkish Women in Turkish Literature of the Nineteenth Century.* Leiden: E. J. Brill, 1969.

Starr, Laura B. "Ladies of the Harem." *The Lady's Realm* 4 (1898): 313–320.

Stevens, Mary Anne, ed. *The Orientalists: Delacroix to Matisse. European Painters in North Africa and the Near East.* London: Royal Academy of Arts and Weidenfeld and Nicolson, 1984.

Stokes, Hugh. "John Frederick Lewis R.A. (1805–1876)." *Walker's Quarterly*, no. 28 (1929): 3–53.

Storrs, Ronald. *The Memoirs of Sir Ronald Storrs.* New York: Arno Press, 1972.

The Sultan's Portrait: Picturing the House of Osman. Topkapı Palace Museum, Istanbul: İşbank, 2000.

Sweetman, John. *The Oriental Obsession: Islamic Inspiration in British and American Art and Architecture, 1500–1920.* Cambridge: Cambridge University Press, 1988.

Thackeray, William Makepeace. *Notes of a Journey from Cornhill to Grand Cairo.* 1846; London: Smith Elder, 1869.

———. *Notes of a Journey from Cornhill to Grand Cairo.* Introduction by Sarah Searight. Sussex: Cockbird Press, 1991.

Thomas, Nicholas. *Entangled Objects: Exchange, Material Culture and Colonialism in the Pacific.* Cambridge, Mass.: Harvard University Press, 1991.

Tickner, Lisa. "Feminism, Art History and Sexual Difference." *Genders*, no. 3 (fall 1988): 92–128.

Toledano, Ehud R. *State and Society in Mid-Nineteenth-Century Egypt.* Cambridge: Cambridge University Press, 1990.

Truman, Nevil. "Empire and the Dandies, 1820–37." In *Historic Costuming.* London: Sir Isaac Pitman and Sons, 1962, 87–92.

Tugay, Emine Foat. *Three Centuries: Family Chronicles of Turkey and Egypt.* Oxford: Oxford University Press, 1963.

Turner, Gerard L'Estrange. *Nineteenth-Century Scientific Instruments.* Berkeley: University of California Press, 1983.

Von Folsach, Birgitte. *By the Light of the Crescent Moon: Images of the Near East in Danish Art and Literature, 1800–1875.* Copenhagen: David Collection, 1996.

Walker, Mary Adelaide. *Eastern Life and Scenery with Excursions in Asia Minor, Mytilene, Crete and Roumania.* 2 vols. London: Chapman and Hall, 1886.

Weeks, Emily M. "About Face: Sir David Wilkie's Portrait of Mehemet Ali Pasha of Egypt." In *Orientalism Transposed: The Impact of the Colonies on British Culture*, ed. Julie F. Codell and Dianne Sachko Macleod. Aldershot, England: Ashgate, 1998, 46–62.

———. "J. F. Lewis 1805–1876: Mythology as Biography." In *Travellers in the Levant: Voyagers and Visionaries*, ed. Sarah Searight and Malcolm Wagstaff. Durham, England: Astene, 2001, 177–196.

———. "The 'Reality Effect': The Orientalist Paintings of John Frederick Lewis (1805–1876)." Ph.D. thesis, Yale University, 2004.

Williams, Caroline. "John Frederick Lewis: 'Reflections of Reality.'" *Muqarnas* 18, (2001): 227–243.

Wilson, Elizabeth. "Oppositional Dress." In *Adorned in Dreams: Fashion and Modernity*, London: Virago, 1985, 179–206.

Woman in Anatolia: 9000 Years of the Anatolian Woman. Istanbul: Topkapı Palace Museum, 1993.

Yeazell, Ruth Bernard. *Harems of the Mind: Passages of Western Art and Literature.* New Haven: Yale University Press, 2000.

Yeğenoğlu, Meyda. *Colonial Fantasies: Towards a Feminist Reading of Orientalism.* Cambridge: Cambridge University Press, 1998.

Zonana, Joyce. "The Sultan and the Slave: Feminist Orientalism and the Structure of *Jane Eyre*." *Signs: Journal of Women in Culture and Society* 18, no. 3 (1993): 592–617.

Index

A page number with n refers to a note; *f*, to a figure.

British women, harem visits of. *See* visits
   to the harem by British women
Browne, Henriette, 10, 53, 60, 124–25,
   PLATE 12
Bugler, Caroline, 162n9
Bukana Hanım, 132–33, 135, 137, 173n17
Burton, Richard, 93, 99–102

Cabouli Paşa, 172–73n13
Cairo. *See* Egypt
cartoons satirizing modern dress, 122,
   123f
Çelik, Zeynep, 5–6, 149, 175n36
Chennells, Ellen, 115
Chlebowski, Stanislaw, 114
Christ in the House of His Parents (Millais),
   32
Çirağan palace, 113
Citadel, 29, 160n30
clothing and fashion, 80–81, 82f; *çarşaf*
   (skirt and cape), 117–18, 122, 123f,
   170n24, PLATE 26; cartoons satirizing modern dress, 122, 123f; choices
   of, for portraits, 112–13, 116–20;
   corsets, 88–89, 167n24; cultural
   cross-dressing, 23–26, 38–39, 66–67,
   93, 146–47, 167–68n1; curiosity of
   Ottoman women about, 80, 86–91,
   167n24; descriptions of, by travel
   writers, 73–74; in Emmeline Lott's
   portraits, 92–93, 94f; eunuch's harem
   masquerade tale, 99–104, 168n11,
   169n19; *ferace* (coat), 118, PLATE 26;
   feredje (cloak), 73–74, 96; fez/tar-
   boosh, 26, 39, 122, 159n17, 160n32,
   161n1; gendered cross-dressing, 99–
   104, 146–49; Lewis's sensual painting of, 74; modern hybrid forms of,
   14–15, 78–79, 112–13, 116–27, 130–33,
   166n33, 172n9, PLATE 26; of Princess Nazlı, 131, 135, 143–44; regula-
   tions governing, 26, 121–22, 159n17;
   of Victorian visitors to the harem,
   80; Walker's illustrations of, 125–26,
   PLATES 27–28; worn in public spaces,

117–20; *yaşmak* (veil), 73–74, 92–99,
   106, 115, 118, 168n8. *See also* portrai-
   ture of Ottoman rulers; portraiture of
   Ottoman women
colonialsm, 5–6, 84, 166n9
Constantinople during the Crimean War
   (Hornby), PLATES 27–28
Coste, Pascal, 160n28
Cotton, Sir Robert, 100–104
Courbet, Gustave, 140
Crary, Jonathan, 52, 148
cross-cultural exchange, 3, 10–11, 139–42,
   151–55, 175n36
Cubley, Lucy, 86
cultural cross-dressing, 93, 167–68n1,
   PLATE 30; by Alexandra, Princess of
   Wales, 66–67; by J. F. Lewis, 23–26,
   29, 38–39; by Nazlı Hanım, 143–44,
   146–49

Davies, Randall, 160n33
Delacroix, Eugène, 87, PLATE 18
DelPlato, Joan, 13, 162n5
dormeuses, Les (Courbet), 140
dress. *See* clothing and fashion

Edward, Prince of Wales, 130
Egypt, 4–7; under British occupation
   and protectorate, 6; during Lewis's
   residency in the 1840s, 21–31; modernization and reform initiatives in,
   6, 28–29, 157n11, 171nn2–3; under
   Muhammad Ali Paşa, 7, 27, 157n10,
   158n13; Ottoman elites of, 7, 25–26,
   159n14; regulation of dress in, 26–27,
   159nn17, 22
Egyptian Pottery Seller Near Gizeh, An
   (Jerichau-Baumann), 147–49, PLATE
   32
Ehrenhoff, Madame d', 128
Elwood, Anne, 86–87, 96–97
Eminé Faika Lutfié Hanım, 169n4
Eminé Hanım, 116, 123–24, 169n4
Englishwoman in Egypt, The (Poole),
   60–61

Griffith, Lucinda Darby, 80–81, 82*f*
Guillemet, Pierre Désiré, 114

Halil Şerif Paşa, 140, 174nn30–31
Halim Paşa, Prince, 140–41, 171n2, 174n30
Harem dans le kiosque, Le (Gérôme), 104–6, PLATE 24
Harem (film), 84
harem literature. *See* travel writing on harem life
Harvey, Annie Jane, 66–68, 73–74
Herbert, Mary, 63
Hhareem, The (Lewis), 20–21, 31–37, PLATE 1; central narrative of, 33–35, 42, 44; critical response to, 31–33, 160n33, 161nn39, 43; exhibit of, in London, 31; fusion of ethnography with fantasy in, 21, 32–35, 55; gendered spectatorship of, 35–37; Lewis's description of, 34; perspectival model of visuality of, 84–85; perspective and composition of, 35, 37, 84–85, 161n43; reworking of, in *An Intercepted Correspondence*, 43–45
Hhareem Life, Constantinople (Lewis), 39–41, 50, 51, 161n2, PLATE 5
Hornby, Emilia, 63–66, 96, 125–26, PLATES 27–28
Hunt, William Holman, 95, PLATE 21

Ibrahim Paşa, 93, 99, 157n10, 166n7
İki Müzisyen Kız (Osman Hamdi Bey), 175n33
Indoor Gossip, Cairo (Lewis), 37, 48–51, 74, PLATE 10
Ingres, Jean, 140, 167n19
Intercepted Correspondence, Cairo, An (Lewis), 43–45, 162nn9–10, PLATE 7
Interior of J. F. Lewis's House in Cairo (Wild), 53, 54*f*
"Interior of the Hharee'm of Mochtah Bey, The" (Griffith), 82*f*, 91–92
interiors, Alpers's art of describing, 43, 162n7
International Exhibition of Vienna, 118

In the Bey's Garden (Lewis), 45–46, 48, 73, 162–63nn13–14, PLATE 8
intimate outsiders, 10–12, 151–55
Ismail, khedive, 115, 129, 171nn2–3, 175n39
Ismail Paşa, 7, 28, 100, 157n10, 166n7
Istanbul, 4–9; independent status of, 5–6; Ottoman archaeology museum in, 8–9; Scutari, 94–95; Topkapı Palace, 9. *See also* modernizing trends in Ottoman culture; Ottoman women
Istanbul: Memories of a City (Pamuk), 5, 157n6

Jay, Martin, 166n31
Jerichau-Baumann, Elisabeth, 128–49, 171–72n3, PLATES 30, 32; critical response to, 136–37, 173nn21–22; display of pictures for Nazlı Hanım, 133–35; fantasy paintings of, 137–39, 147–49, 174n23, PLATES 30, 32; homecoming experience of, 150–52; on hybrid fashions of Ottoman women, 130–33, 172n9; New Bond Street Gallery exhibition of 1871, 129, 136–37; portraiture of Princess Nazlı by, 2–3, 133–37, 173n15; "princess thief" story, 1–2; relationship of, with Nazlı Hanım, 15, 130–33, 139–40, 172n12, 174n23; success and reputation of, 130, 138–39, 172n7, 174nn24–25; transformation of Orientalist values of, 130–33, 152–53, 172–73n13; views of, on European feminism, 133
Jerichau-Baumann, Harald, 140
Jervas, Charles, 69–70
John Frederick Lewis in Oriental Dress (unknown), PLATE 4
Journey across the Desert, from Ceylon to Marseilles, A (Griffith), 82*f*

Kargopoulo photography studio, 144
khedives of Cairo. *See* Egypt
Kingsley, Ben, 84
Kinski, Natassja, 84

Kitchener, Lord Horatio Herbert, 142, 175n40

Lacan, Jacques, 82–86, 166n11, 167nn15, 21, 26
Lane, Edward, 34, 61, 63, 165n11
Language of Flowers, The (Bugler), 162n9
Lecomte de Noüy, Jean Jules Antoine, 76, PLATE 15
Leeks, Wendy, 167n19
Leighton, Frederic, 22, 90, PLATE 19
Lewis, John Frederick, 20–21; aestheticist views of the harem of, 39–56, 163nn17–18; art affiliations of, in London, 30–31; art of describing of, 43, 162n7; Cairo house of, 53, 54f, PLATE 13; expatriate authority of, 20–21, 24–25, 29–30, 34, 160n33; Oriental dress of, 23–26, 29, 152; outsider status of, 11–12; photographic portrait of, 152, PLATE 4; *The Portfolio* article on, 30; realism of, 10–12, 21, 30, 34–37, 40–41, 48; return of, to England, 37, 39; Rochard's portrait of, 24, 25f, 38–39, 161n1; role of mashrabiyah for, 97–98; Ruskin's views of, 31, 48, 161n39, 163n19; Spanish career of, 22; Thackeray's portrayal of, 11–12, 19–31, 34, 36, 55–56, 159n6, 160n33, 161n1. *See also* Lewis's Orientalist paintings
Lewis, Marian, 39, 51, 77, 161n3
Lewis, Reina, 12, 14, 61
Lewis's Orientalist paintings, 9–10, 21, 30, 49–54, PLATES 1–2, 4–11, 13, 16, 22–23; botanical inaccuracies in, 48, 163n20; composition and perspective of, 35, 37, 40–41, 42, 164n31; critical responses to, 31–33, 44–49, 51, 55, 160n33, 161nn39, 43; emphasis on surfaces in, 43; fusion of ethnography with fantasy in *The Hhareem,* 20–21, 32–35, 55; harem garden paintings of, 45–48, 73, 162n13, 162–63n14, 163n16; *Portrait of Mehemet Ali Pasha,* 26–29; repetition in, 49, 164n23; stereo-

scopic effects of *The Reception,* 51–53, 164nn26, 29; synaesthetic effects of, 45–48, 73, 74, 76–77, 163n16, 166n31; treatment of detail in, 34–35, 41, 48, 56, 62, 162n5. *See also* spectatorship in Lewis's work; and under names of specific works, e.g., *Hhareem, The*
Life in the Harem, Cairo (Lewis), 39, 41–43, 50, 51, 74, PLATE 6
Light of the Harem, The (Leighton), 90, PLATE 19
Lilium Auratum (Lewis), 45, 46–47, PLATE 9
Lott, Emmeline, 15, 83–84, 92–94, 99–106, 155, 166n7, 168nn9–10; attitude of, toward eunuchs, 103; eunuch's harem masquerade tale, 99–104, 155, 168n11, 169n19; goal of, of unveiling the harem, 99; portrait of, 92–93, 94f
Lustful Turk, The, 83

Mahmut II, Sultan, 113, 114, 122, 159n22
Manasie, Rubens, 113–14, PLATE 25
marriage customs, 112–13
mashrabiyah (lattice screens), 28–29, 34–35, 97–98
matriarchal authority, 135
Mecidiye mosque, 113
Mehemet Ali (Wilkie), PLATE 3
Mehmet II, Sultan, 113
Melman, Billie, 12, 61
Mendurah in My House in Cairo (Lewis), 53, PLATE 13
Merleau-Ponty, Maurice, 77
Midday Meal, Cairo, The (Lewis), 98, PLATE 23
Millais, John Everett, 32
Mills, Sara, 12
Mochtah Bey's harem, 80–81, 82f
modernizing trends in Ottoman culture, 3–4, 78–79, 152–53; architectural reforms, 28–29, 160n28; in clothing and fashion, 14–15, 26, 78–79, 112–13, 116–27, 159n17, 159n22, 166nn32–33, PLATE 26; interest in European culture, 5–9,

also clothing and fashion; Fatma Sultan, princess; Nazlı Hanım; portraiture of Ottoman women

Outdoor Gossip, Cairo (Lewis), 49

outsider roles of Western observers, 10–12, 151–55

Pamuk, Orhan, 5, 157n6

Pardoe, Julia, 59–60, 70–72, 77, 152

Peirce, Leslie, 8

perspectival model of visuality, 84–85

photographic portraiture, 143–49, 175n42

Poole, Sophia, 60–61, 83

Portrait of Abdülmecid (Manasie), 113–14, PLATE 25

Portrait of J. F. Lewis, R. A. (Rochard), 24, 25f, 38–39

Portrait of Mehemet Ali Pasha (Lewis), 26–29, PLATE 2

portraiture of Ottoman rulers, 113–14; of Abdülaziz, 111; of Abdülmecit, 113–14, PLATE 25; balcony portrait iconography, 114; clothing choices in, 113; of Mahmut II, 159n22; of Muhammad Ali Paşa, 26–29, PLATES 2–3; public and diplomatic role of, 114; setting choices in, 113

portraiture of Ottoman women, 13–16; clothing choices in, 112–13, 116–20; of Fatma Sultan, 109–14; Hamdi Bey's paintings of women in public spaces, 8, 117–20, PLATE 26; impact of miniature tradition on, 115–16; modern projections in, 14–15, 116–27, 153–55; parodies of, 143–49, 155, 176n47, PLATE 31; photographic portraiture, 115; public exhibition of, 129, 136–37; restricted visibility of, 114–15, 127, 129; role of, 123–24. See also Jerichau-Baumann, Elisabeth; Lewis's Orientalist paintings; Nazlı Hanım; Walker, Mary Adelaide

Pre-Raphaelite movement, 31–32, 47, 161n39

Prettejohn, Elizabeth, 161n39

Princess Nazili Hanum, The (Jerichau-Baumann), 137–38, 174n23, PLATE 30

Princess Nazlı Hanım (Sébah photography studio), 136, PLATE 29

Princess Nazlı Hanım (unknown), PLATE 31

privileged access. See visits to the harem by British women

Quataert, Donald, 7–8

realism, 9–12. See also Lewis's Orientalist paintings

Reception, The (Lewis), 48–49, 51–54, PLATE 11

Riza Paşa, 123

Riza Paşa harem, 63–66, 68–69, 73–74, 169n4

Roberts, David, 22

Rochard, Simon Jacques, 24, 25f, 38–39

Rogers, Mary, 74–75

Romer, Isabella, 88, 89

Ruskin, John, 31, 48, 161n39, 163n19

Said, Edward, 101

Sait Paşa, 157n10

sartorial practices. See clothing and fashion

Sébah photography studios, 136, 144, PLATE 29

secondary narcissism, 89–90

seeing and being seen, 80–91, 167n19; in Delacroix's Femmes d'Alger dans leur intérieur, 87; in the eunuch's harem masquerade tale, 99–104, 168n11, 169n19; in Gérôme's Le Harem dans le kiosque, 104–6; Lacan's theory of gaze, 82–86; in Lewis's The Hhareem, 84–85; role of mashrabiyah (lattice screens) in, 28–29, 34–35, 97–98; role of the veil in, 92–99, 106. See also clothing and fashion; spectatorship in Lewis's work

Selim III, Sultan, 114

Şeni, Nora, 122, 123f, 171n32

Mary Roberts is the John Schaeffer Associate Professor in British Art at the University of Sydney. She has coedited three volumes, including *Edges of Empire: Orientalism and Visual Culture* (2005) and *Orientalism's Interlocutors: Painting, Architecture, Photography* (2002).

Library of Congress Cataloging-in-Publication Data
Roberts, Mary
Intimate outsiders : the harem in Ottoman and orientalist art and travel literature /
Mary Roberts.
p. cm. — (Objects/histories)
Includes bibliographical references and index.
ISBN 978-0-8223-3956-4 (cloth : alk. paper)
ISBN 978-0-8223-3967-0 (pbk. : alk. paper)
1. Harems in art. 2. Orientalism in art—England. 3. Art, Turkish—19th century.
4. Travelers' writings, English—Turkey—History and criticism. 5. Harems—
Turkey—Istanbul—History—19th century. 6. Harems—Egypt—Cairo—History—
19th century. 7. Women—Turkey—Social conditions—19th century. 8. Turkey—
Relations—England. 9. England—Relations—Turkey. I. Title.
NX650.H37R63 2007
700'.455—dc22   2007021173